CW01630667

All the best,
Arna

Arna's Song

My Finnish Life 1931- 1955

Arna Davis

All rights reserved. No part of this publication may be reproduced, stored in a retrieval system, or transmitted, in any form, or by any means, electronic, mechanical, photocopying, recording or otherwise, without the prior permission of the author.

This book is sold subject to the condition that it shall not, by way of trade or otherwise, be lent, resold, hired out or otherwise circulated without the author's prior consent in any form of binding or cover other than that in which it is published and without a similar condition, including this condition, being imposed on the subsequent publisher.

ISBN: 978-1-9997129-2-1

Copyright © Arna Davis 2020

Cover design by Colin Robinson, based on a painting by Arna Davis

Dedication

This book, my song to Finland, (Lauluni Suomelle) is written with gratitude to the country of my youth, dedicated with love to my children Martin, Karin and Kim, their partners, and my grandchildren Callum, Hamish, Annelie and Oscar.

Contents

Prologue

In the late afternoon sunshine of August 1955 Baltika, the Russian ship, sailing between Leningrad and London, was slowly gliding out from Helsinki harbour, preparing to manoeuvre her way through the narrow corridor past Suomenlinna fortress to the open sea.

I stood on the deck, a petite young woman, my long blonde hair blowing over my face, concealing the tears streaming from my eyes. Clutching an enormous bunch of deep red roses to my bosom, I waved frantically with my free hand, hoping to catch one last glimpse of the man waving, blowing kisses and running along the quay. As the ship gained more distance, he became gradually just a tiny speck. I asked myself: What am I doing voluntarily leaving the man who loves me more than I have ever felt loved? What am I doing abandoning all that is important, my family, my country, and my friends? What am I running away from? Decisions I am not able or ready to make about my life?

Yrjö and Karin Pelkonen
with Rainer and Arna,
Autumn 1931

Mamma and Arna
Summer 1934

Family photo with
baby Laila, early in 1935

Chapter One

Years of Innocence (1931-1939)

Life in Kuopio

March, for me, is the most beautiful month in the Finnish calendar. The world is white, the air crisp and clear, the sun shines from a cloudless sky, and the bare trees cast long, blue shadows and geometrical patterns on the snow. Days grow longer; dusk lingers on and on, colouring the landscape with delicate pastel shades even after the sun's gradual disappearance beyond the horizon. Metamorphosis has begun, the stillness of the frozen world is giving way to the noises of nature's awakening: shrill, crashing sounds of icicles tumbling from the roofs, rhythmic dripping of snow, and the crackle of ice on the lakes, as the solid white changes to a translucent pale blue and the solidity to flowing.

Into this beautiful world, ready to embrace it, eager to feel and smell it, I, Arna Karin Helena, was born twenty minutes before midnight on 31st March 1931, apparently, in a hurry to come out of the darkness of my mother's womb before midnight. Who would wish to be an April fool?

On that evening, my parents Karin and Yrjö, on their leisurely evening stroll in the town of Kuopio, had to quicken their steps to reach the maternity hospital in time; made it. I have no memories of my life in Kuopio, a town that had many family links for both of my parents. Nor could I, as a baby, be aware of the dramatic events that drastically changed Karin's and Yrjö's stable existence. All my baby self needed was safety and to be cared for with love in order to gain trust in the world I had entered.

My mother, Karin Nylenius, had qualified as a dentist in 1925. Joining her aunt, a teacher, and her newly married younger sister, Eva, both already settled in Kuopio, she decided to open her dental surgery in the thriving market town in centre of Finland. My father, Yrjö Pelkonen, newly qualified Forestry Officer, had also arrived into Kuopio in 1925 to find work in the timber business. He was invited to be one of three partners in a small firm 'Savon Puu', set up by Kaarlo Dahlström, his future brother-in law.

Yrjö, needing a dentist, became Karin's patient. Very soon a passionate love affair developed between the patient and his dentist. Karin claimed that she fell in love with Yrjö's beautiful mouth. Yrjö simply fell in love with this attractive Swedish-speaking young woman. The couple decided to marry without delay, thus avoiding the temptation of sinning. Their simple marriage ceremony took place on 18th September 1926 in the small German Church in Helsinki, witnessed only by their two widowed mothers, Amanda and Elin.

On 19th April 1928 baby Rainer was born, prematurely. Struggling to survive, he was weak, would not feed, and caused his learner-parents great anxiety. Mummi Elin, Karin's mother, was called from Helsinki to take care of Rainer. It took no time for the baby to thrive in Mummi Elin's expert care, and for the anxious parents to relax, be delighted and proud of what their love had given them.

Rainer was less than two years old when disaster struck. The financial crisis of America also affected Finland;

exports ceased, particularly the timber trade to Russia. Savon Puu went bankrupt, and Yrjö, in his financial naivety, was made to carry the main loss. He not only lost his job, but the furniture from their home was removed to be auctioned. Karin, not even knowing that she was pregnant, miscarried. A shock but also a relief in their difficult financial circumstances; there wouldn't have been room for another child. The couple were heading towards a major crisis in their marriage. Yrjö, jobless and penniless, sank into a deep depression, locking himself into a space that Karin could not enter. He had failed as the provider for his family, repeating the pattern of his own father, who had died aged 37, leaving his wife to bring up seven children on her own.

Karin was now in charge. They had to survive with her earnings. She, determined not to be defeated, went to the auction rooms, and bid back their furniture with money she had put aside to pay some of her student loan. The home was saved; life had to go on.

In November 1930 Yrjö faced the loss he had most feared: the sudden death of his mother, Amanda Helena, from a heart attack. Strong, beautiful, and courageous Mandi, widowed at 37, was idealised, admired, and deeply respected by all. After her husband Gustav's death, Yrjö, not even five, had been her support and advisor in many matters. He, of all her children, had been particularly close to his mother, and she to him. Yrjö grieved deeply at his mother's death, and withdrew into silence, unable to share his sadness, leaving Karin, now pregnant with me, alone and unsupported. The death had separated them even deeper into two souls unable to reach each other's worlds. Between them they had little emotional space to enjoy the arrival of the new baby. Karin continued working full time until the last minute before I, a healthy, pretty baby girl, was born.

Karin, as soon as allowed, went back to her dentistry. The surgery was part of their flat, so it seemed safe to leave the new-born baby and Rainer, now three years old, in the care of Tyyne, their young maid. Rainer, having been called 'Poju' (little boy), insisted now on being called Rainer, saying, 'I am big, not Poju!'

Karin's breast feeding had to be fitted into the short gaps between her patients. She, her thoughts still with her patient, rushed to the nursery, took me from Tyyne, offering her breast for me to suck, then speedily returned to continue her dentistry work. The mother/baby couple had no time to bond, no time for leisurely reveries, and Karin had no time to just be, holding her baby to her breast. My guess is that young Tyyne gave me a sense of security, and a basic trust in life. She had time, she held me, and looked at me with her loving brown eyes. My fantasy is that the name Tyyne, 'serene' in Finnish, suggests the quality of her care.

Move to Helsinki

In the autumn 1932 Yrjö had begun a pioneering, new career as a forestry officer, specialising in reclaiming swampland an anxious time for him, except for the security of earning a regular salary from the State. He would never have to go through bankruptcy or unemployment again. His new job meant that he spent his summers in the Kainuu area, north Finland, overseeing the reclaiming projects.

During the months from November to May he was in Helsinki working with the Forest Administrative Board.

The move to Helsinki was difficult for Karin. She had a well-established dental practice in Kuopio, now she would need to start again from scratch. As luck would have it, her colleague, May, my godmother, was moving her dental practice into a more prosperous part of the city. She offered Karin the chance to take over her old surgery in a working-class area of Helsinki, thus Karin had a few patients straight away.

For me, a little toddler, the move from Kuopio to Helsinki meant separation from Tyyne, my lovely nanny, who had looked after me from birth. She was my first attachment figure, and her loss, an earthshattering abandonment. I only understood the significance of this abandonment years later through my psychotherapy training. The search for a loving face, and for Tyyne's kind brown eyes continued for years and years, without me consciously knowing what I was searching for. I had cried and cried, and according to Karin it was, 'All Tyyne's fault for having spoilt you.' My loss coincided with Karin's depression, caused not only by the move to an unknown future, but also by Yrjö, struggling with his job, and, for the couple, by the long separations the new job necessitated, not only physically but also emotionally. I was already an adult when Karin told me:

'Deeply unhappy, my eyes filled with tears, I used to push you in your pram. You, my baby Arna did not exist for me, I was in my own sad world.'

What did it mean for the baby in the pram to see a face with tear-filled ice-blue eyes replacing the brown eyes in a smiling, loving face? There was nothing I could do to make Mamma see me. I had to adapt, to fit in, and to survive, convincing myself: 'I do not need anyone. I can manage.'

In the search for somewhere to live in Helsinki, Yrjö's Aunt Milma came to our rescue. She, the Headmistress of the School for the Blind, offered us the top floor of the School, with its high gothic windows, and the view over Töölö Bay.

One vague memory I have from that time is from a cold winter's day, standing looking at the frozen bay, its edge fenced with a barbed wire. I decided to lick the frosty metal wire. My tongue got stuck. I tried to pull it free.

'Ouch, ouch! It hurts. Help!' I cried.

No one came. I pulled harder, felt a knife-sharp pain, and saw blood on the snow, my tongue was free, and I had learned my lesson, never to lick metal on a frosty day again.

In the summer of 1933 God entered our family in a big way. Karin, depressed and unhappy, began seeking help from on high. Having heard that the charismatic preacher Ole Hallesby, from Norway, would be present at a Scandinavian Christian Students' meeting, she decided to attend the meeting. Karin returned home, liberated, having found her Saviour, and she was 'a born-again Christian', having gained a childlike faith in a God always present, always loving and always forgiving. From then on, all her problems were safely put into God's almighty hands. He would give a solution; all you needed was to trust Him. Mamma began preaching at home and outside, using every opportunity to proclaim the wonder of being saved by Jesus. Even using the helpless position of her patients, tied to the dental chair with mouth open, to 'feed' them with

'God's love'. If the poorer patients were unable to pay for their treatment, she reassured them: 'God will pay me in His way.'

Mamma's absolute, unconditional, and irrational belief in God, affected me. I grew up to be a fearless risktaker.

Our home at Museonkatu 37

In the spring of 1934 Karin discovered that she was pregnant with her third child. It was not a good time to have another child; the pregnancy was not planned. In addition, it was marred by a strong pressure from both Yrjö and other close relatives for Karin to have an abortion. She, a Christian, could not even begin to contemplate that option. Feeling let down and unsupported by her husband and wider family, Karin concentrated on finding the family a bigger flat during the summer months when Rainer and I were in Kaihoniemi, looked after by relatives.

The move into our new home was completed in August 1934, and Rainer and I came back from Kaihoniemi to a new home in Helsinki. The building was on a corner site, facing open, wooded land with a path through trees leading to the sea. Mummi Elin now lived within walking distance of us in a small flat and became more involved with our family after the baby was born. Our rented, ground floor flat had three rooms and a kitchen, in a four-storey apartment block. Yrjö used the large living room as his office, Karin and Yrjö also slept there, Rainer and I shared a small room with a bunk bed, and the third room was a dining room with a bed for Alina, the maid.

I remember my early years as happy ones. I was allowed to do my own things and spent time with my imaginary friends or with Rainer. There were grown-ups around: my hardworking, tired or absent Mamma, Isä sitting at his desk, glued to the papers in front of him, and then there was Alina, a small thin girl, fond of me, giving me special goodies, and also providing me with a safe hiding place in the kitchen. The only big disturbance was my brother, Rainer, tall and bossy, teasing me relentlessly, though by now the teasing had become a game, and we were most of the time good friends.

In the autumn of 1934, I had an inkling that something was not quite as it had been. The grown-ups were whispering or speaking in Swedish, Mummi was fussing around Mamma, Isä looked gloomy. Mamma was always tired when she came home from her surgery.

Laila Marit Aurora was born on the third of December 1934. The birth had been long and difficult. The baby cried a lot, she would not feed, she had eczema, an itching, milk allergy, and Mummi decided to look after Laila in her flat. With Laila's birth my world, as I had known it, was shattered. I was three years and eight months old. I, this happy, cute, pretty girl, amusing the grown-ups with my funny sayings, was now ignored. Why were all the grown-ups fussing around this crying little creature? I wondered. I wish they would take her away. Then I got whooping cough. I coughed and coughed. I could not breathe. I felt strangled and was sick. Perhaps now I'll be noticed, I hoped. But instead Mamma just warned me: 'Do not go near the baby.' I didn't understand. What was the point of having a sister, if you were not allowed to go near her?

One day I sneaked to Laila's crib, had a good look at this little bundle, and thought: I might as well try to get on with this little monster. Bending over the crib, I gave Laila a sisterly kiss. The angry grown-ups hurriedly pushed me away.

'We told you not to go near the baby,' they said.

'I only wanted to give Laila a kiss.'

My loud protest was ignored. Of course, it was then my fault that the baby started coughing and became seriously ill. I felt angry with everybody. Nobody loved me. I was bad and sad. Even God punished me; I became cross eyed.

Squinting was part of the process of the pretty princess turning into an ugly frog. I had to start wearing horrible, black-rimmed glasses, and to train the 'lazy eye', a black patch was put over the good eye for an hour each day. Isä, working from home, decided to make this ordeal more pleasant by taking me for a walk along the leafy path leading to the sea, stopping en route to teach me about trees, plants, birds, and squirrels. I was skipping and jumping of joy, so happy to be with my Isä. Taking hold of me, he said: 'I want to show you the correct way of walking. Put your hands behind your back like this, and hold your head high. This will help you in having a good posture.'

My joy was gone, I felt ticked off. Why didn't Isä understand that I was jumping because I was so happy to be with him? I loved my Isä. These daily walks with him are amongst the treasured memories from those years; I was his girl.

Very soon Mamma went back to work. Returning home dead tired, she would lie down on the settee in the living room, closing her eyes and falling asleep almost immediately. Rainer and I, having eagerly waited for her return, felt deeply disappointed. One day Rainer said: 'Let's pretend that mamma is dead'. I agreed. Rainer continued: 'I'll be the vicar; I'll perform the funeral service'.

We found a flower pot, and not to wake Mamma up, we placed it very carefully on her tummy. We knew the procedure in funerals, having quite recently been to Great Aunt Betty's funeral, and began our ceremony with singing a hymn 'Levolle lasken Luojani' (a hymn sung as a lullaby). Rainer then took his place behind mamma's head. Taking a wooden spoon in his hand, he pretended to put soil over Mamma, and uttered the words: 'From earth you have come, to earth you shall return.'

At that point the play had become too serious for me. I was panicking: What, if Mamma is really dead? I jumped up from my seat, and rushed to her, still lying absolutely still. With outstretched arms and bending over Mamma, I pronounced: I am Jesus Christ, I am waking you up from the dead. Karin, rise from the dead. Go to your children.'

By now Mamma could no longer keep still and she burst out into a laugh. I was joyous; Jesus had performed a miracle, and Mamma was back in the land of living.

About that time Mamma became involved with the Oxford Moral Re-armament Movement. Meetings of 'Silent prayers' and 'Listening for God's messages' were held in our home. Rainer and I were allowed to join the group. One day we decided to pray that God would make us into angels. It would be fun to be able to fly. We were kneeling next to each other.

After a while Rainer whispered: 'Do you feel anything happening?'

'No', I replied, but when he asked again, I said: 'Now I can feel a tickle in my back.' We waited and waited; no wings were appearing.

Rainer teased me and fought with me; our play was often quite physical, we would wrestle, have fist fights. Rainer always winning. He could be sadistic and cruel. If I dared to cry, he would mock me: 'You little cry baby, your lips are trembling, ha, ha, ha.'

We shared a bedroom, and had bunk beds, Rainer sleeping in the top bunk. Often in the evenings Rainer begged me to join him in his bed. I refused and refused, but Rainer insisted; eventually I gave in, and climbed up to his bed. It was cosy to be there, close to my big brother. I think there was a need to be physically close to somebody, as our parents gave few cuddles to us. There was also curiosity about each other's bodies. Rainer was keen to show me his little willy, and touch my bottom.

Working at home, Isä was the parent coming to say good night to us. He had on a few occasions discovered that we were both in the top bunk. With a stern voice, he had ordered me to climb down and go immediately into my bed. One day, discovering again, both of us in Rainer's bed, Isä became extremely angry. He ushered Rainer to the bathroom and gave him a good hiding. Then it was my turn to get a few lashes from his belt. His fierce reaction to our innocent 'sex play', made me feel we had committed a great, punishable sin, and that we were thoroughly bad children. Why otherwise would my loving Isä be so horrible and beat me? Isä's disproportionate reaction to our need of cuddles and hugs affected my attitude to sex into my adulthood.

Another incident, affecting me greatly, is from the same time. Aged four, sitting at the dining table, I was refusing to eat the food put on my plate. Angrily, Mamma said:

'Finish your meal, Arna. How many times do we have we ask you?'

'I am not hungry,' I insisted.

'You must be ill, if you are not hungry,' said the grown-ups.

I remember several people forcing me to eat.

'I am not ill; I am not hungry.' I repeated, now shouting. But my protests were ignored.

'Hurry up and empty your plate'.

Then, the threat was repeated: 'If you are not eating, you'll be put to bed.'

I shouted at the top of my voice:' I AM NOT HUNGRY!'

My protest was again ignored. The grown-ups simply picked me up, carried me to the bedroom, and, undressed me by force while I kicked and continued to protest: 'I AM NOT ILL!!'

My clothes were removed. I was naked, but managed to free myself from the grip of the holding adult, dart to the front door, open it, run down the stairs out to the street, and carry on running some three hundred metres or so before being caught. Screaming, I was carried in, and put to bed.

I was never allowed to forget this incident; the story was repeatedly told. Rainer taking special pleasure in telling the tale to other children in the flats: 'Arna was running NAKED along the streets of Helsinki.'

I call this event 'The taming of the wild horse' and see it as a turning point. Yes, the wild horse was tamed, but at what price? My free spirit was squashed, I was forced to accept the power of authority. I became obedient, had to ask to be forgiven, and had to make a promise to be good. I lost trust in the grown-ups. The truth was, I was not hungry and I was not ill.

Laila, having been in Mummi's care, returned home looking like a little princess. Mummi had made her a white coat, a white bonnet, and a scarf. My coat was horrid green, I had black-rimmed glasses, and was feeling like a beggar's daughter.

Maybe I am an orphan that my parents have adopted out of pity. These thoughts were part of the disappearance of my happy world. I was stealing, being naughty and rebellious. Alina was my only friend.

Rainer started in the elementary school at the age of seven, and I lost my playmate. A year later, aged five, I expressed a wish to learn Swedish. Mamma found a Swedish nursery school, not too far, except that there was a busy main street to cross. It was taken for granted I would walk there on my own. One day, just as I had started crossing the road, a bus full of passengers appeared from nowhere. The driver managed to slam the breaks on; an accident was avoided. I could see a mass of angry looking faces, all pointing their fingers at me and scolding me:

'You, naughty girl, why didn't you look before you started crossing?'

I had looked! I was longing for just one person to say something kind, but there was no-one.

Mamma, feeling sorry for me, decided to give me a little treat.

'Let's go to the shop, and buy the ring you wanted.'

I had chosen one with a blue stone, but Mamma decided to buy a different one. I tried to protest.

'I don't like that one. I want this one with a blue stone.'

Of course, Mamma ignored me, went ahead, and bought her choice.

This is not fair, I thought as I slipped the ring of my choice into my pocket. The theft, the terrible crime, was of course discovered as soon as we got home.

Mamma was horrified. 'How can you, my child, be a thief?'

The consequence of this great crime was a journey of repentance. Mamma dragged me back to the shop, where I had to return the ring, confess my sin, beg for forgiveness. Back at home, Mamma and I prayed to God for forgiveness; Mamma always accepted herself as a co-sinner.

Move to Käpylä, Sampsantie 40, in 1937

Käpylä is a garden suburb east of Helsinki, with a tramline running through its main, tree-lined street. Behind the trees there were rows of pastel coloured, small wooden, semi-detached family houses. Our new home was not one of these houses; instead a flat in one of the four-storey apartment buildings on the edge of the garden suburb, at Sampsantie 40; another rented property, a three bedroomed ground-floor flat. Our maid, tiny, kind-hearted Alina moved with us. She slept on a wooden bed in an alcove that was part of the kitchen. I spent a lot of time sitting at the kitchen table talking with Alina.

For a while Mamma kept her old dental practice, a tram ride away, but soon she managed to rent a two-roomed flat for her surgery within a walking distance from our new home. Mummi agreed to move to live in the flat, and to become Mamma's receptionist. She rented out her flat in the centre of Helsinki, and earned a little extra money to top up her meagre widow's pension. These arrangements worked well, she helped Karin, and was easily accessible to us.

The apartments' residents were mainly families with young children. Behind the building we had open countryside, grassy fields and a mound of large rocks. All you needed was to run out and you would find plenty of playmates. Mirja, two years older than me, a thin, unkempt, pale girl from a poor, single parent family, soon became my best friend. She had a rich and wonderful imagination. Together we invented and played out many long-lasting stories. A favourite play started by a simply overheard sentence, spoken in Swedish, by two teenaged girls: 'And I danced with him four, five dances.'

Seeing these excited girls and hearing that sentence, Mirja and I started repeating these words every time someone passed us. Before long, our fantasies had created a complicated story from that simple starting point. We became two beautiful daughters of a count. Our stately home was created from the highest rocks in the field. We spoke in a posh way, we went to dances in stunningly beautiful gowns, and we were full of our own aristocratic importance. Gradually, we became bored. It was not much fun being so perfect all the time.

So we invented a parallel story: Two ugly, naughty and horrid daughters, Manta and Miina of a butcher Makkarakoski (Mr. Sausagemaker). He was a widower, and these two girls were out of their father's control. Their humble home was at the edge of the playing field, amongst the small rocks. In this play we used freely, and with great pleasure, forbidden words like 'shit' and 'piss'; foul language, and swearwords like 'perkele' (devil) 'helvetti' (hell). We did bad things: we stole, threw stones at windows, we fought with boys, winning every time, and we ate as many sweets as we wanted.

Having enjoyed my nursery school, I was ready, and wanted to go to a proper school. Being only six I was not accepted to the large Finnish school, where the starting age was seven. There was a Swedish elementary school on the other side of the main road. The story told is this:

'Arna walked into the classroom of this little school, sat down and announced:

"I want come to be a pupil, and come to this school." The amazed teacher accepted her.'

It did not take long before my Swedish improved, and at home I spoke Swedish to Mamma. In September 1938, I wrote to Isä in Swedish:

'Kära Pappa. När kommer du hem? Jag har ledsamt efter pappa. Lämna inte bilen dit. Vill du komma snabbt hem? Kom så snart du bara kan. Gud välsigne dig pappa. Din egen flicka Arna' (Dear Daddy. When are you coming home? I miss you, Daddy. Do not leave the car behind there. Are

you coming home soon? Come as quickly as you can. God bless you, Daddy. Your own girl, Arna)

The two years from 1937 to 1939 were happy times for the whole family. Karin's new surgery was close to home, and Mummi gave us a feeling of security we had not experienced before, and we each found new playmates of our own age. Laila had by now grown much stronger, and was fun to be with. She, wanting to be a boy, found her friends among the little boys living in various flats.

Learning to know so many other families, I became aware that our family was quite different: our mother was not at home, she worked, and she was a dentist. Our mother spoke Swedish and we spoke Swedish to her, we called her 'Mamma', not 'Äiti'. Our father, with whom we spoke Finnish, was only at home for the darkest winter months, then disappeared for months and months. The most important thing was that our Isä was the only one who had a car.

When Isä was at home, he liked being with his children, teaching, guiding and taking an interest in us. He taught Laila and me to skate and ski; we would make long skiing excursions to the surrounding forests and hills. There was a ski-jumping hill quite close. Rainer, of course, had already managed to do the jump, and came down the hill without falling. Now Isä was challenging Laila and me to be brave enough to ski downhill without falling. As a prize he promised special bindings to be fitted into our skis. I can well remember how scared I was the first time I stood on top of the hill, looking down at the steep slope, and into the distance to the ground. I'll never manage, I thought. The speed was fast, I fell, and came tumbling down, but was keen to try again. Eventually, I managed to stand up all the way and won my new bindings. Laila failed.

There was also an ice-skating rink near the flats, and again Isä was there, guiding us through the first wobbly steps on the ice. The ice rink, with music blaring from the loudspeakers, was a natural meeting place. All you needed was to skate around, sooner or later one of your friends would catch up with you and skate with you. Or we would skate into a corner to practise figure skating.

Winter was a fun time. Not only did we skate and ski, we also had sledges. Joining many chair-sledges into one long train, then the last person gave a kick start before jumping on the sledge, and down we would go, shouting and laughing as the 'train' was gathering faster and faster speed. Often, we would crash, no serious injuries, just part of the fun.

Another new discovery was the library. Mirja, a regular user, took me there. Week after week I borrowed and returned children's books. Then one day I borrowed a book from the adult section *'Mylly joen Rannalla'* **(**'Mill on the Floss'**)** by George Eliot**.** I can to this day remember how impressed I was with the girl Maggie. I thought, here is a writer, who knows what it is to be a child, and who knows how to describe what a child feels.

By the end of April, Isä began his preparations for his fieldwork up in Kainuu, where he would stay until the end of October. His car, a grey Ford, was taken out from its winter garage. Parked in the back yard, it drew both admiration and envy from children and adults.

The month of May was a transitional time, often warm; a metamorphosis to summer life with the light increasing daily. Thick long, prickly stockings were exchanged for white knee-socks, woollen underpants stored away in moth-balls, winter boots exchanged for pretty shoes, and new summer dresses were bought or made. People looked happy and were light-hearted. Summer was on its way.

This metamorphosis was marked with 'Vappu' (the first of May) celebrations. Having started as a labour day, Vappu had become not only a day for workers but also a feasting day for students, ancient and young, all wearing their white caps. In my childhood the whole nation joined in celebrating the increasing light and warmth. Even the cows joined in; on the first of May they were let out from their sheds to the fields.

Partying started already on the Eve, carrying on all night, and continuing the whole Vappu Day. Already jolly from their parties, early on Vappu morning the students marched to the Market Square, near the harbour. They stopped in front of 'Havis Amanda', a statue of a nude woman, standing in a pool of water, with fountains sprinkling her beautiful body. The annual challenge was for one of the male students to jump into the water, take his shirt off, and dress Havis Amanda's nude body with it.

As the sun was rising, the march carried on towards the top of the hill near the harbour, where the male students, joining the birds in their dawn chorus, burst into song, and marched, singing and merry making, through the streets of Helsinki.

How I loved Vappu. Our whole family headed towards the centre of town to join the celebrating masses. Isä and Mamma, having dug out their yellowed white caps, looked so young, happy and free, and would tell tales of their student days. We drank 'sima' (mead), ate 'tippaleipiä' (a special Vappu treat made of cake mixture poured through a funnel into hot fat, making a 'bird's nest'), and had ice creams. Isä bought us balloons and paper whisks.

One special treat Isä offered us, as well as the children from the flats, was a Vappu outing in his car. I do not remember how many he managed to squeeze in, but I do remember the car bulging with children. On those occasions Isä was one of us, joking, laughing, so obviously pleased in pleasing us. A great way to end celebrations.

In the Finnish year, springs changing to summers are magic. In May the white nights are there, and with the school holidays beginning on the first of June, a mass exodus to the country begins. Every Finn wants to make use of this annual wonder of nature, heading for their cottage on the shores of one of the thousands and thousands of lakes.

For us, the end of the school year meant the long, annual separation from our parents, and from town life. We, Rainer, Laila and I, were heading to Isä's childhood home, our summer paradise, 'Kaihoniemi', in Karelia.

My grandmother Amanda Helena with her six children: Juuso, Yrjö, Jaakko, Kaarlo, Amanda, Laina and Ester, 1904

Kaihoniemi, the main house. built 1901

Chapter Two

Kaihoniemi, my Summer Paradise

My grandparents, Gustav and Amanda Pelkonen, had barely had ten happy years together when Gustav, the vicar in charge of the Finnish Parish in Narva, Estonia, died aged 37 of tuberculosis, in early May 1902. During those ten years eight children had been born, one of them, a baby girl, lived only two weeks. Amanda Helena (Mandi) alone, sad, lost, and bewildered, was now a single parent of her seven children: Ester, the first born not even nine, then came Laina, eight, Kaarlo, six, Yrjö, not yet five, Juuso, four, Martta, three, and baby Jaakko, only one year old. The enormity of Gustav's death hit her with full force, and she realised the full consequences of the family's loss, saying to herself:' I am 36 years old, a widow. In a few months' time a new vicar will be arriving, and I'll be homeless with my seven children.'

Amanda had no other choice except to move with her children to their newly built summer house in Karelia. In May 1903, with sorrow in their hearts, she and the seven children left the Narva vicarage. The move did not go as smoothly as Amanda had planned and hoped. The little sunshine girl, three-year old Martta, had caught TB from her father and, in spite of all the tender care, she, 'God's little angel', joined her father within only a few months from the onset of her illness. Another heart-breaking loss for the family to face before they had arrived back in Finland.

With all their belongings, they were heading for Jaakkima, a small town on the shores of Lake Ladoga, where several of Amanda's siblings had already settled. As soon as the seriousness of Gustav's tuberculosis was understood, he and Amanda had bought farming land in 1901. A large timber villa, meant for summer use only, would be the orphaned family's new home. Amanda named it '*Kaihoniemi*' (the cape of tender longing). The memories of love and loss were so tangible in Kaihoniemi even I could sense them.

Amanda and her children stayed in Kaihoniemi for the first few years after Gustav's death. Soon after their move two tasks seemed to have priority for Amanda. Firstly, she planted trees around the peninsula, as a protection from the cold north-easterly winds. Secondly, in Gustav's memory, she created a most beautiful flower garden.

It's not difficult to imagine how hard these initial years must have been: an orphaned family in a cold, large, and strange building; no running water, no electricity. In the winter months log fires provided the only heating, which ate up huge piles of logs. These had to be chopped daily, and then carried to the house. Luckily, milk and farm produce were available from the farm close by, and owned by Amanda's brother Jussi, a teacher. In my childhood the farm was managed by his son Esko, and Laura, his wife. Mandi was surrounded by members of her large extended family, and with their support the family survived. The two oldest, Ester and Laina, needed to continue their education, but there was no school within a walking distance. Mandi found a solution by persuading her niece Aino, aged seventeen, to leave her own studies, and become a home tutor. Aino agreed, providing her two brothers Aito and Eino were allowed to join the tutoring group.

After a couple of years life became easier. Mandi obtained a teaching post in Viipuri, the main town of Karelia. The family moved to Viipuri for the winter months. From then on, their life followed the normal Finnish pattern: winters were lived in towns, and summers at their dachas in the country. Kaihoniemi remained a shared, much-loved summer home for all the family. In my childhood the house was run by Great-Aunt Auroora, Mandi's older sister, already retired, and Aunt Laina; two spinster-teachers with three months' long summer holidays. My grandmother Mandi had died before I was born.

'There is always summer in Kaihoniemi,' was my enthusiastic, eulogising remark on returning home to Helsinki after one of the long summers spent in Karelia. Even today I think with love and yearning of those long, sunny, innocent childhood summers, lost forever, but sealed in my heart as precious memories. For Rainer, Laila and me, life in Kaihoniemi was an immersion into an exciting, wonderous, at times mysterious world of both sunshine, love, and happiness as well as many stories of loss, sadness, and danger.

As the end of May approached my parents began to make the necessary arrangements for handing over our care to Aunt Laina and Great Aunt Auroora. Our maid would be accompanying us to give the aunts practical help in caring for us. Mamma came to Kaihoniemi for part of her short summer holiday; the other part she spent with Isä up in Kainuu. Isä, in his turn, came for two or three short visits during the summer months.

Our travelling arrangements were as follows: Rainer, Laila and our maid travelled by train. I was the privileged one, accompanying Isä in his grey Ford, sitting next to him, as his 'dame', heading first to Viipuri to pick up Aunt Laina and Great Aunt Auroora.

The journey from Helsinki to Viipuri was on winding country roads and took long enough for us to need an overnight stop in a small guest/farmhouse. One journey, when I was four years old, is still vividly in my memory. In the early evening Isä pulled into the yard of a large farmhouse, surrounded by several outbuildings. We were taken into their guest room. It had only one double bed for us to share. I was given a glass of fresh milk and a sandwich. Exhausted by the journey, I went straight to bed and fell asleep.

As I opened my eyes the next morning, I couldn't remember where I was; all looked strange. I noticed a folded blanket on the bed. Someone had slept next to me. But who? Then I remembered our journey. Where had Isä gone? Had he abandoned me, left me behind, and resumed the journey on his own?' Fear and panic arose in me.

'Isä, where are you?' I cried.

No answer. My heart jumped to my throat, the panic and dread increased. I opened the door: silence. Nobody there.

'Help, Isä has left me, he has abandoned me!' Still in my night dress, I ran like a frightened animal out to the yard, shouting, 'Isä, Isä, where are you?' I could not see him in the yard, so I ran behind the buildings. Then, finally, in the back yard, I saw him, bent over his car. Running into his arms, I burst into tears.

He seemed bemused by my panic, gave me a hug, and said in his calm, reassuring manner, 'Arna, all is well, I was just checking the car. Hurry up, get dressed, we are leaving for Viipuri.'

I was so relieved and happy, I rushed back and got dressed. Travelling in my new pale blue coat with a matching hat, I was looking forward to showing off the outfit to the two aunts.

Isä's home town, Viipuri (Vyborg), the capital of Karelia, has a long history. As we approached the city, we could see the massive Viipurin linna (Vyborg Castle) on a rocky island. The castle was built in 1293 during the third crusade, then new parts had been added. Isä pointed out many fine buildings, we drove past his school, and the modern library, which did not impress me. Only later I found out that it was designed by Alvar Aalto, Finland's most famous architect. Isä did not think of telling me.

The two aunts were pleased to see us. Neither of them noticed my new outfit. I was simply ordered to take my coat and hat off. I did not remove my beautiful hat. Aunt Laina, hunchback, with her bulging fish-eyes looked at me sternly.

'Arna, take your hat off.'

I refused, still hoping she would say something nice, at least, about my hat. Aunt Laina repeated her demand, I refused, and said, 'Ladies are allowed to wear a hat indoors.'

Amused, Great Aunt Auroora smiled, nodding her approval. My hat stayed on. Aunt Laina looked furious; her authority had been undermined. I was scared of her. She became 'Lain täti' (aunt of law's), my 'witch' godmother, always critical, always displeased with me.

We had a light lunch, then the journey continued. Looking old and dignified, Great Aunt Auroora, in her black long dress and starched petticoat, filled the front seat. Even Aunt Law looked a different person, happy and smiling, so pleased to begin her long holiday.

Our journey took us to Jaakkima, some 150 kilometres from Viipuri, and glimpses of Lake Ladoga became visible. Excited, I knew that we'd soon be in the summer paradise.

'Isä, can I go swimming?'

'We have to heat the sauna first, the water is too cold to just rush in,' said sensible Isä. 'You can help by bringing some logs to the sauna.'

Driving through Jaakkima to Lahdenpohja, the small town on the shore of Lake Ladoga, we turned onto a sandy, narrow road. There was the lake on the left side, and soon a bay on the right side became visible. On the other side of the bay stood a high, steep, vertical cliff, called 'Annan Riutta' (Anna's cliff), named after a young maiden, who was chased by a Russian solder. In desperation Anna, in fear of being raped, jumped from the cliff and drowned. Anna's sad story was one of the many stories that filled my imagination. Kaihoniemi to me seemed a mysterious place, surrounded by fairy stories that became alive.

We had reached the cape of 45 acres of land, all part of Kaihoniemi. Facing us was a large, red log building; what a wonderful, welcoming sight for each of us. The house had eight spacious rooms. On the ground floor the large drawing room had doors to the hall, to the library room, and to a roomy glass veranda. The veranda was furnished with a rocking chair, a table, chairs and a wooden settee, and had steps leading to the garden.

The living room had windows facing both the lake and the garden, and held the furniture brought from the home in Narva: an antique table, settee and chairs, a grand piano. The room looked more like the parlour of a vicarage than one in a country dacha. Above the grand piano hung large, framed photographs of my grandparents and my two uncles, Kaarlo and Juuso who had both died in their late teens. Behind the settee on a pedestal stood a white statue of Christ with open arms, offering his blessing to the house and its occupants, a smaller version of the famous 'Christ' statue by the Danish sculptor Thorvaldsen. The timber walls had been covered with a rose-patterned wallpaper. Upstairs were four bedrooms, and a spacious landing, leading to a large balcony, overlooking the garden.

Lingering in each room, imagining the life of the Pelkonen family, I could see the six children running around, trying to settle into their new world; the two oldest, Ester and Laina busily helping their mother the best they could. Music gave the fatherless family solace. Ester was an excellent piano player, Yrjö played the violin, and both Amanda and Yrjö, with their beautiful singing voices, sang duets. Isä's childhood, though not talked about, was alive and pulsating in my mind: the rooms, the furniture and the walls all held within them secrets, memories, and the untold stories of loss, of bravery and of happiness.

Now, as an adult, I can understand why these stories were never voiced. The enormity and the depth of their loss could not be shared. There can't be a greater loss for a young family than the loss of the father, or for a young wife the loss of her husband. Everything changed with that one event; the impact lasting through their whole lives, and continued to the next generation. Gustav became a saint. The horror and anger of his death was carried within the hearts of the survivors. The story tells that, once a week, Amanda walked the ten-kilometres to the cemetery, using these lonely journeys as her silent grieving process. The remarkable Amanda Helena struggled as a single parent over the first difficult years. Then, just as she thought the family's path was safe, fate gave her two more heart breaking losses: first, her firstborn son Kaarlo, in his teens, died suddenly of meningitis, and then Juuso, a year younger than Yrjö, gave his life for Finland in the civil war 1918. How I wish I would have heard more of what my two of my uncles were like, or would have known my grandparents, especially my grandfather, the enigmatic Gustav, the father my father never had.

The memory of Amanda Helena, my grandmother, was still acutely felt in my childhood. The trees she planted had grown high, her garden, with its winding paths, was full of colour, and a rich variety of flowers. I could sense the tender longing and sorrow held in Kaihoniemi, and the solace Amanda found working on her garden.

Kaihoniemi was surrounded by houses belonging to the Pelkonen clan. Mandi, my grandmother was the youngest of nine siblings, and all of them had houses quite close. Our closest neighbour was my great uncle Jussi. He had a farm,

'Toivoranta' from where we picked up our milk each day. His son Esko with his wife Laura and their only daughter Pirjo shared the house. Pirjo, who was my age, and I were inseparable during the summer months. The rest of the clan had their houses on the other side of a narrow sound, on the land that had belonged to the family since 1860. Once in the summer months, on 31st of July, on Helena's name day, they all arrived with their rowing or motorboats across the lake to Kaihoniemi. It was the highlight of the summer, a day of remembering their sister Amanda Helena, and a great opportunity for the whole extended family to come together. Coffee, lemonade, cakes, strawberries and home-made ice-cream was served. We, about thirty second cousins of all ages, had a real fun day. Rainer arranged running competitions, we played ball games, some of us went swimming, the older girls stayed together gossiping, ignoring Pirjo and me. We did not mind; we joined the boys in their games. Pirjo was pixielike, full of fun, and always ready for some pranks. Her blonde, fine hair was almost white, her eyes light blue. Whenever we were allowed, we had 'sleepovers' in each other's houses.

Mamma, after her short visit to see us, wrote in a letter in 1934 to Isä:

'The day before I left for Helsinki, we and many other relations had all gathered to celebrate Helena day in Kaihoniemi. Arna created lot of attention, and she conquered every one's hearts. She had her new light blue dress on, she looked so pretty, lovely in fact, and she was so free. One of the guests asked her: 'Whose girl are you?' 'I am my Mamma's girl.' 'Who is your Mamma?' 'She has a blue dress on, come with me, I'll show you.' They came to

the room where I sat, and Arna came close to me and said: 'Here is my Mamma.' Before we said our goodbyes, we sang, Arna joining in the singing. When it ended, she carried on singing solo, and all the guests started laughing. Many of the ladies were asking could Arna come and visit them.'

I have always loved my third name, Helena, and wished I would have been called Helena not Arna. When about six, I decided simply to become Helena, and also to have a new surname: 'Karikoski', a translation from the Swedish surname 'Holmström'. Helena Karikoski sounded so much better than Arna Pelkonen, particularly as Arna was a name not heard of in Finland, and frequently confused with Arno and Arne, both names for boys.

Back to Kaihoniemi. The plot of land had, in addition to the main house, several smaller buildings: two smaller buildings for people managing the farm to live in, a children's playhouse near the main building, the sauna, a log building on the lakeshore. Quite close to the house, some 150 meters away up a gentle slope, was a two-storey building, containing the woodshed, and on the top floor, the privy, with four small holes for children and, on a higher level, four for adults. I never understood why the privy had so many holes and had to be on the first floor. (Apparently, it was so that the muck could be emptied by using a horse and a cart.) For a child in a hurry, the distance to the privy seemed extremely long, and accidents happened. One day, when I was perhaps five, this happened to me. I had delayed and delayed. The shit came out, filled my pants before I reached a hole. Oh, dear, what will Aunt Law say? I thought to myself. Rather than face her scolding, I decided to just drop my dirty pants into the faeces below, then run to the lake and wash my bottom. I sneaked in, picking up clean pants, and pleased that my 'crime' had been sorted out neatly. But, oh no, of course Aunt Law had been watching me.

'Arna, come here,' she shouted, taking hold of my hand. Together we marched towards the privy and climbed the stairs. I was scared. I guessed what was going to happen. Aunt Law and I were now at the level of the small holes. She lifted the lid, and made me look down.

'What do you think I can see down there? Might it be your pants?' Without waiting for my answer, Aunt Law gave me an order. 'Fish the pants out, take them to the lake, wash them, and present the cleaned pants to me.'

Feeling humiliated, and angry with Aunt Law, I had no option except do what I was told. Picking up a long stick, I managed to separate the pants from all the surrounding shitty mess and to fish them onto the stick. Holding my nose with one hand, I carried the pants with the other, dangling at the furthest end of the stick, to the lake. Dumping the pants into the water, I put a big stone on them, hoping waves would do the first cleaning, then fetched a piece of soap from the sauna.

A contrast to the critical, strict, humourless Aunt Law, was my Great Aunt Auroora. She was my replacement 'Mummi', my other grandmother. She was gentle, kind, and wise, and to my eyes, very old. I have a dear memory of seeing her, sitting in the rocking chair in the glass veranda, holding me on her lap, Laila in her pram close to her, Rainer nowhere to be seen. Great Aunt Auroora was telling us stories or reading her Bible aloud. One day, reading the Sermon on the Mount, she decided to dedicate a verse to each of us. Laila's was: *'How blest are those whose hearts are pure; they shall see God'*. Mine was: *'How blest are the peacemakers; God shall call them his sons'*. I treasured my verse, and tried to act as a peacemaker in situations where opposite sides were arguing; I was even a go-between Mamma and Isä.

Great Aunt Auroora was one of the first qualified female teachers, teaching in a Finnish language co-educational secondary school. As her retirement present, she had received a beautiful gold watch to be worn like a medallion around the neck on a gold chain. Each evening she performed the same ritual: She removed her watch and chain slowly and carefully, holding them for a while in her hand, then lovingly, as if putting a baby into a cot, placed her watch and chain onto a stand on the bedside table. One evening, as I was watching her, she took the watch from the stand, put it gently into my hand, and looking at me with her wise, kind eyes, she said, 'When I die, this watch will be yours.' Pointing to the engraved initials *A.P*, in the centre of the flower garland, she added, 'Look, your initials are already there.'

In late October Pirjo, aged five, lost her Mummi, Great Uncle Jussi's wife Iines. The funeral was in Toivoranta and I accompanied Isä. Up to then, there is always summer in Kaihoniemi, had been my belief. What a shock to see the dark, grey, sunless sky and the muddy puddles left by rain. No flowers, no leaves on trees, only a few yellow leaves still hanging on the birches. The world looked depressingly sad, echoing how sad Pirjo must have felt. Her grandparents had been caring for Pirjo and shared the house with Pirjo's family since her birth.

Mummi had knitted me a white dress to wear for the funeral. I had travelled in a navy-blue skirt and a striped jumper, and Mummi had instructed me to leave changing into the white dress until just before the funeral. On the morning of the funeral, with still some hours to go, I begged and begged Isä, 'Please, please, let me put the white dress on now. I promise to be careful.'

'It's still hours before the funeral, you'll have time to make the dress dirty,' said Isä.

'I promise, I promise to be careful,' I reassured him.

Finally, Isä agreed, stressing the importance of keeping the dress spotless. Delighted and excited, desperately wanting to show it off to Pirjo, I quickly changed into this lovely, white dress. I ran out to the farmyard, skipping happily, carefully avoiding puddles, looking for Pirjo, but she was nowhere to be seen. Then I saw her walking towards the house. She noticed me, and rushed towards me, and I began running towards her. Disaster happened, I stumbled and fell into one of those muddy puddles.

'Oh, please, please help! What do I do now?' I cried. My white dress was ruined, wet and grey. I started to sob, feeling so ashamed, so miserable, and so afraid. Of course, what I had been warned about had now happened and of course, as I walked in, there was Aunt Law, finger pointing and scolding.

'You naughty girl, why did you put your white dress on? You had been told not to. Go and change back to the dress you travelled in.' Turning to Isä, she ticked him off. 'You should have known how careless Arna is. What made you give in to her thoughtless request?'

I felt so bad that, in addition, my lovely daddy was being blamed for my sins. My punishment and humiliation was to attend the funeral in my plain navy skirt and striped top. The memory of the shame still makes me blush!

That same winter, some six months later, Great Aunt Auroora died. I was not told when she died or who went to the funeral. In vain I waited for the promised gold watch. Great Aunt had made a promise, she had kept it, that I knew, but what had happened? I never dared to ask Aunt Law. I felt angry and let down: this was another confirmation that grown-ups couldn't be trusted. Gradually, I forgot the watch.

When I was fourteen, I was confirmed. On that day, as my confirmation present, Aunt Law put into my hand a pretty, blue heart shaped pocket, embroidered with flowers, and on the back, there was a pin to fix the pocket to my skirt. Inside the pocket was Great Aunt Auroora's golden watch, without its chain. Aunt Law knew, and was right, that I, a young girl, wouldn't be willing to wear a watch on a chain around my neck. She had found a solution. I was so proud to show off the gold watch and point out my initials on it. Finally, Great Aunt Auroora's promised gift was mine.

Some weeks passed, then, out of the blue, Aunt Law came marching in, holding something in her hand, and calling me to come and look: a wrist watch with a brown strap.

'Arna, I can see you are not taking good enough care of the gold watch. I am going to take it back into my care. I'll give you this wrist watch instead,' she said.

I had no say in the matter. She took what was mine, and presented me with a cheap wrist watch as a replacement. I was speechless. Stupidly, I assumed that at least after Aunt Law's death, the watch would be handed back to me. Not so, instead I discovered from Laila what had happened. As a present from Aunt Law for passing her matriculation examinations, Laila had received a golden locket with a chain. The locket turned out to be the outer case of my watch. Aunt Law had had the audacity to remove the clockwork, presenting Laila the empty case as a medallion. How I hated Aunt Law for her theft and betrayal.

During the summer, Kaihoniemi was full of spinster aunts, second cousins, and their friends, many of them teachers. The special highlight was Isä's sister, Aunt Ester's arrival for her holiday from London. Ester had had a fairy story life; she had worked in America and Russia, now she was in London, working as a senior clerk in the Finnish Legation. Ester was tiny, delicate, with green, laughing eyes. She had a slightly humped back like her sister Laina; the reason given for the humps was all the starching and ironing of clothes Ester and Laina were responsible for as the two girls in the family.

Ester, totally different from Aunt Law, was free. She smoked, wore nail polish, was beautifully dressed, had a modern hairstyle. She was 'a woman of the world'.

Ester brought us expensive, special gifts. I remember Laila's soft donkey with a yellow waistcoat, and green velvet trousers, her favourite, always to be carried with her. 'Rippe' was my toy dog, a fox terrier, so lifelike that other dogs came to sniff it. The most precious gift was my baby doll, with the head made of china, eyes that closed, and she could say, 'Mummy'. I called her Elizabeth, as pictures of the two British princesses were seen in many magazines. Rainer, her godson, always received some special presents. How I envied him for having Ester, a real fairy godmother as his godmother.

Each summer Pirjo's father, Esko, arranged an over-night fishing trip to the outer islands of Lake Ladoga for those who were staying at that time in Kaihoniemi. Pirjo's mother Laura came to help with the catering. Rainer, the only one from us children, was allowed to join the grown-ups in these over-night trips. Esko had a big, powerful motorboat with a cabin to take shelter from high waves and rain. Second in charge Rainer sat very proudly next to Esko, and was allowed to steer the boat in the calmer waters.

Finally, in the summer, when Pirjo and I, were six, we were given permission to join the overnight fishing party. We were so excited, jumping of joy, helping to carry baskets containing essential paraphernalia: enamelled mugs, plates and a coffee pot, another one with bread, butter, milk etc. to the boat. We also needed several blankets to lie on for the night. Pirjo and I made ourselves a cosy little place on the boat in the prow, wrapping ourselves in 'Molander's coat', a black, warm winter coat, big enough for both of us to crawl under it, and be lulled by the waves. We did not care who this Molander was; it kept us warm. Much later I discovered that the coat had belonged to Amanda Molander, my grandfather Gustav's mother. Having delivered her baby from the safety of her womb, she had herself returned to the black womb of the Mother Earth, abandoning little Gustav.

As the journey proceeded, Pirjo and I joined the party outside, being in the blackness was no longer fun. The boat was passing island after island, some with summer houses, going through narrow sounds, the speed was cut down, and then, in front of us was the open, vast, immense grey green sea. What a sight; I had never been so far out on the Lake Ladoga, no land visible, just water and sky melting into one. Big waves were rocking the boat, hitting it, and splashing us with icy water; the sky was clear, some white clouds, a typical hot summer's day, but chilly on the open sea. After a couple of hours, we could see on the horizon a rocky island, and, coming closer, the dome of Valamo monastery, the Russian Orthodox monastery. The first monk, a Greek, had settled on the island in 992, and was followed by monk Herman; they two had brought with them Christianity.

After Finland's Independence in 1917, Valamo became part of the Finnish Republic. The monks deciding to remain there and received the Finnish citizenship. They developed Valamo to a sought-after pilgrimage and tourist destination. Daily boats from Sortavala ferried tourists and pilgrims to Valamo. I had asked Aunt Law to take me there, and had been told, 'Not until you are ten years old.' In the end, I had to wait until I was 82 years old for my visit to Valamo, and for a swim, once again, in Lake Ladoga.

After we had passed Valamo, other new outer islands began to appear. Esko, knowing the islands, steered his boat towards the one he had chosen for us. He began circling around it for a good landing place in a sheltered bay with a small sandy beach. Rainer, Pirjo and I jumped off the boat, ran up the smooth cliffs to the top, and then searched for a flat enough surface where we could spread our blankets. Back down the cliffs to the boat helping to carry our belongings. It was now early afternoon, the cliffs were hot, burning our bare feet.

'Can we go swimming?' we implored.

Aunt Law, the spoilsport's reply, 'Not until you have collected sticks for the campfire. I assume you want to eat?'

Of course, we were all hungry. As the fire was burning, we were allowed to run to the lake.

First in the water, I shouted, 'Fie! Icy cold.'

That didn't spoil our fun. We jumped from the cliffs into the water over and over again, until the charred smell of the burnt sausages reached our nostrils. Quickly drying ourselves, up the cliff we ran; we were starving. The blackened sausages were manna from heaven. Strawberries for dessert, what more could you wish for? A coffee pot was hanging from a fork, brewing a heavenly drink for the grown-ups.

The women busied themselves clearing up, Rainer went to help Esko with the fishing nets, and Pirjo and I were given the freedom to explore the island. Initially, just running wildly, we soon slowed our steps.

Pirjo, looking worried, said, 'What if there are wild animals?'

'Don't be so stupid,' I said.

Pirjo did not give up. 'They might have walked across in winter and got trapped when the ice thawed.'

'Ok, let's go and look. Take a strong stick,' I said.

We found sweet blueberries, stopped to eat a few mouths full, and wandered on. We found a better beach between high cliffs, and decided to have another swim, leaving our clothes on the sand.

'The water's warmer here,' I assured Pirjo, as I was running full speed into the water. 'Help!' I screamed, 'I am nearly out of my depth. Pirjo, take care, come slowly.'

Now we were scared; neither of us could swim properly. Our fun came to a quick end. 'Best not to tell the grown-ups,' we decided as we hastened our way back to the campsite. Soon we could see the red glow of the embers and feel the warmth of the log fire; we were safe!

It was already evening. 'Fishing would be best soon after sunrise,' Esko informed us.

'We want to stay up and wait for the sunrise. Please, please, say yes,' we begged.

For once, no obstacles were put in our way, not even by Aunt Law. 'If you think you are able to stay awake all night, feel free to do so,' she said.

The Aunts were sitting round the fire, telling stories, and laughing aloud. What a different Aunt Law, I thought, seeing her happy and laughing.

As the night was approaching, we began singing melancholy Finnish folksongs, telling of the longings for loved ones, praising the beauty of the summer nights, and the eternal longing for faraway places.

Meanwhile, Esko and Rainer had made a small raft with a bonfire on it, ready to be lit and to be pushed to out to sail.

'Come and look, Lake Ladoga is burning,' Esko raised his voice to be heard by the women.

Pirjo and I were the first ones to run to the water's edge. What a sight: Lake Ladoga calm and still, only gentle swells, coloured by reflections of the twilight sky, and the small burning raft slowly making its way further and further into the vastness of the waters. As we stood there watching, we saw the sun sink into the depths of the lake; twilight would remain. After only a couple of hours dusk would melt into the dawn; a new day was to be born. Fishing would commence.

Pirjo and I, with our fishing rods and the tin of worms, were ready to cast our rods as soon as we saw the fish jumping and leaving rings behind them. It did not take long before we had a good catch of small perches, and had had enough of fishing. In any case, as the sun was rising, the fish stopped jumping. We were tired and hungry, time to crawl under Molander's coat. Soon we would get up for porridge and milk, wait for Esko and Rainer to return from their more serious fishing, and then back to Kaihoniemi.

Saturday was a day of baking, and the sauna night. I can still see Great Aunt Auroora busy in the kitchen baking Karelian pies. There she was waiting with freshly baked 'piirakka', butter melting on it, and a glass of milk on my return from sauna, clean and ready to go to bed. Saturday sauna, the taste of the warm piirakka, and the homely figure of Great Aunt Auroora, giving me a hug, these are memories and provisions in my knapsack for life.

Summer 1939 was the end of my secure, safe, and innocent childhood. Kaihoniemi remains a place of love, and tender longing. Locked into my heart, are the many, many happy memories of long, endless, sunny summer days in my summer paradise.

Family Pelkonen,
Christmas 1941

Chapter Three

The Winter War, 30.11 1939 - 13.3 1940, and the Truce 13.3.1940 - 21.6.1941

Evacuation to Kuopio

Rainer, Laila and I returned home at the end of August after a summer full of events, and adventures; a sunny, full of fun, and an exceptionally hot summer. There had also been some fierce, powerful and frightening thunderstorms. One happened when I was alone in the big house. Suddenly, the wind strengthened, the sky darkened to almost black, I heard first some distant rumbling, then within minutes the booms became louder, the thunder closer. Lightning was flashing across the sky, illuminating it like sparklers at Christmas. No time to count the distance, the thunder was just above. The house was shaking, and I was panicking, crawled under the big kitchen table, trembling, convinced lightning would strike the house, and I, with the house, would go up in flames.

Were the thunderstorms nature's warning, and a foreshadowing of things to come? Had the fear and worry in the atmosphere added to my panic? There had been serious talk between the adults during the summer months. I had seen them glued to the radio, and had heard the anxiety in their voices without understanding their concerns.

As eventful and enjoyable as the summer had been, I was keen to return to our life in Käpylä. I had missed Mamma and Mummi. I looked forward to seeing my playmates, and was most excited about my move to the big Finnish junior school, the one Rainer and my friends were already attending. I would be joining the third-year class as the youngest pupil.

Within the first days at school I made a new friend, Kyllikki. I soon discovered that she was the top pupil in my class, clever and serious. She had dark, thick hair, plaited into pigtails. She was taller than me, her movements were clumsy. I was pleased that she wore glasses. The most important thing about Kyllikki was that she carried her books in a rucksack. I had been begging and begging Isä to buy me a satchel, similar to the one all the other girls had. He had not given in, instead he'd insisted that books need to be carried in a rucksack to strengthen the back, and to give a good posture. He might have been worried that I would end up with a humped back like his two sisters.

Kyllikki and I shared the best part of the journey home. She lived in one of the pretty, pastel-coloured wooden houses off the main road with her parents and two sisters, one just a year older, and a little sister about Laila's age. We would linger a long time at the point where we parted. Kyllikki and I continued to be friends in the Grammar School, she always the top pupil. Kyllikki never married, she studied History at Helsinki University, and first, teaching history in one of the Helsinki Grammar Schools, she ended up by becoming the headmistress of the same school. We remained friends until her death at the age of 89.

That same day, the first of September when we began our autumn term, the war in Europe started. Finland was put on high alert in fear of an invasion by the Russians. I sensed the fear around, and took in the general panic in the air, but I had no understanding of what being in a war might mean.

Evacuating children away from Helsinki became an official concern. Many parents, including mine, were turning to their relatives living away from Helsinki, in the country. For us the Dahlström family was the obvious choice, and Kuopio a safe place in the centre of Finland. My mother's sister, Eva, was married to Kaarlo Dahlström. My uncle was the owner of a lemonade factory and a brick works. He offered us a small vacant workers' cottage with one bedroom and a large living room/kitchen. A huge farm stove provided all the heating and was used for cooking and baking. First, for a week or two we had the use of the Dahlström's summer villa before we moved to the small cottage.

The Dahlströms had four children, similar in age to us; we looked forward to getting to know our cousins.

Mamma carried on her dentist work, and Isä was up in the north, still doing his own job.

Heading to Kuopio, Mummi, Rainer, Laila and I left Helsinki by train in late October. We were given few details or explanations and did not ask many questions. Spending time in Kuopio was going to be an exciting adventure for me. On the 30th November 1939, Russia declared war, and Finland was drawn into the war against its will. On that day the Russian troops crossed the border at Suomussalmi, invading the area where Isä was doing his forestry work. As soon as the war was declared, he was called up to the reserve troops. Thankfully, Isä would be working at the headquarters, and not sent to fight. What an enormous relief.

Winter was approaching fast. The winter of 1939-40 was an exceptionally cold one, some days the temperature went down to minus 39 centigrade in Kuopio. I had never experienced such low temperatures. I remember my nose and toes freezing, and the excruciating pain of them thawing.The cottage we stayed in was not meant for winter use, so we had to move. It was nearly Christmas when we, Mamma had now joined us, moved into a farmhouse, eight kilometres from Kuopio. We were given one large room that was to be our home; the enormous farm kitchen was shared with the farmer's family. Rainer and I attended a local school, skiing some three kilometres to the small village school, where about forty pupils were taught in one large classroom by one teacher.

There was deep concern for the fighting soldiers in these extreme conditions. How would they be able to fight? How would they survive? Parcels with warm clothing were sent to the frontier, simply labelled: 'To the unknown soldier.' Everyone, including the children, wanted to be part of this home front effort to help the brave soldiers. Mummi supervised me in knitting thick woollen socks. I was taught the tricky manoeuvre of making the heel. My socks were put into our parcel with a note: *'I have made these for you to keep your feet warm, Arna, aged 8'*. A couple of weeks later, by army mail, a letter, simply addressed: Arna, arrived. The 'Unknown Soldier' wrote: *'Kiitos, pikku Arna'* (thank you little Arna). He continued: *'The socks are keeping my feet warm, and your kind thoughts are warming my heart,'* signed *'Matti'*. I kept the letter hidden under my pillow. Each night I read it again and again, praying that Matti would be safe. In my imagination I was there on the front line as a nurse, caring for the wounded, giving them hope. By now I was fully aware of the seriousness of the war, and listen to the news on the radio.

I have no recollection of how we spent Christmas that year, except the journey across the frozen lake by horse and sledge to attend the Christmas morning service in Kuopio cathedral with Mamma. It was one of those freezing cold winter mornings: clear pale blue sky, the sun rising, the snow hard and crisp, making cracking noises as you walked on it. The farmer in his fur coat and fur hat, covering his ears, was waiting with his horse as Mamma and I stepped into the sledge, warmly dressed in our winter gear. The sledge was lined with a fur blanket, and the farmer wrapped us up in another. My first and only sledge ride. How well I remember the excitement and the thrill, as off we went, the horse galloping, accelerating, and almost flying across the frozen lake. His nostrils were white with icicles, and his breathing leaving a trail in the air as he was speeding. My face was freezing, my body cosily warm under the blanket. This was Christmas 1939.

Behind the farmer's fields there was a dense forest, a magical winter land, to which I would escape after school, even in the bitter cold, forgetting the horrors of the war. The snow sparkled like diamonds in the winter sunshine, the tall, snow-laden trees became white pillars of the stately palace where I lived as the snow princess. One special white birch tree became my Prince Charming, bending its branches to greet me. As the light faded, the blue twilight and the dark shadows transformed the landscape to magic and mystery, signalling that it was time to return back to the farmhouse.

One day, on these escapes to my imaginary world, something quite extraordinary happened. Just as the light was beginning to fade, I looked up to the sky, and to my bewilderment the dark sky was getting lighter, I was perplexed, couldn't understand: 'What is happening?'

Bright coloured shapes, in a rhythmic movement, were darting across the sky, filling it with an incredible drama of purple, blue and green shapes. The light was intensifying, forming a wide white band above the horizon. Looking at the show with amazement, I also began to feel frightened. I remembered vividly how often Mamma had talked about 'Christ's second coming'. Was that what was happening now? I saw the sky filled with angels, and, proclaiming, I thought, that the Heavenly Forces were coming to assist David-Finland in his fight against Goliath-Russia. Right in the brilliant centre, I saw Christ, surrounded by this incredible light. I was truly petrified, paralysed with fear, and totally convinced that this was indeed the second coming of Christ. According to Mamma's belief, Christ would take his followers to heaven, and the unbelievers would be left behind. Here I was, Christ had not taken me. By now I was feeling desperate and crying. Jesus did not want me but Mamma must be one of the chosen ones; Jesus was the centre of her life. The sky was still flashing with light and colour. I felt utterly forlorn. What is the point of me skiing back to the farmhouse? I thought. Mamma won't be there. I just want to die. The tears on my cheeks were turning into ice. Removing my skis, I sank into the deep, soft snow. It felt comfortable and cosy to lie very still, fall into sleep, never wake up.

I do not remember how long I might have been lying in the snow, but eventually the cold and hunger forced me to get up; the life-force had kicked in. Picking up my skis with frozen fingers I managed to fasten the bindings to my boots. Still very frightened, my heart beating fast, I pushed the ski-sticks deep into the snow, and slowly began to ski towards the farm. By then the show had ended and the dark sky was starlit. Standing outside the front door I, quietly and hesitantly, pushed it ajar, just a tiny bit, enough to peep in. A welcoming warmth hit me, I pushed the door a bit more, looked around, and could not believe my eyes: There my beloved Mamma stood alive and well at the stove cooking something that smelt delicious. A miracle had happened; Christ had not taken her. My relief was indescribable. Perhaps He decided to be merciful as we needed our Mamma. Mamma had not even noticed that I had gone skiing. I did not see any point in telling what had happened; all was well.

But the terror I had gone through on that winter night stayed with me for years and years. Every time I tried to tell the story of what I had experienced in seeing *'Aurora Borealis'* for the first time, I burst into a flood of tears. I was back in the frozen forest, an abandoned and petrified little girl, evacuated from her home, aware that Finland was fighting for its survival, and never having seen the drama of the Northern Lights, I had given the display an interpretation, coloured by Mamma's biblical stories and the terror of the war.

As the winter war progressed, Finland's defeat began to loom as inevitable. There was great concern for the children. Sweden felt obliged to offer a place of safety, and a rescue package to children. The Finnish state encouraged families to take up the offer. In this mass evacuation, 70,000 children were sent, from various parts of Finland, to Sweden. My parents decided that Rainer, Laila and I were to be sent to Kuopio's twin town, Jönköping for our safety. Isä had requested, if at all possible, our placement should be with a family where the father had a similar occupation to his.

The fact that bomb attacks had increased, Kuopio was bombed, and we had only very basic living quarters on the farm, helped my parents make their heart wrenching decision to send their three children to a foreign country. Many years later when I queried mamma, 'How could you send your children away?' Her answer was, 'In the circumstances, we saw no other option. We could not return to Helsinki. Our accommodation was only a temporary one. I left you in God's care.'

War child in Sweden

In the middle of February 1940, we joined a large group of Kuopio children and boarded a train going north. Mamma had volunteered to be one of the escorts travelling with us to Tornio, the Finnish/Swedish boarder town. There we said our goodbyes. Mamma, holding back her tears, hugged each of us, saying, 'God will take care of you,' adding her standard phrase at each parting: *'Mötas och skiljas är livets gång, mötas och åter mötas är hoppets sang.'* (To meet and to part, is the pattern of life; to meet and to meet again, is the song of hope.)

There we stood, like sheep, following orders with name plates dangling round our necks, bewildered and sad. Rainer, almost twelve, tall and gangly, had objected to being sent away, but he understood fully the seriousness of the situation. In his clumsy way he attempted to console us, saying that he would be our protector. Laila cried, as did so many other of the children, I tried to be strong, but there was a lump in my throat, and the tears in my eyes were hidden by my spectacles.

We crossed over to Sweden and were transferred to a Swedish train; the journey to an unknown destination had begun. Would any of us see our parents or Finland again? The train journey from Haparanda to Stockholm seemed to last forever and ever; we spent at least two nights on the train. We slept in bunk beds, we were given soup and rye bread to eat. In Stockholm each child was seen by a doctor before they were sent to their Swedish family. Rainer, Laila and I, with some of the children, carried on our journey to Jönköping, a small town at the southern end of the Lake Vettern.

On arrival, we were herded like cattle into a big assembly hall of the local grammar school. We stood waiting, surrounded by Swedish women, all busy doing something; nobody seemed to be paying much attention to us. I was hungry and tired, and needed to go to the loo. After some time, Rainer and Laila were taken aside. Rainer had time to whisper to me, 'It looks like Laila and I are going together.' I saw a blonde, nice looking lady holding Laila's hand, and Rainer next to her, all three leaving the assembly hall.

'Wait!' I shouted. 'I want to say goodbye.'

Nobody turned.

I wet my pants.

As I stood there, miserable and sad in my wet underwear, I thought, I'll never see my brother and sister again. The waiting continued. Didn't anybody want me? I was getting upset and was tearful. Then one of the women who had been busy organising the other children, walked towards me, took hold of my hand and my small suitcase.

'I am Märtta Hallander, my family is going to look after you,' she announced.

My first suspicious thought was, you don't look very friendly. How I wished that I could have gone with Rainer and Laila, and their foster mother. Aunt Märtta was as tall as my mother, with dark straight hair and a fringe almost to her eyes. She wore round, dark rimmed glasses, making her look like an owl.

The Hallanders lived in a large detached house with a big garden in the suburbs of Jönköping. On the other side of the road was a park with a path leading down to the Lake Vettern. My parents' wish had been noted: Åke Hallander was a 'Jägmestare' (Forestry Officer). He was slim, shorter than his wife, had dark hair and a moustache. I noticed his friendly smile, and the benign look in his brown eyes. I felt instantly happy that this kind man would be my Swedish foster father.

Åke and Märtta had three children Brita, aged 11, Inga, 9 and Håkan, aged 6. Brita was small for her age, the same size as Inga, but already showing signs of her breasts developing. She had her father's brown eyes and short dark hair. She was lively and fun to be with. She had already a boyfriend named Pelle. Brita took me under her wing; looking at me in a motherly way, she promised: 'Arna, I'll take care of you, you'll be alright with us.'

Inga was quite different from Brita, both in looks and in temperament. Serious and awkward in her movements, she was short-sighted and wore glasses. This pleased me. Her mousy hair was braided into a single plait. We three girls would be sharing a bedroom. Brita and Inga had a bunk bed, a third tier had been added for me to sleep in. Håkan had his own room. He was so much younger, I did not have that much to do with him, mainly, we played games together.

I settled well with the Hallanders; I enjoyed playing with all three children and having Brita and Inga as my older sisters. Climbing up or coming down from the top bunk was quite difficult. The horror was to wake up in the middle of the night needing to go to the loo. I delayed and delayed the climbing down and, half asleep, I imagined or dreamt that I had reached the bathroom. Too late, the accident had happened; fully awake now, I discovered something wet and warm under me. I tried to cover up the shame, and hoped that the stain on the sheet would dry and disappear by the evening. Aunt Märtta was good, she never ticked me off, perhaps she never climbed up to the top bunk. Wetting my bed was hard enough humiliation for an eight year old, being scolded would just have driven me to despair.

I quickly discovered, and was relieved to find out, that Rainer and Laila were very close, just around the corner, living in a large modern house with their foster parents Mr and Mrs Trotting and their only child, a teenage daughter.

Rainer did not settle with them or in Sweden. He felt angry with our parents. 'I am too old to be treated like a helpless child,' he would complain. 'I should have been allowed to stay in Finland.' Laila, only five, was homesick and unhappy; she could not speak much Swedish. She protested by refusing to eat.

We had not been in Jönköping even a month when we heard that Finland and Russia had made a truce agreement, on the 13th of March. We were jubilant. Now we could travel back home to Finland. Then we heard what the price for peace was: a heart-breaking shock, the loss of Karelia. Our summer paradise Kaihoniemi would now be in the hands of the Russians, our arch enemy. It was just too, too dreadful to think about. Rainer, Laila and I wanted to return home to Finland immediately; to be with our countrymen in our shared, deep sorrow.

Immediately after the truce agreement had been declared, we received Isä's letter:

'My dear children, Rainer, Arna and Laila, the loss of Kaihoniemi was extremely sad and hard. Maybe Kaihoniemi had not had time to become as greatly loved by you as it was by us adults, into our lives it was deeply engraved, and many plans for future were made, at least by me...'

In spite of all the dangers and difficulties, Isä was determined to make his farewell trip to Kaihoniemi before Karelia was handed over to the Russians. As a military officer he managed to hire horse and sledge from the withdrawing army and was speeding back to Jaakkima and Kaihoniemi. His aim was to salvage at least something from the treasured objects, and to have his private moment to grieve. He filled the sledge with almost random items:

silverware, photos, a samovar, special china, carpets and the harmonium. The contents of the sledge were put into a container, and then transported by rail to Helsinki; initially taken to our flat in Käpylä, later, Aunt Law took care of the distribution of the items.

We heard later from Mamma, that Isä, who seldom showed his feelings, had burst into inconsolable tears. The loss of Kaihoniemi was not only the loss of the land and house, but the loss of his childhood, his father and mother, once more. Our hope of instantly returning home was stifled. We had to accept that it would take time arranging the transport back for the thousands of evacuated children.

The end of March was approaching, and my ninth birthday. For the first time in my life, I would not be at home. Birthdays had always been something very special in our family. The tradition was that late on the eve of a birthday, Isä would bring his brass tobacco table into the centre of the living room, and Mamma would arrange the presents on it, still in their wrappings, before going to bed. Before anyone else was awake, even in the middle of the night, I used to tiptoe to the room, just to ensure myself that there were parcels, then happily to go back to sleep.

On this, my ninth birthday morning, the sun was shining brightly. I woke up early, climbed down from the top bunk, looking around for a table with presents. There was nothing there and my happy, hopeful mood sank like a stone into a well, tears filling my eyes. 'Mamma, Mamma, I need you,' I cried. 'Take me home, I don't want to be here any longer. It's horrible to be away from Finland, horrible not be at home on my birthday.'

I soon discovered that the Hallanders had not forgotten my birthday. Aunt Märtta had invited some of the local children for a birthday party. I did not know these children but was eager to join them in the various games. My cheeks were burning, I was running around excited, but did not feel at all well. Then suddenly, I just collapsed. Aunt Märtta rushed over, took one look at me, felt my burning, hot forehead and deduced that something was drastically wrong. Perhaps diphtheria? Some local children had contracted the disease. Rushing out from the room, she phoned for an ambulance. It all happened at speed. Without giving me any explanations, I was carried into an ambulance, and rushed to an isolation hospital. There the doctor on duty examined me and made his diagnosis. 'This child does not have diphtheria, she has scarlet fever.' Back into the ambulance, and to another isolation hospital, a single-storey low building on the outskirts of the town. I was met at the door by a nurse, and escorted in.

Aunt Märtta waving goodbye, shouted, 'Arna, be brave.' She had time to explain. 'I am so sorry; we are not allowed into the ward. I'll come each day, and wave to you behind the window.'

There I was, just nine years old, in a foreign country, bewildered, scared, feeling feverish and really ill. The nurse took me by the hand, undressed me without saying a word. She put a horrible hospital gown on me, and ushered me to a big dormitory, putting me into a bed, like a baby's cot, and she pulled the sides up. I wanted to scream, 'I am not a baby!' I could see that there were many other children in their beds. I was by now really scared. What was going to happen to me? Would I just be rotting there, forgotten?

Soon Rainer and Laila would be returning to Finland, but what about me?'

Aunt Märtta visited me almost daily, standing behind the window, telling what had happened in their lives, and showing me letters that had come from Mamma. I was not allowed to have them. Letters were burnt to avoid spreading infection.

One day Aunt Märtta came, looking awkward. 'Arna, I am so sad to tell you, Rainer and Laila left the Trottings yesterday. They'll be joining a group of children leaving from Stockholm to travel back to Finland.'

I burst into tears. 'This is not fair. I want to go home. I hate you all. I wouldn't have got scarlet fever in Finland.' I ran to my bed crying, pulled the bed clothes over my head, rolled myself to a ball, and just sobbed and sobbed. I wanted to die. The news of Rainer and Laila leaving broke my courage; I did not want to be brave, I felt so utterly unhappy, trapped in a cage like an animal.

Twice the nightmare of those weeks in the hospital has returned to haunt me. First at age fifteen, when a joint in my small finger developed a deep abscess, and I had to be anaesthetised in order to clean the puss round the bone. During the anaesthesia, probably mild enough for me to feel pain, I was back in the horror of the isolation hospital.

The second time, years and years later, was on my fiftieth birthday. Peter, my husband, and I made a trip to Sri Lanka, where my two colleagues were working for the 'Save the Children' charity. We had visited many children's homes during our stay. I had been deeply upset by seeing many young and beautiful polio victims permanently paralysed, sitting on the floor, unable to walk or stand up. Seeing my upset and sadness, my colleague John suggested, 'Let's make an all-day boat trip tomorrow. We'll show you the happy island.'

The next day I woke up with a serious stomach upset, I was not able to go on the trip, and was left behind. I had seen the doctor, had been given antibiotics, and the doctor had warned, 'There is a chance that you might get a mild allergic reaction to this medicine.'

I was resting on the beach most of the day, feeling sorry for myself, alone, just waiting for the return of Peter, John and Meg. I waited and waited, constantly looking to see their boat approaching. As they were not back at the expected time, my anxiety level began to rise, feeling panicky, abandoned, and my imagination running wild. I knew I was being irrational with my fears and panic.

Finally, they returned; they had had a fantastic day. Nobody asked, 'How are you feeling? What have you done?' That night I woke up, feeling funny. I touched my face, I could not feel it; my legs were stiffening, getting numb. Am I getting paralysed? I panicked. Is this the allergic reaction the doctor had hinted might happen, or is it a stroke? I shook Peter.

'Peter, wake up, something frightening is happening to me. You must call a doctor right away.'

He was calm, took hold of my hand and said, 'I'll get a doctor, but let's wait a minute or two to see if the symptoms increase.'

His calmness settled my fear somewhat. 'I am happy to wait, but, please, promise to stay awake.'

In that stillness of the night, firmly held by my Peter, the frightened nine-year-old girl in a Swedish isolation hospital came to my consciousness. I had had to travel to Sri Lanka, to be so far away from my home in UK to get in touch with what that little abandoned girl in a Swedish isolation hospital had been feeling. That memory allowed the panic to recede, and slowly the sensation returned to my legs and face. Without making this link, I probably would have been frightened to travel long distances.

Returning home

Back to the isolation hospital in Sweden. In May 1940, after six long weeks, the day eventually arrived when I was discharged back to the Hallander family, while the journey home was being arranged. All I remember is, I travelled alone from Jönköping to Stockholm, spent a night there with Märtta's sister-in-law. In the morning she escorted me to the boat heading for Turku, where Mummi was meeting me. She was in Turku helping her youngest daughter, Ruth, in caring for Ruth's new-born baby, Frank. Mummi escorted me to the railway station and put me on a train to Helsinki.

My parents, Rainer and Laila were very happy to welcome me home. I know they had missed me and had worried about me. Isä wanted to see me safely back home, hug me, and hear my tales, and had delayed his departure to his new, difficult job. He with many other Forestry Officers had been appointed to map out plots of land to be compulsorily taken from landowners for the relocation of Karelian farmers.

The Arna returning home, was not the same happy, carefree, innocent and ignorant little girl she had been only few months previously. It took time to feel at home, to speak Finnish, and to understand that the Finland I had returned to, was a deeply wounded, mutilated and grieving Finland. The young, independent 'Maid of Finland' had lost her left arm, and a large section of her skirt had been ripped off; she had been attacked and robbed.

The cost of the Winter War was enormous: 24,000 Finnish lives had been lost, the number of wounded was over 43,000, the majority of these were front line soldiers, in addition, nearly 400,000 civilians from Karelia and the Hanko Peninsula had to be evacuated and relocated. Immediately after the truce, the Parliament passed a law permitting speedy colonisation by compulsory expropriation of land, and giving the displaced farmers rights to new land, in an attempt to ease their situation.

The state had used up its funds; the coffer was empty; money was urgently needed for reconstruction. The Government's 'first aid' idea was to encourage married citizens to exchange their golden wedding rings for iron ones to top up the low gold reserves. This voluntary act of patriotism and sacrifice became the norm with nearly all married Finns, including Isä and Mamma.

The Helsinki 1940 Olympic Games had been cancelled, but the Olympic village had already been built. The Karelians moving to Helsinki were given homes in the Olympic village, situated within a walking distance of us, in Käpylä. Aunt Law, having lost her flat in Viipuri, was one of the lucky ones, obtaining a two-roomed flat there. Living so close, she now became part of our winter life.

It was now the end of May, the time when we would normally head for our summer holiday in Karelia. But, with no Kaihoniemi, what now? There was no problem with

Rainer. He would be working near Helsinki on Isä's cousin's farm, but where would Laila and I spend our summer holiday, and where would Aunt Law go for her vacation? She had worked out a solution. We three would travel up north to Raahe, a small northern coastal town, Mamma's birth town, and spend the summer months with cousin Lyyli, one of the spinster Aunts, who had been visiting Kaihoniemi each summer.

Lyyli, a lecturer in Botany and Biology at the Raahe Teachers' Training College, lived with her widowed friend Gerda, also a teacher, and Gerda's slightly retarded, musical cantor son, Erkki, in a detached, wooden house overlooking the sea. Together they also shared a small summer place on an island, a short boat ride from Raahe. This was going to be our summer home for 1940.

Laila and I were well received, bringing life and colour to their adult, childless life. Aunt Lyyli, her wonderful housekeeper Aino, a marvellous cook, and Aunt Law, now submissive and resigned to her role as a guest, all took excellent care of us, each in their own way.

Aunt Lyyli, a true teacher, enthusiastic, knowledgeable and patient, used the opportunity to teach Laila and me about the birds around us, and the wild flowers in the woods and fields. She also had a small loom. On rainy days she taught us to weave, and we returned home, each with a small bathroom mat we had woven. Laila enjoyed fishing with Aunt Lyyli, and we all went for motorboat rides and picked berries and wild mushrooms.

The summer was pleasant, but so different, lacking in excitement and adventures. I missed Pirjo. There was an aching longing in our hearts. Our summer paradise was lost, the mystery and history of Kaihoniemi. There could not be a replacement; we were homeless, driven out by heartless Russians. How well I could understand, and feel with Isä, with his tears, with his sadness. Kaihoniemi, so dear to me, meant so much more for him. The house and land had been a haven and safety for his childhood family in their distress. Kaihoniemi had witnessed life getting better, and had, each summer, welcomed them and us, the next generation, with sunshine and warmth.

Schools in Helsinki opened their door in September 1940. What a joy it was to see my friends: We looked at each other, saw the changes: we had grown taller, had become 'little adults', each with our unique stories from the period of evacuation. All of us had been affected by the war. Some of us had sad news: Maija's father had been killed in one of the fierce battles up in Suomussalmi, Esko's father had been seriously wounded, and was still in a military hospital. A Karelian girl, Ritva, joined our class. We heard her sad story, and rejoiced with her, that her family had been given a new home in the Olympic Village.

Yes, in just over a year so much had happened. We had lost our childhood innocence. We were acutely aware of the price Finland had paid in making the peace treaty, and the effort now required by every Finn in our country's reconstruction. What could I, nine years old, and my two friends Kyllikki and Liisa, both ten, do to help?

We decided to meet in my home once a week, discuss ideas, and each of us put one mark (about 5 old pennies) into a box for a fund we would use later. The plan we came up with was this: On Christmas Eve we would ski to the

Military Hospital, some five kilometres away, and give each of the war invalids a small present.

By Christmas, with small donations from our parents, we had saved enough money to buy a big bag of sweets, and a couple of boxes of small candles. We would give each soldier some sweets, and put on his bedside table a candle in a homemade candleholder. Our hope was that by lighting the candles and handing out the sweets, the soldiers would feel a little joy in their sadness at having to be separated from their families and that they would sense that we did care.

Early in the shadowy hours of the morning of Christmas Eve we set off on our skis. The world was silent, sky grey, and huge snowflakes were falling, creating a picture postcard.

'Perhaps we'll be turned away or laughed at for being stupid little children?' we wondered to each other.

We entered the reception area hesitantly, explaining to the nurse why we had come. Surprise, surprise, the nurse smiled warmly, welcoming us, and said, 'The soldiers will be delighted to see you, thank you so much for coming. Just follow me, I'll take you to the ward.'

There we stood, embarrassed, with snow dripping from our clothes, not knowing what to do next.

The nurse then announced, 'These three girls have come specially to wish you Happy Christmas.'

As we were removing our outdoor clothing, we noticed, to our horror, the big puddles on the floor from the melting snow on our anoraks. We glanced at the men. There were men in their beds and needing a great deal of nursing care, some men were moving around in wheelchairs, and some limping along with their crutches, all now looking at us.

Kyllikki had agreed to be our spokesperson. Confidently she told them a little about us. Then Liisa and I joined in wishing the men, *'Hyvää Joulua'* (Happy Christmas). One man began clapping his hands; soon they all joined him. Liisa handed over some sweets, I put the candles on their tables, and, with the help of the ward sister, I lit them. The injured men were looking happy and smiling broadly, one of them suggesting, 'What about you singing us a Christmas Carol?'

We started, quietly and hesitatingly: *'No onkos tullut kesä nyt talven keskelle? Ja laitetaanko pesä myös pikkulinnuille....'* (a very well-known carol: 'Has summer arrived in middle of the winter? And shall we build a nest for the small birds?')

Almost immediately the men joined us in singing, and asking us to sing more of the well-known carols; some of the men had powerful, fine voices.

Before leaving we went around, shaking hands with each of them, once more wishing, *'Hyvää Joulua'.*

They shouted in unison, *'Kiitos, kiitos. Hyvää Joulua pienet tontut.'* (Thank you, thank you. Happy Christmas, little goblins).

Pleased and proud with the success of our mission, we returned to our homes in time for each of us celebrate Christmas with our families. We had done our tiny bit for Finland. This was the end of our charity work for now; the skating rink and the ski tracks were waiting.

I had noticed during the autumn months that Mamma was getting rounder, and then one day she told us that she was expecting a baby to be born in March. I knew nothing about how babies were born or about pregnancy but was curious to find out what was going on in Mamma's body. In the bookcase, amongst the forbidden books, books we were not allowed to touch without permission, I had seen a medical book. After school it was not too difficult to sneak to the bookcase, make off with the forbidden book, and disappear into the wardrobe, reading all about pregnancy, and discovering an illustration of a baby upside down in the womb. I could now follow the progress of Mamma's pregnancy. It was almost as if the baby inside Mamma became my baby, and I already had a pram.

For years I had longed to receive a doll's pram as a Christmas present, but year after year I had been disappointed, and had been told they were too expensive. Now, this Christmas 1940, Isä had managed to get hold of a second-hand, silver-grey doll's pram, big enough for a real baby. I hadn't been too bothered about the pram, I no longer played with dolls. But now I felt quite excited by the thought, maybe I'll be able to put our new baby in my pram?

Mamma, being already 41 years old, and having had a difficult time giving birth to Laila, was questioned about her decision to have one more child. Her answer was, 'Finland has lost thousands of young men in the war, it's my duty to give a son to Finland.' She was absolutely convinced that the baby she carried would be a boy. Indeed, on the 20th March 1941 she had a healthy, strong baby boy, named Juha Kristian. (Juha literally fulfilled Mamma's promise to Finland; he became a soldier, rising to be a high-ranking officer, lieutenant colonel). Juha, a lovely, contented and happy baby, my baby, immediately won everyone's heart.

It turned out that my doll's pram was indeed big enough to put my little baby brother into it, showing him off to the children living in the flats.

Summer was approaching, and arrangements for our care needed to be made. Juha, naturally, would stay with Mamma; his care was to be shared by Mamma and our new, homely, middle-aged housekeeper, Hilda, who had fallen in love with Juha at first sight. Laila was happy to go back to Raahe with Aunt Laina to stay with Aunt Lyyli, whom she really liked. They shared a love of nature and animals. There would be a little kitten waiting for Laila. Rainer would be spending another summer helping Isä's cousin on his farm.

Inga and Arna,
Sweden 1942

Laila, Rainer, Juha and Arna,
Autumn 1944

Chapter Four
The 'Continuation War' 1940-1945

June 1941 – August 1942, second time in Sweden

The plans for me were different. Märtta Hallander had written to my parents, offering me the chance to spend the summer holiday with them in Sweden. This suited everyone, including me as it would be much more fun to be with the Hallander family than the adults in Raahe. Before I left Finland Isä insisted that I see the eye specialist, Dr Teittinen, Mamma's friend from her student days. She had been following my squint since it was first noticed. There had been a long gap since the previous visit. Dr Teittinen was pleased with my eyes; the squint was almost corrected.

'Let's have another check-up in a year's time,' she said to Mamma, and turning to me, 'I think you'll be OK without glasses by then.'

I was very happy, did not forget what she said, and decided to stop wearing glasses as soon as I arrived to Sweden. What a relief to be like everyone else, not to be called names. In the beginning of June, I set off, excited, eager, and confident. The journey by myself did not scare me. The route would be a reverse from the previous year's return journey home: by train to Turku, and by boat to Stockholm, then a train to Jönköping. In Turku Aunt Ruth would see me to the right boat, and in Stockholm Aunt Märtta's friend would assist with the change from boat to the train.

The travelling went well. Uncle Åke and Inga were waiting for me at Jönköping station. Inga was glad to see me, and uncle Åke hugged me.

'Hej, Taggen Naggi,' (my nickname by him, meaning 'Cuddly Teddy'), 'so good to see you, you have grown.'

Only three weeks of my holiday had passed when, on 22nd of June, the truce ended and the 'Continuation War' began. This war was seen from the outset as a follow-up to the Winter War. (Much later I read: *'In January 1941 a plan had been drawn up in complete secrecy for Finno-German co-operation in the great push to the east. The Germans would have responsibility for the offensive from the northern half of Finland. The Finns would attack the Karelia Isthmus and north of Lake Ladoga. There Finns would meet up with the Germans, who were aiming to take Leningrad. The Finnish army did not open its attack until the Soviet air force had started its bombing raids on southern Finland and the government had confirmed that Finland was at war again.* (Henrik Meinander: A History of Finland, p. 152.)

The mood in Finland was totally different in this war: The aim was to conquer Karelia back. Aided by the Germans this would be achieved, and with 'sisu' (guts, intestinal stamina, courage). In every home Finns were glued to the radio, following with suspense the daily progress of the army. Each step in retaking our land was a jubilation. After five months of victorious fighting, the Finnish army was able to dig into positions that lay several hundred kilometres to the east of the 1939 border. At the same time Russian bombing attacks increased all over Finland; special targets were Helsinki and Oulu. The nation was yet again on high alert, and mass evacuation of children back to the safety of Sweden began.

Having been so happy to come to Sweden for the summer holiday, I now felt horribly homesick, frightened, anxious, and isolated from what was going on at home. Isä had been called to the front to fight. What if he is injured, or he might even be killed, I panicked. Letters were infrequent, some writing was blacked out by the censor. I was not able to share my worries, as the day to day life was full of fun, and the Hallander children had no interest in a war far away.

The family spent their holiday at an agricultural college in the Swedish countryside. The headmaster was Åke's good friend, and he offered the Hallanders the use of a school building for the family's holiday. The part of the school we had access to was full of interesting places to hide in and places to play our imaginary games. We had the large school grounds, a lake to swim in, and on rainy days we escaped to the enormous loft for our endless Monopoly - and other games.

Being away over the summer months was a pattern I had been used to. In many ways staying in Sweden was not all that different, except for the constant underlying worry about the war, waiting for letters from home, and between letters living with the fear that something has happened to Isä.

By August I had begun to count the days to my departure, eagerly longing to go home, and completely unaware of the letters that had been exchanged between Mamma and Aunt Märtta, questioning the safety of my return to a country at war.

Märtta wrote to Mamma on 21st August 1941:

*'Om inte fru Pelkonen har något emot det, ville vi gärna att Arna stannar här tills vidare. Hon får gå här i skolan i samma klass som Inga, som börjar första klassen i flickskolan. Jag har talat med rectorn här och det möter inga hinder.' (*If Mrs Pelkonen does not have any objections, we would like Arna to stay with us for the time being. She can attend a school here, and be in the same class as Inga, who is starting in the first class of the Girls' Grammar school. I have spoken to the headmaster, and there is no hindrance.)

My parents' decision to take up this offer was helped by the government's ruling: 'For the time being it is not safe for the schools in Helsinki to open their doors.'

When I heard that I was not going home, my first reaction was anger and fury.

'It's not fair,' I cried. 'I do not want to stay here. I do not want to go to a Swedish school. I want to go to Käpylä Grammar school; all my best friends will be there. I have a place there.' In the spring term I had passed the entrance examinations with good marks. By the first of September I had accepted the grown-ups' decision, and was both keen and excited in joining Inga at the Grammar school.

Living on the outskirts of Jönköping we travelled by tram to the school, going home for our lunch each day. Managing the short lunch break was a real rush, more often than not we had to run as fast as we could to catch the tram. In this fast running I managed to drop my scarf, then my gloves, and even my hat; there was no time to stop and pick them up, I just left them behind. Naturally, I got into serious trouble as soon as Aunt Märtta discovered the losses. She demanded to know what I had done. 'How is it possible to lose a hat or a scarf?'

I knew that both Inga and Brita had lost gloves, so that was forgiven. I tried to explain that they had just vanished in school, and that most likely somebody had nicked my pretty scarf. She did not believe me.

'Arna, you are an ungrateful, careless, and lying little girl,' she scolded.

She was right, I knew I had been careless, and I knew I had been telling a fib, and in an attempt to cover up one sin, I had committed another. Still, I hated Aunt Märtta for ticking me off; she, usually kind, became another nasty Aunt Law.

Being in an all-girls school was a new experience; girls, with no boys around, seemed to be behaving better, none of the rough games nor fights that I was used to in a mixed school, and with my big brother Rainer. Of course, there were arguments, nasty remarks, teasing, and name calling. Luckily, I no longer wore glasses. It was great to have Inga in the same class; her friends from the junior school also became my friends. I had no difficulties in coping with tuition being in Swedish, but I struggled with the written work and spelling.

Having never in my life experienced normal family life with a mum who stayed at home looking after her kids, a dad who went to work in the morning and came home in time for us all to have dinner together, life with the Hallander family felt so different, good, safe and secure. I was part of the family, loved and cared for, especially by Brita, who had taken me under her wing already on my first stay, and now continued to be a real big sister to me.

Every Saturday evening Uncle Åke gathered us children around the log fire in the large hall upstairs. We had a light supper: a drink of hot chocolate, and special sandwiches, prepared by Aunt Märtta. Then Uncle Åke wanted to know from each of us in turn, 'Is there any reason why your pocket money should be reduced this week?' Naturally, we claimed to have been well behaved, and the money was now dished out. The evening ended with Uncle Åke reading aloud from 'Robinson Crusoe' or some other book, before we said, 'God natt. Sov gott.' ('Good Night. Sleep well.')

On Sundays, leaving Aunt Märtta to prepare the lunch, Uncle Åke took us for a walk along the shores of Lake Vettern. There we ran, chasing each other, played ball games, and threw flat stones across the surface of the lake, competing to see whose stone would make most 'rings'. The highlight of the walk was the stop at a café, serving hot chocolate with whipping cream, and most delicious homemade pastries and cakes. Uncle Åke allowed each of us to choose our own special cake; mine was a shortbread tart filled with buttercream and topped with pink icing.

As the term progressed, in spite of being well cared for, I was feeling more and more homesick. In my letters I was begging to be allowed to return home, although I knew that the war was still going on. Isä, having had to work away from his family, was the one who understood my homesickness. He wrote to Mamma, instructing her to arrange my travel home: *'It will be too upsetting for Arna to spend Christmas away from home'*. The Hallanders understood well that being away at Christmas time would be sad for a child, and Märtta began to arrange the Swedish side of my journey. She was also looking for possibilities for

Laila to come to Sweden with me after the holiday. The Trottings had moved away, but there was another family, with a boy of Laila's age, living a few houses away, willing to take her.

The knowledge that I would be back at home and see all my family, filled my whole being with joy, especially to see little Juha; how he had changed, and wondering would he remember me. It had been tough to be in a foreign country. I had blocked off my fears and sadness, kept it all inside me, perhaps the occasional bedwetting told of the tears that could not be shared. I knew that I ought to be grateful being looked after by good people, but inside I couldn't feel any gratitude, simply an enormous longing to be back with Mamma and Isä.

What a thrill when, a few days before my departure, Mamma's letter arrived with tickets. The envelope had been opened by the censor, some of Mamma's writing had been blackened. Checking the various tickets Aunt Märtta was shocked to discover that the tickets for my boat fares were missing; all that was left were simply my meal tickets for the boat journey. My heart jumped to my throat; full of panic, alarm bells ringing, I asked, 'Will my journey now be cancelled?'

Aunt Märtta, sensing my panic, assured me that the matter would be sorted out. She immediately contacted her sister-in-law, Mrs Gisten, in Stockholm, asking for her help. She had already promised to take care of my transfer from the train to the boat. As planned, I travelled to Stockholm, and was met by Mrs Gisten. As she was hugging me, she told me that all would be ok.

'I have contacted the Finnish Embassy. They have advised us to go to the ship in good time before the departure and discuss the matter of your lost ticket with the captain. He is going to sort it out.'

Mrs Gisten, a tall, elegant, beautifully dressed lady, lived in a large apartment in the centre of Stockholm. I loved staying with her, she treated me more like an equal than a child. Her beautiful home, full of exquisite art objects and wonderful paintings, was a glimpse into another world.

The next morning, we set off to go to the harbour. There 'Vellamo', the ship sailing between Stockholm and Turku, was ready to sail later that day. On the deck I spotted the captain standing to attention. He, a sturdy, average sized man with a reddish complexion and a beard, welcomed me.

'Hei pikku neiti, tervetuloa. Olen kuullut, että minulle on kunnia saada pitää sinua vieraanani matkalla Turkuun.' (Hello little miss. I have heard that I have the honour of having you as my guest for the voyage to Turku). He smiled warmly.

Looking up to his blue eyes, I saw in him the familiar face of so many Finnish men, and thought to myself, he is trustworthy, my trip will be safe.

Indeed, I was treated as a special guest, taken to the captain's cabin. Adjacent to it was a small cubbyhole, my bedroom with a put-up bed.

At the captain's table I met other guests; all curious about me. I sensed their unspoken questions: 'How is it that a little ten-year-old girl is travelling on her own back to a country at war?' Each lady in the party wanted to mother me, offering sweets, even money. It was fun to have all this attention.

The sea was frozen, a narrow passage of clear water had been made by an icebreaker for the ship to plough through. Its sides were hitting blocks of ice at regular intervals, making a loud bang. I was scared: 'What if the ship is so badly damaged that we all end in the icy water?' Certainly, the loud noises made it impossible to sleep.

We arrived in Turku in the morning. Saying my thanks and goodbye to the captain, and wishing him a happy Christmas, he took hold of my hand, pressing a twenty mark note into it, and said, 'You gave us joy, you were a very special guest, thank you.' I was thinking, God had sent this captain to be my Guardian Angel. That's how God cares.

I do not remember who came to meet me, but I do remember how wonderful it was to be back in Käpylä, to see my whole family. Isä was at home, he had been given leave over the Christmas period. He and Mamma hugged me, Rainer and Laila just said, 'Terve' ('Hi'). Seeing Juha, I could not believe my eyes; he was no longer a baby in a pram. He was standing up, holding onto the bars of his cot, babbling in his own language. I had a feeling he remembered me. Now I would have time to play with him, get to know him. And there was Mummi waiting to greet me, showing the new midnight blue velvet dresses she had sown ready for Laila and me for Christmas Eve.

On the morning of Christmas Eve, I was sent to buy the Christmas tree from a farm about three kilometres away. Being used to walking long distances I soon reached the farm and saw the pile of trees. Choosing a symmetrical tree, with dense branches, and as big as, I thought, I would be able to drag behind me, I set off for the return journey. It did not take long before the weight of the tree made itself felt, and my walking proceeded at a snail's pace. A car drove past me, then decided to stop.

The driver, a well-dressed middle-aged man, came out, and asked, 'Can I offer you a lift? It looks as if you are struggling with that big tree. Where are you going?'

I replied, 'Just to Käpylä. I can manage.'

The man said: 'I can see you are a strong girl, but as I am going that way, jump in, I'll take you there.'

'Never, never accept a lift from a stranger,' Mamma had repeatedly warned me. In my head I heard her words, but the invitation was too tempting. With my heart throbbing, I let the man fix the tree behind the car, and accepted his lift with, '*Kiitos*'. (Thanks.)

As soon as he started the engine my fears came back, grew and grew: What have I done? Is this man one of those bad strangers who offers children sweets and then does horrible things? What now, I am trapped in his car. We were still some distance from my home, now really worried, and fantasies running wild in my mind, already standing up, I said, 'I need to get off here.'

The man looked at me surprised, with a slight smile on his face, and said, 'We are not quite in Käpylä.' I think he sensed my panic, as he did not argue. He just stopped the car, and handed me the tree, wishing me, '*Hyvää Joulua.*'

Now I was embarrassed, sensing too late the man's goodwill, and simply said, '*Monet kiitokset ja oikein 'Hyvää Joulua.'* (Many thanks and have a really good Christmas).

I dragged the tree home, never telling anyone about the lift from a stranger. I just accepted Isä's praise for having chosen such a big, beautiful tree, and for coming home so swiftly.

During the holiday I met Kyllikki. Together we decided to go and have a look at the new school building for the co-educational Käpylä Grammar School, some distance from our junior school. The building would be ready to receive pupils in the beginning of September 1942. I was going to join in the second year with many of my friends.

The two weeks disappeared, and I had no option but to return to Sweden to finish my school year. With this knowledge, and the knowledge that Laila would follow me as soon as all her papers were in order, I returned to life with the Hallanders. Laila arrived a few weeks later. First, she stayed with a family living on the same road, but for the summer holiday she joined the Hallanders. Laila and I were longing to return home, but as we did not have a place in Finland to go to for the summer holidays, our parents decided that we should remain in Sweden until the autumn term began. The happy day came in late August 1942 when we joined a group of other children returning to Finland.

Being back home felt like a stone had fallen from inside me. It had been tough to be so far away, and for so long. Juha was now taking his wobbly steps, and saying a few words; a delightful little toddler.

The only time I saw Uncle Åke and Aunt Märtta again, was in the autumn 1946. As a small return for all their care and kindness given to Laila, Juha and me during the war years, my parents invited them to come to Finland for their Silver Wedding celebrations on 18th September1946. Uncle

Åke and Aunt Märtta were astonished to see the changes that had taken place in us; having not seen Rainer since spring 1940, now a 182 cm tall sportsman, and I now no longer a child but a teenager, last seen in 1942.

Uncle Åke hugged me, looking at me again, as if he had seen me for the first time, and said, *'Taggen Naggi, du har så vackra ögon'* ('Taggen Naggi, you have such beautiful eyes'), giving me another hug.

Nobody had ever given me compliment about my looks. His words were special, warmed my heart, and gave me confidence. I remember Uncle Åke with great fondness. Mamma and Märtta continued to send each other annual Christmas letters for years and years. Mamma died in December 1988. When I returned from her funeral, I had a parcel from Sweden waiting for me, labelled, 'Children's drawings'. In fact, it was Mammas' letters to Märtta. Co-incidentally, Märtta had also died in December 1988. Clearing her belongings, Brita had come across the letters, and sent them to me.

Inga and I kept in touch for many, many years, sending each other Christmas messages. She and her first husband even visited us in the 1970s.

Autumn 1942- December 1944, the war continues

Laila and I arrived back home in late August. Mamma had arranged both Laila's and my schooling. Laila, now seven, would begin at the junior school with some of her friends, and I had a place in the Grammar school, in the second year, with the condition that I had extra lessons in Finnish grammar. This was arranged. I was excited and happy to be joining the class 2A and seeing some of my friends from junior school in the same class.

The brand-new school building, purpose built, was ready and waiting to open its doors in September. It was situated some distance away, on the other side of the hill from my home, the hill onto which the Finnish army had placed their anti-aircraft guns. New teachers had been appointed, most of them quite young. The art teacher Mrs Lucander ('Lukki'), only thirty-one years old, and a war widow with a young child, was our form teacher. She was strikingly beautiful, tall and slim, her black hair pulled tightly back to a bun. She took both her subject and us seriously, had a sense of humour, but was strict and demanding. We felt lucky having her as our form teacher. She stayed with us all the years of our Grammar school education, even afterwards joining us in our annual re-union gatherings.

In the autumn term she decided to teach us perspective drawing. I found it quite impossible to draw straight lines, no rulers were allowed. Each week she criticized my drawings, until finally she was so fed up that she burst out, 'Arna, if you do not throw your drawings in the wastepaper basket, I'll be sick.'

The class laughed, I felt humiliated.

At Christmas we received our end of term report, and to my utter amazement I saw the number 8 for drawing (10-9 'excellent', 8-7 'with praise', 6-5 pass, 4' fail'), I had expected 6, at best. I asked her, 'How is it that you have given me such a good number when you have been continuously finding fault in my drawings?'

I have never forgotten her reply: 'Even a blind hen *sometimes* finds a corn.'

In a twisted way Lukki had awakened my interest in art. To be fair to Lukki, she had also praised me for my good colour sense, and with her encouragement I decided to take art as an extra subject in the sixth form, gaining a 9 in my final certificate. When I started my art studies years and years later in UK, I sent Lukki a note: 'The blind hen is still looking for a corn.'

Our headmaster, Mr Perttilä, teaching Mathematics and Physics, was an average size, slim man in his late forties. His reddish hair was thinning, and his green, cold eyes would stare at you intensely, waiting for your response to his questions. He was strict and could be cruel and sarcastic. He held the firm belief that girls were no good in Maths or in understanding Physics; we proved him right. One day he called me to the blackboard, asking me to explain how a piston works in a cylinder to make steam. Feeling Mr. Perttilä's stare burning my neck, I stood there in silence with a piece of chalk in my hand, frightened and completely at loss. He put his hand around his ear, as a mockery of wanting to hear better, and rolling the R in my name to an exaggeration, 'Arrrrrrrrrrrrrrna', I can't hear a thing.'

The whole class was finding the show amusing, but no one would have dared to laugh. I was allowed to go back to my seat, and a clever boy was called to show his knowledge. I hated physics from then on, and certainly didn't have any wish to know how steam was made. There was another side to Mr. Perttilä; his piano-playing was of concert standard, and from time to time he became a different person, a true musician, totally involved with his whole being in his playing. I have not forgotten the thrill of hearing him play

Liszt's 'Campanella' or the power in his playing of Chopin's 'Revolutionary', pieces that I had never heard before.

The war continued with optimism in the air. The Finnish Army had advanced beyond the lost part of Karelia and was moving further into Russian Karelia, to the delight of the Finnish speaking tribes living there. The dislocated Finnish Karelians were beginning a move back to their homes, bravely facing the devastation of their houses, and with 'sisu', hope and determination, rebuilding their destroyed homes.

As Karelia was now back in the hands of the Finns, it was obvious that my Aunts Ester and Laina, my Uncle Jaakko, and Isä were keen to make a journey to Kaihoniemi. In the spring of 1942 Isä made an exploratory trip there. In spite of hearing his stories of the state of the buildings, Aunt Laina was the first on deciding to face the devastation, spending part of her summer holiday there with Aunt Lyyli. We heard the main building was not inhabitable but that the foreman's cottage, some two hundred meters from the main building, had been saved, and could, with small repairs, be used.

None of us children went to Kaihoniemi in the summer 1942. Laila and I were still in Sweden, Juha stayed in Helsinki with Mamma and our maid, and Rainer, already leading quite an independent life, involved in sports, needed to stay in Helsinki. His running potential had been discovered, and he was under the wing of HIFK (*Helsingfors Idrots Föreningen Kamraterna,* a Swedish-speaking sport organisation.) Isä had by now been ordered to leave his military duties, and he was transferred to the compulsory expropriation of land programme. He was stationed in

Savonlinna; a small, beautiful spa town, famous for its medieval stone castle on an island almost adjacent to the town. He stayed until the war ended.

When, in the following summer of 1943, a summer place was again needed for the school holidays, Isä managed to obtain a couple of rooms from a farm close to Savonlinna. This meant that for the first time since the winter war had started, we as a family were together, even Rainer, now a 6-foot-tall teenager, already competing in running events, joined us on and off.

It felt so good to be together. The war seemed far away, no bombings and no cannons were heard, just perfect summer days such as those long ago in Kaihoniemi. Mamma was able to rest and relax, as Isä was there. He loved putting down the fishing nets; I was his rower. We lay the nets in the evening, the lake often mirror-calm, then lifting them up early next morning with mist lingering above the surface of the lake, and the sun rising higher and higher as we proceeded; Isä issuing his instructions. *'Souda eteenpäin, pidä vene paikallaan'* ('Row forwards, keep the boat still') or '*Huopaa hitaasti*' ('Row backwards slowly.') By the time we had gathered the nets the morning had advanced, the air was warm, it was time for a swim. If we caught some fish, we cleaned the catch before presenting them to Mamma.

The farmer and his wife were typical people of the Savo region, talkative, always joking, easy people to get along with. The only enemy on the farm was their angry cock, keenly protecting his harem. Juha, playing in the yard where the hens were running around, must have been a threat to the cock. One day the cock suddenly dashed towards Juha with the clear intention of attacking him. Isä saw the danger, managed to stop the cock, in full spurt, and with one strong movement, broke its neck. Juha could not forget the drama.

The farmer's wife was keen to teach me how to milk the cows. Having managed to squeeze a few drops from the udders, and mostly missing the bucket, I gave up. I had tried.

Savonlinna, only two kilometres away, was where we did our shopping. One day Isä, as a special treat, decided to row us across the rapidly flowing torrent to the castle. It was quite a manoeuvre, the boat was spinning around; instead of going forward, we seemed to be pulled backwards. Eventually, Isä managed to zig zag his way in the current, and found a sheltered landing place. The climb up the slippery rock surface was tricky, but worth it. Olavinlinna (St Olaf's castle) built in 1475 by Eric Tott as a defence against attacks from the east, was a well-preserved stone castle with many corridors and passages. Walking through these spaces it was easy to move back in time and imagine the life that might have been lived within the castle walls. There were many legends that had survived, living on and creating new stories. One that came to my mind, was the tale of a young maiden, who fell in love with an enemy officer. She helped him have access to the castle, and as a punishment for her treason, she was immured alive into the castle wall. The legend added that a rowan tree grew at the location of her execution. The white rowan flowers were seen as symbolizing the maiden's innocence, and the red berries her blood. We saw no sign of a tree, but the maiden's tale became alive.

The castle lost its military importance in the eighteenth century, and was, from then on, a significant tourist attraction as well as popular location for festivals. The first five opera festivals in the castle were organized at the beginning of the twentieth century, but it took until 1969 for the renowned International Savonlinna Opera Festivals to commence, an annual event taking place each July.

Following Great Britain's declaration of war against Finland in 1942, the Finnish Embassy in London had been evacuated to Lisbon, and Aunt Ester was one of the personnel transferred there. As she was on holiday from Portugal in August 1943, a Pelkonen family gathering was arranged in Kaihoniemi. Ester, the oldest of the Pelkonen siblings, was the most exciting of our relatives. She, a petite, small boned, elflike woman with a small, delicate, beautiful face, smiling green eyes, fine brown hair, and a slightly hunched back, was an enlightened, open minded person, highly regarded in her post, and loved by her brother's children. Ester never married, but she certainly had admirers. She left Finland in her late twenties, heading for America, where she worked as housekeeper for a wealthy family. The family soon discovered Ester's skilful piano playing, and promoted her to a lady in waiting, expecting her to entertain the family's dinner guests with her piano playing.

On her return from America she obtained a post as a clerk at the Ministry of Foreign affairs. Her first foreign posting was to Moscow, where the movements of the Embassy staff were strictly limited, and they could be spied on at any time. While there she managed to obtain some precious art objects, like the portrait of the Russian girl with sorrowful brown eyes, hanging on the wall of Aunt Laina's flat, a painting I stood in front of often, and I now own. From Moscow Aunt Ester was transferred to London in 1937, and back there again from Lisbon at the end of the war.

Rainer was the lucky one to have Ester as his godmother, but she was fond of all of us, and supported my parents with money as well as sending food and clothes. Her life-story probably was an encouragement to me when the time came to explore options in my life.

The August day we had been anxiously waiting for arrived. We crammed into Isä's car, heading to Kaihoniemi, driving along through Lahdenpohja, the small town we knew so well, now with destroyed buildings and burnt houses, then on the country lanes past Toivoranta to the peninsula of Kaihoniemi. Rainer, Laila and I had been warned that Kaihoniemi was no longer the place we treasured in our memories: 'Prepare yourself to face the havoc and devastation of the Russian occupation'. The car had hardly stopped when Rainer, showing off his fast speed, ran down to the main building, Laila and I followed, Juha, only two, was just bewildered.

The reality facing us was much worse than we could ever have imagined. The beautiful house had been brutally vandalised, windows on all sides were broken, the entrance hall was covered in bird droppings. A musky smell hit us as soon as we pushed the door ajar. The elegant drawing room was barren, every single piece of furniture had been removed; smashed picture frames, shattered glass and broken crockery covered the floor, even the rose-pattern wallpaper had been ripped off the walls. We discovered later, peeping into the playhouse, that Russian children had saved a piece of the wallpaper for a picture on the wall there. The upstairs rooms had been used as a hen house; the floors covered in straw, bird shit and feathers. The lovely garden, Amanda's pride and love, was overgrown, some flowers still blooming in the wilderness. There was nothing to remind us of Kaihoniemi, our precious summer paradise. It had been raped, cruelly wrecked and destroyed. What there was left was disgusting, unbearably ugly, smelly and revolting. We had no words to share; each of us walked away with anger, a heavy heart, and an unbearable sadness.

The sleeping arrangements for so many of us caused some headache. There were not enough beds or rooms in the small cottage, so it was decided to use one of the outbuildings for Uncle Jaakko, Rainer and I to sleep in. An enormous mattress filled with straw was put on the floor, and we were each given a blanket and a pillow. My place was next to the wall, then Rainer, and then Uncle Jaakko.

In the middle of the night I woke up feeling that my blanket was being raised, and Rainer was touching my bottom. I tried to pretend to be a sleep, but memories returned from Museokatu: Rainer insisting on me climbing up to his bed. Then we were small, innocent children; now the situation was different. Anything to do with sex was an absolute taboo for me; touching below the waist was a sin, strictly forbidden. The warning bells were ringing. My body tensed up. Rainer was fifteen, he already had a steady girlfriend, and was used to being admired by girls. He was not afraid to fool around with them or me. I was his slave, proud to have him as my brother.

As Rainer's touching became braver, my panic increased, and my fears became uncontainable; I ran out to the yard, screaming with the top of my voice. Of course, my screaming woke everybody up, anxious to find out what was the matter with me. I can remember the deep, deep sense of shame I felt when I tried to explain what had happened. Mamma, taking the blame for having been so thoughtless with the sleeping arrangements, was amazingly supportive.

'I should have realized that Rainer was in his puberty, and his sexual hormones are running wild,' she said.

All stared at me, and, I was sure, were thinking, Arna has been making a fuss about nothing. No one spoke to me, nor did Rainer. The shame of it, stayed in my mind as a dirty secret. I kept asking myself, had I allowed my fantasies to blur my thinking? Or, perhaps had I encouraged Rainer?' I recalled the boisterous, physical games we had played when he spent few days with us in Savonlinna: Rainer wanting to show his strength, picking me up, putting me down, chasing and catching me. For me it had been just fun, but for him? (Many, many years later I wrote to Rainer reminding him of this event, and its long-term affect in my life. I was hoping for an apology or at least an acknowledgement. Rainer did not reply.)

During these couple of days when all the descendants of Gustav and Amanda Pelkonen were together there had been an optimistic mood, and plans were made to improve the foreman's cottage for our summer use. The same optimistic mood prevailed amongst all Finns, particularly Karelians, many already living in their new-built houses. Finland was on the winning side in the war. The thought of this being the last time we would all be together in Kaihoniemi, did not exist.

The End Game

Summer over, ready to start a new school year, we returned home. In Helsinki the Russian air raids continued with regularity. The bombing attacks came mainly during the nights. We became quite used to being woken up by the warning sirens, and then jumping out of our beds, quickly grabbing some clothes, and running as fast as we could to the shelter in the cellar of our building. These air raids were part of our life. The most powerful and frightening noises came from the Finnish anti-aircraft battery, the cannons firing away at full blast, and placed on top of nearby hill. Windows in nearby buildings, including ours, were rattling, some even shattering with the force of the power of the guns. On the other side of the hill, our school was an equal distance from the defence guns. Our lessons could suddenly be interrupted by the sound of the warning sirens, and all pupils ordered to gather at a specific point.

In February 1944, the Russians decided to carry out intensified bombing attacks on Helsinki to soften the Finnish government into accepting their demands for a peace treaty. There were three massive bombing raids on Helsinki on 6th, 16th and 26th, resulting in schools again being shut, and the civilian population being advised to move out from Helsinki.

The 6th of February was a beautiful winter's day, clear blue sky, about eight degrees below freezing, and a perfect day to go skating. Most days, after school, in the early evening, my friends and I would head to the skating rink, just a short walk from the flats, across the main road. We could hear the music blaring full blast after crossing the road. We would hasten our steps, running into the wooden changing hut, where we left our shoes, and put on our skates. All one needed to do was to start skating around the rink, and soon someone would join you. Once there was a group, one of us started skating as fast she or he could, shouting, ‘Catch me if you can.’ The first one to catch the skater was the next one to make a speedy spurt, shouting, ‘Catch me.’ Of course, the boys were usually winning. It didn’t matter, it was fun in any case.

I had been skating nearly two hours; it was getting dark, stars were twinkling, I was hungry, and decided it was time to go home. Laila had already gone. Just as I began skating towards the hut, the sound, louder than the music, of the alarm siren was heard, getting even louder, and continuous. The caretaker of the skating rink, using the loudspeaker, shouted, ’Hurry, hurry, return to the changing hut immediately.’

All skaters were cramming into the hut, hunting for their shoes, falling over each other. I managed to find my shoes, and as quickly as I could, put them on. The canons fired nonstop, and we could hear the roar of the Russian bombers. We were all panicking. I grabbed my skates, starting to run home at full speed. Just as I opened the main door, I heard something like an enormous stone falling from the sky. I dared not look; then I heard glass shattering somewhere close. I rushed to open the door of our flat looking for Mamma, then remembered that she had planned to go to the church with Vieno, and that Mummi was taking care of Juha. Laila was at home; she was lying on the floor petrified and crying. Rainer was trying to calm her down. Each time we heard the bombers approaching, he ordered me to lie down too. The air raid seemed to be lasting for ages and ages; the sky was flashing with light and the skyline was red; there was shattering of glass and heavy thumping sounds of the bombs falling on the houses.

'Why have Mamma and Vieno not come home? The service should have finished a long time ago,' we wondered. The three of us were seriously worried. Finally, we heard footsteps. Mamma told us what had happened in the church, and added, 'The air raid is over. Go to bed. I think it's best if you keep your clothes on; we might have another raid.' Mamma decided to sit up and finish the letter to Isä that she had started writing, but left it unfinished before going to church:

'Dear Yrjö,..... This evening I'll go to Käpylä church to hear Muromaa preaching, I'll finish this letter on my return. It is nearly six in the evening, Juha is with Mummi, Arna and Laila are skating. I'll take Vieno with me'. She continued when she was back home, several hours later: *'It might have been that this letter would forever have remained unfinished. Much has happened in a few hours. I arrived home around 10 pm. A most terrible bombing raid began in the middle of Muromaa's sermon. We did not even get a warning alarm, but an order that no one could leave the church, and as many as there was room for were ordered to go to the shelter under the church. The canons were firing fiercely, a bomb fell on Sampsantie* (our road)*, making a large crater. One bomb landed close to the church, hitting the rock. All windows of the church were shattered. The caretaker's flat collapsed totally with air pressure. In the vicarage all windows were broken, and their furniture*

scattered all over. We who were left in the church, were covered by soil, pieces of glass; smoke made breathing difficult. The whole building was swaying and it felt as if the roof would collapse; as if we were living our last moments. Poor Vieno, she was praying and crying. Many went down on their knees, screaming for God to help. I was praying for all the mothers, who had small children alone at home, and that God would protect us. We sang hymns to relieve the panic. God heard our prayers. A calm descended, and even the fear for the children lessened. We were freezing, the broken windows did not protect us from the perishing frost. The air raid lasted two and a half hours. It was with suspense that we returned home. All windows had been saved in our flat, even though the windows of the shops, and several in our building had been broken. Mummi had been with Juha at the surgery. All the windows of the bank were broken and plaster had fallen off the walls. Juha had been remarkably calm, simply wanting to go to the air raid shelter. Rainer and Laila were at home when the alarm sounded. Arna was at the skating rink, but just changing into her shoes. There had been panic, as everyone was looking for their shoes. Arna managed to get home in time. Poor Laila had for most of the time been lying flat on the floor and praying. Arna and Rainer stood at the window looking at the Russian phosphor balls lighting the whole city, and they had seen a bomb falling. One of the wooden houses close to us was flattened to the ground. When Rainer heard the whistling sound of bombs, he had ordered the girls to the ground but had himself remained standing. Even though it's midnight now, we have not undressed, it feels that there will be a new alarm. The following morning, she continued her writing:

'Yes, we did have another alarm. After an hour, terrible bombing again, and the air defence firing away. The walls were swaying and the beds shaking. The terrible drama lasted until five in the morning. Juha slept through it all. Laila was so afraid that I took her to my bed. I read the Bible aloud, that calmed us. God promised to give us His protection. Arna was aware of the bombing, but was so tired that she slept through most of it. Rainer sat up and did his homework, not now needed. The schools are closed. The junior schools are used to accommodate the homeless. Children have to be evacuated. At five in the morning the terrible drama ended and I went to bed, slept until Juha woke up at seven. If you intend to come, come quickly. Laina is of the opinion that we should not wait for you, just leave as soon as we can, and she said Lyyli has promised to take her and the children. Vieno does not want to leave us, she is willing to stay here or go wherever we go. I need to pack now, perhaps I can send something to Kuopio. Oh, if one would be able to receive God's wisdom and advice. One's own wisdom is not sufficient now. People are leaving the town, lorries full of furniture and people, and sledges packed with people's belongings. At Käpylä station masses of people with their belongings are queuing. Many lives have been lost. People are out of their minds; they don't want to come to the surgery as we have air raids even during the day. I wonder what will happen to the treatments that are in process? Payments will not be received from most.

Rainer just came in from his adventure trip into the town, among other things he had seen was part of a man's scalp with his earlobe just lying on the street.

May God be with you. May the Lord himself guide us with the evacuation of our children. Loving greetings. See you soon,

Karin.

There was an urgency to flee from Helsinki to a safer location. Where could a family with four children, a mother, grandmother, maid and aunt go? This was the problem my parents, separated from each other, tried to find a solution to. I do not know how they managed to find and rent two rooms from a farmhouse in a village called Röykkä, 90 kilometres west from Helsinki. The house was quite close to the main road; long distance busses passing hourly between Turku and Helsinki. This was important, because Mamma needed to earn money from her dental practice, travelling back to Käpylä several times a week.

Röykkä was a short-term sorting out place. From there Rainer was sent to Kuopio to Dahlströms to continue his interrupted schooling, I was sent to Aunt Lyyli in Raahe, to continue my schooling, Aunt Laina was placed as an extra teacher in a local infant school, and she was given a room for her private use, Laila was able to attend her school in Röykkä. Juha was looked after by Vieno and Mummi.

My parents started negotiations with the Hallanders for Laila and Juha to be sent to Sweden. It took until the end of August before they left with a big group of other children. Laila and I, having spent the summer of 1940 in Aunt Lyyli's summer cottage, this time I would be staying in her town house, jointly owned by Aunt Lyyli and her widowed friend Gerda.

Raahe, a small town on the north-west coast of the Bay of Bothnia, was historically important to us, being the town where my maternal grandparents settled as newlyweds. It was also Mamma's birth town. In 1905 when my grandfather had been appointed the lecturer of Finnish in the Swedish Lyceum, and Swedish in the Finnish Lyceum in Oulu, the family moved from Raahe. Oulu became the town where Mamma and her three sisters grew up, went to school, and where she and Mummi worked as volunteers during the Civil War in 1918. Close to Raahe, Oulu was bombed fiercely during the Continuation War; German troops, fighting in the North of Finland and Lapland were stationed there.

Aunt Lyyli's house, a typical turn of the century, pastel coloured, wooden villa, with the façade facing the sea, was situated on a corner plot of the street coming from the town centre towards the sea, and the street running along the shore. Lyyli and Gerda were an unlikely pair, both teachers. Gerda short, plump, dark haired, moving awkwardly; Lyyli tall, slim, fair haired, with kind, blue, and wise eyes. Gerda's grown-up, organist son, Erkki, lived with them. Part of the household was Maija, their homely housekeeper, and their cat, just about to give birth to kittens, on my arrival.

I was made very welcome: Maija had some freshly baked buns to offer me, and Aunt Lyyli had already been in touch with the headmaster of Raahe's co-educational Grammar School. I was able to continue my schooling without delay. On the first day in the new school, I met Eila, a girl slightly older than I, also evacuated from Helsinki. We became instantly great friends, spent a lot of time together, but never meeting after we returned to Helsinki.

The three months spent in Raahe were safe, happy and special. In the adult household I was an only child, and the three women, each in their own way, enjoyed having me there, spoiling me, and keeping me under observation. It was the first time in my life that I had been so far north in the winter. I now had the chance to observe the miracle of the light, increasing daily, made even more dramatic by the sun making the frozen sea glitter like a carpet of diamonds. Each evening I observed the changing drama of the sun lingering longer and longer, before finally fusing with the horizon, leaving a play of colours in the sky.

During the war there was a shortage of firewood to heat houses. To help the shortage, the government encouraged able bodied people to go into forests, where trees had been felled, sawing the logs into one-metre lengths, and assembling them into one cubic meter stacks. Firewood was sold by cubic metre. A small sum was paid for a cube of wood, and a metal axe, to be worn on your lapel, was given as a reward.

Erkki, Aunt Lyyli and I took part in this project. We made several skiing trips into an allocated forest, some five kilometres from Raahe. The terrain was quite flat, easy to ski on. Trees in the forest had already thrown off their snow coats, the sounds of spring were audible: crackling, dripping, and birds singing with joy. Bare patches were appearing in the sunny spots, and the trees were casting long, blue shadows on the yellow snow.

We had a division of labour: Erkki did the sawing, Aunt Lyyli and I the assembling. After an hour or so we had a break, collected dry wood for a fire, lit it, and dug a sturdy tree branch into the snow, filled the coffee pot with snow and pitched it on the branch over the fire. Once the snow melted, we added the ground coffee to the water. Maija had packed some delicious sandwiches and buns.

Aunt Lyyli knew all the wintering birds. As we were sitting relaxed, having our coffee, she pointed out the birds, listened to their singing, and explained which bird was making each particular sound. I learned so much from her. She was able from the marks in the snow to tell which animal had been walking there.

One extra pleasure of my stay in Raahe was Erkki teaching me to play the piano. This had been my dream. In the short period I stayed in Raahe, I managed to learn enough to be able to read music and play simple tunes.

The shadow side of this happy period was Lyyli's worry about my safety as a young teenage girl. She kept a sharp eye on my movements outside school hours, demanding that I came straight home, and that I did not loiter on the High Street.

Walking up and down the whole length of the High Street was what teenagers in Raahe did. It was a way for boys to meet girls and girls to meet boys. Of course, I wanted to join them, but managed to avoid her wrath by telling her that I was going to Eila's house. Together we then made our strolls on the High Street.

When the term ended, I travelled by train from Raahe to Savonlinna to be with Isä. The train was packed with soldiers, returning back to the front from their leave. It was embarrassing and overwhelming to be surrounded by so many young men, all joking, chatting and flirting with me. I was blushing, wanting to disappear under the earth; both excited and flattered. Boys had become interesting.

Isä had only one room in Savonlinna. I had reached the age when sleeping with my father in the same room felt awkward for both of us. He recognized that I was no longer a little child but a teenager. He had bought a put-you-up bed, placed it in the corner of the room, and had screened it off with a chest of drawers, to give a little privacy. Before bedtime, he disappeared for a walk, allowing me to change into my nightdress unobserved.

To highlight this change in me, Isä took me out the next day for lunch at Hotel Tott, the best and most famous eating place in town. I remember how happy I was to be escorted to a window table, and how proud to be Isä's 'lady'. He wanted to buy me summer shoes as a late birthday present. I chose pink ones; the soles were made from wood and the top from paper, woven to a cloth. No leather shoes were available. Aunt Ester from Portugal had sent me shoes that were the envy of all my girlfriends. These were bright red, of soft leather, and had wedged heels made from cork, fantastic.

After lunch we set off to drive to Kaihoniemi, where we would meet up with Aunt Laina, Vieno, Laila and Juha. Once again Aunt Laina would take care of us during the summer holidays. The foreman's cottage was now equipped with essential furniture, crockery and household goods. I felt uneasy being there; the memories from the previous summer's event was still too fresh in my mind, and this place was nothing like Kaihoniemi. Even Lake Ladoga had lost its appeal; the water seemed dirty, and I could not help thinking of the dead soldiers, Russian and Finnish, who had lost their lives fighting, and now their bodies were at the bottom of the lake. Swimming was no longer a pleasure. Already on our arrival we could hear the sounds of canons, the sounds getting louder day by day; there was nervous tension in the air.

On the 9th of June the end game had begun: A major offensive was launched by the Russians on the Karelian Isthmus. The Finnish troops, determined to hold on to the original pre-war border, were fiercely and with 'sisu' resisting the advancing Red Army, but they ended in a bitter retreat. Finland lost thousands of young men in this final stage of fighting; amongst them three of my second cousins, one aged 22 and two brothers aged 20 and 22.

It was just after midsummer when an officer knocked on the door at the cottage giving an order, 'Be ready to leave in a couple of hours, it is no longer safe for you to remain here. A horse and carriage will fetch you and take you to safety.'

There was no time to feel fear or panic; we simply had to gather the essentials we needed; everything else had to be left behind. Aunt Laina gathered the newly bought crockery, and other non-perishable small items, I carried them to a deep gully close by and buried them, still hanging on to the hope or dream of one day returning to Kaihoniemi, and us finding the items there.

In the early evening the five of us were picked up by a man with a horse and cart. We clambered on to the cart with our belongings. Juha was crying, sensing our panic. Aunt Laina tried to reassure him by picking him up and lulling him to sleep. Being rocked by the steady trot of the horse, I also fell asleep. A sharp pain woke me up; my hand had been dangling down and had been caught in the cart wheel. We stopped to see if any serious damage had been done. Luckily not, so the journey continued.

Our flight to safety was accompanied by the increasing noises of cannons and shootings. Finland was losing the war. What would happen to us, and all the Karelians who had returned to their homes? A fear, a sense of anger and hopelessness, as well as a deep sadness filled my heart. This was the last time we saw Kaihoniemi.

We were heading to Uncle Jaakko's home, close to the border. This would be the first step to safety. After resting a couple of days, we carried on from there to Kuopio by train, and spent the rest of the summer in the same cottage to which we had been evacuated during the Winter War, returning to Röykkä in late August. Mamma, having given up her surgery in Käpylä, had opened up a surgery in Röykkä, where she had a busy, thriving practice. She carried on working there from Käpylä until we moved to the centre of Helsinki in 1945. Rainer and I returned to Helsinki to continue at Käpylä Grammar School.

Autumn 1944- spring 1945

Juha and Laila left for Sweden at the end of August. It was a heart-breaking decision for my parents to send Juha, only three and a half years old, and Laila, nine years old, to a foreign country. Laila, by nature shy and reserved, now took on her shoulders the responsibility of caring for the safety of her little brother. Juha, bewildered by all the changes that were happening in his little life, and not being able to speak Swedish, relied entirely on Laila. The close bond that they made in their months in Sweden remained there in their adult life.

We all missed them both, particularly Juha, a delightful sunshine child, the apple of Isä's eye, and at a lovely age, making us laugh with his pranks and funny sayings. He had developed a great sense of humour, and his imagination was flourishing. I was responsible for telling him bedtime stories; his favourite one was 'The Red Riding Hood'. Together we invented variations to the story; she became 'The Blue Riding Hood' and 'The Big Bad Whale' became the terrifying villain.

Only as an adult and a mother can I begin to understand the impossible decisions that Finnish parents were asked to make; abandoning their children in the hope of saving their lives. We were lucky, the Hallanders had proved to be a truly caring couple.

A ceasefire was announced on 4th September and a peace treaty two weeks later. The war ended in the south of Finland but fighting went on in Lapland until late spring of 1945. I want to end this chapter by trying to give you an understanding of Finland's position in the war by using quotes from Henrik Meinander's book *A History of Finland*: pages 155-157.

'When Germany's fortunes of war had taken a definite turn for the worse in the winter of 1942-43, Finland's political leadership began to prepare for a dismantling of the coalition and for peace negotiations with the Soviet Union. But this was more easily said than done. Germany's grip on Finland and the entire Baltic region remained strong through to January 1944, when the Red Army managed to break the siege of Leningrad.'

'In the summer of 1943 hopes were being voiced that the government would intensify its efforts to get Finland out of the war between the great powers. Germany's reaction was one of anger towards such expressions of opinion, and so peace soundings were not initiated until the spring of 1944, when the situation was becoming increasingly threatening, even for Finland. Exploratory peace talks began in Moscow in March 1944 but were soon broken off because the Finnish government could not see any way it could meet the Soviet demands for 600 million dollars in war reparations and the rapid expulsion of the Germans. Germany was judged to still be far too powerful. The Finnish political leadership therefore decided, jointly with Mannerheim, to await the Allies' landing in the west in the hope that that would reduce the pressure on Finland and open up possibilities for a more acceptable peace. A few days after the landing in Normandy had commenced, all Finnish wishful thinking collapsed. Stalin had made up his mind to force Finland into a separate peace before the race for Berlin began.'

'When the front lines had stabilised in mid-July 1944, fresh and even more secret exploratory talks were set up with Moscow. Finland was keen to negotiate a peace treaty with Russia. Having given the Germans his personal assurance that his government would not enter into peace negotiations with Russia, President Ryti decided to stand down from his presidential office in favour of Field Marshall Mannerheim. Mannerheim, not being bound to Ryti's promise, was able to negotiate a ceasefire that was put in operation on 4th September; an armistice treaty followed two weeks later, on 19th September.'

'The treaty not very different from Moscow's original peace demands. The result was return to the 1940 frontiers and the loss of Petsamo, where nickel mines and ice-free harbour had been of some significance for the Finnish economy. War reparations halved to 300 million dollars, but in compensation the Porkkala Peninsula, only thirty kilometres west of Helsinki, had to be leased out as a Soviet military base. To top it all, the former coalition troops were to be disarmed or expelled from the country, and this led to a war against the German troops in Lapland in the winter of 1944-45.'

The remarkable achievement for Finland of this three-part war was that, in contrast to all other minor states involved in the war in Europe, Finland was never occupied, in spite of its thousand-kilometre-long land border with Russia.

Finland lost 94,000 lives, was badly lacerated and cut down, but remained independent. With 'sisu' and hard work Finland would rise again, stronger, and united; determined to show the world its metamorphosis to a successful modern industrial state.

After the peace treaty

There was now ceasefire, but the end of 1944 and the beginning of 1945 were a turbulent, troublesome period for Finland and all Finns. The regular payment of war reparations had begun and would continue up to the autumn of 1952. By accepting a reduced standard of living the Finns managed to fulfil this obligation.

There was still the Lapland War to be fought against our former brothers-in-arms. No deadline for this task was set, but it took months to drive the German troops to Norway. In their retreat they laid waste to most of the buildings and infrastructure in Lapland. The transition from a Finno-German coalition to a Soviet-dominated armistice was abrupt.

Considerable internal difficulties were caused by the accusation against war criminals, amongst them was President Risto Ryti, accused of his role in starting the Continuation War. Ironically, ten years earlier, in 1934, Risto Ryti had been awarded the honour of Knight Commander of the Victorian Order for his work in improving Anglo-Finnish relationships. In the trial President Ryti was given a ten year prison sentence. He was pardoned in 1949 for health reasons and died in 1956 from the chronic ill health caused by the imprisonment.

For our family the autumn of 1944 was a period of turmoil and fragmentation. We remained scattered, living in different locations: Juha and Laila in Jönköping, Isä in Savonlinna, Mamma travelling between her surgery in Röykkä and our home in Käpylä, Mummi still in Kuopio with the Dahlström family, and Rainer and I in Käpylä, cared for by our new maid, with Aunt Law's critical eye watching over me.

She invited me to share meals with her, not without first having an inspection. 'Arna, show your hands. Look, they are dirty. Go and wash them! Scrub your nails!'

'Take your shoes off! Look, there are holes in your socks.'

I dreaded these visits, except that Aunt Law was teaching me to play the harmonium that Isä had rescued from Kaihoniemi. Our home felt empty. We missed the family members, especially Juha, who had charmed us all from the moment he was born with his happy disposition, and large blue eyes. Mamma was worn out and losing weight with her long working days, and then travelling by bus the 90 kilometres between Röykkä and Käpylä several times a week. Isä was very concerned for us, encouraging us to write to him almost daily.

Following the chaos after the peace treaty, the government had decided to delay the commencement of the autumn term in Helsinki schools until the first of November. The main reason for this was the use of schools as assembling points for the returning Ingrians, our kinsmen from the Russian part of Karelia. The Russian government was forcing the return of all Ingrians back to their homeland, many of them had migrated to Finland when their land was conquered by the Finnish troops. Scouts and Guides were mobilized to help with their transition.

Each morning, at eight, we reported to our leaders in the allocated schools, waiting to be told what tasks we would be helping with. Girls worked in the kitchen, preparing food, serving food, washing up and doing other household task; boys were consigned to assembling fold-up beds, moving desks and other furniture, helping with jobs that required strength.

Ingrians, speaking good Finnish with a Karelian dialect, were well settled, and reluctant to be leaving Finland. Life, even during the war, had been good. They hated their forced returning to the far harsher life in Russia. For years the Ingrians had been free to wander between Karelia and Ingria until, with Finland's declaration of Independence in 1917, it became necessary to make a clear border with Russia.

In early October the owner of our rented flat in Käpylä informed my parents of his daughter's forthcoming marriage in the late spring; the newlyweds would need our flat. The prospect of having to move from Käpylä, a happy and safe place, was a big shock, an unexpected, crushing blow. Where could my parents find a suitable, rented flat, and another surgery for Mamma? This was now an all-consuming problem, especially an enormous headache for Isä, the head of the family. What chance would he have to search for a new flat from a distance, and with no spare time? There was a serious shortage of available rented accommodation: many buildings had been affected by the bombing, Karelians needed homes, and there had been no chance to begin new building projects.

Mamma, as always, turned to God, trusting that something would turn up. It took some months before Mamma was happy to announce to Isä, 'I told you, God has come up with a solution, you too should believe in Him and trust Him.'

God's answer to Mamma's prayers was a startling surprise, a surprise none of us would ever have dreamt of, a miracle solution offered to our approaching homelessness. One day a new patient, a tall, distinguished looking gentleman entered Mamma's surgery in Röykkä, introducing himself as Hans Brummer, addressing Mamma in Swedish. He needed urgent dental treatment. Mr Brummer was the wealthy owner of Hiiskula Manor house, situated not far from Röykkä. As his treatment proceeded, Mr Brummer and Mamma found a good rapport, sharing worries about the peace treaty, and discussing their personal concerns; Mamma using the opportunity to proclaim her faith in God. In their discussions Mr Brummer revealed that after his wife's death, he had moved to the manor house in order to take care of his country estate. His town house in Helsinki stood empty, except for his old housekeeper, still occupying one room and the use of the kitchen. He had recently had a letter from the Helsinki Housing Department, threatening to take over the vacant house for accommodating homeless people. The threat gave Mr Brummer sleepless nights and nightmares. He was alarmed by the thought of a large number of homeless people moving into this historically important building, built by his ancestor Court Counsellor Carl Brummer in 1816.

Aleksanterinkatu 14

Karin with her sisters:
Verna, Eva, Ruth (1923)

Verna
(1923)

Family photo: Mummi,
Arna, Mamma, Laila,
Rainer, Isä and Juha,
February 1948

Chapter Five
The Teenage Years 1945-1949

Before we moved into this wonderful apartment, I decided, with Mamma's approval, to attend 'The Confirmation School', religious classes required to be completed by all members of the Lutheran church, and a requirement for having a Christian wedding. These classes were held in each parish for teenagers from fifteen upwards. I was almost fifteen, and wanted to be with my friends, already fifteen. We would be confirmed together in our local Käpylä church, receiving Holy Communion for the first time.

The girls wore white long dresses (black ones were also allowed), and boys wore dark suits, white shirts with a tie. Mamma insisted that my dress should be black. 'That will help you to concentrate on the meaning of the confirmation.' I wanted to have a white dress. Mamma could not see that being the only one in a black dress would make me stand out, embarrassed, and simply thinking about the dress. It was useless to argue with Mamma, she was not listening to me. I decided to take the matter into my own hands; I borrowed a dress from a girl who had already been confirmed. I told Mamma and Aunt Law; they did not object.

Aleksanterinkatu 14

This fine house was the second oldest stone house in Helsinki, situated in the centre of the city in a prime position diagonally across from the Senate Square, and opposite the

Council of State building. At the end of the street was the sea. Mamma learned that during the Civil War in 1918, General Gustaf Mannerheim, after his appointment as the commander-in–chief fighting the Red Guards, had been using the house as his official residence. The top floor apartment of the house was already occupied by a family, known to Mr Brummer, and the ground floor had been converted to a shop, with a totally separate entrance. Mr Brummer had been given the option of finding his own tenants to fill the huge first floor apartment, but he had not been successful. Mamma quickly saw God's answer in Mr Brummer's dilemma, and suggested that we, a family of four children, grandmother and maid, would easily fill the apartment and satisfy the Housing Department, particularly as she also needed additional space for a dental surgery.

Isä was not at all happy about the prospect of us living in the centre of the city on the main street of Helsinki, with busy traffic and a noisy tramline. In his opinion it was not a suitable environment for children; no playgrounds, no nature and very few outdoor opportunities; in addition, he worried about the extra renting and heating costs. What he did not admit was his suspicion about Mamma's relationship with Mr Brummer. Ever since his bankruptcy Isä had easily felt inferior in the company of successful, wealthy, particularly Swedish speaking, men. Being far away in Savonlinna, it hurt his pride not to be in a position to offer alternative solutions to the urgent demand to vacate our Käpylä flat. What else could he do but protest? Nor was it easy for him to see his family in such a grand apartment, obtained thanks to Mamma.

Towards the end of January 1945 Mr Brummer invited Mamma to come and inspect the Aleksanterinkatu apartment. She took me with her, hoping that I would support her, and write to Isä a favourable report, urging him to accept Mr Brummer's offer. Entering this magnificent apartment, I was utterly amazed, I had never in my life seen anything like this: elegant, enormous rooms, high ceilings, tall windows, hand-painted tiles on the wood-burning fireplaces - one of them had two cherubs on the sides of the fireplace- one room had paintings above each of its doors. The layout of the apartment was amazing: you walked through one room to the next; in the centre was the enormous bathroom with one door leading to a bedroom and the other door taking you to the dining room. The dining room lead to a study/drawing room with large French windows, opening up to a long wooden balcony, facing the courtyard. Standing there, looking at the cobbled yard and the old lime trees, I was back in time, some three hundred years, to the time when the first building had been erected on this site. The prospect of moving to this fantastic flat was exciting. I had no difficulties in singing its praises to Isä. Mamma, in her turn, wrote:

'The matter is now settled, the rent, including logs for the heating is 3000 Mk, very reasonable. You, who have always cared so wonderfully for your family, you have been quite blind in this matter. God will open the eyes of a blind man, providing he asks. You'll then become even a better father, responsible also for the souls of your children.'

We moved in the spring of 1945 to our new home, Aleksanterinkatu 14, and stayed there for the next eleven years until autumn 1956. By then our family no longer needed the flat. Rainer was married, had two children, and they had their own flat. Mummi had died in 1948. Mummi's flat was rented out until her death, then owned by my parents. Laila and I were living there, I for a short period only. Juha was the only one still at home, attending the Lyceum for Boys, the best single sex Grammar School. He moved with Isä and Mamma to Kajaani when in 1956 the Ministry of Forestry issued a direction for Forestry Officers in charge of swamp drying projects to relocate into the area they covered. After we left the house, Mr Brummer's older son took charge of the building. He decided to vacate the house, giving notices to quit to the family upstairs, and the shop owners. Unoccupied, he offered Helsinki City the possibility to buy this historically important building, an offer the City could not refuse. Aleksanterinkatu 14 was renovated to its original glory, and it became the official residence of the Lord Mayor of Helsinki City in 1959. When the Presidential Palace, in turn, went through a renovation in 2012-2014, the Lord Mayor moved out temporarily from the building for President Sauli Niinistö to use the house as his official Residence.

Juha and Laila returned back home from Sweden in early June 1945. Both had changed and grown. Laila was much more confident and talkative. Juha had forgotten his Finnish, so Swedish became our home language. He surprised us with his good, polite behaviour, and how quickly he settled being back with us in our new home. He talked very little of his time in Sweden; we didn't ask. It was just lovely that we were all together. Isä was still working on the relocation of Karelians but had now been transferred from Savonlinna to much closer to Helsinki, making his coming home easier and more frequent.

There was one snag for Rainer and me. The journey to our school in Käpylä was going to be quite long and would mean catching a bus from a stop about half a mile away. We gained assurance from Isä and Mamma that we would be allowed to continue our education at Käpylä Grammar School.

Each morning, as I set out to walk to the bus stop, Rainer would tease me, 'Ha, hah ha, are you leaving this early?'

The result of this teasing was that I delayed my leaving, missed the bus, whilst Rainer, the sprinter, flashed passed me, catching the bus. Having to wait for the next bus, I was late for school, and was not only ticked off but this was noted in the end of term report; all Rainer's fault.

Having attended her final year in the Junior School in Sweden, Laila now needed to move to a Grammar School. All her friends were in Käpylä. She was hoping to begin the autumn term in Käpylä Grammar school, joining Rainer and me. Mamma had different plans and stuck to them. Laila was going to be enrolled into a Girls' Grammar School within a walking distance from our new home. The headmistress was Mamma's Christian friend. Laila's protests, anger, and the fact that she had always preferred boys to girls as her friends, was ignored. She felt hard done by, unfairly treated.

'Why are Rainer and Arna allowed to continue in Käpylä Grammar School?' she stormed.

But she was not heard and was enrolled to the Girls' Grammar School. Laila carried a grudge to the day she died against Mamma for not listening to her.

Luckily, as the autumn term started, she soon discovered a girl called Helena sharing the same walk to the school, and she was in the same class with Laila. Helena, full of fun, humorous and cheerful, was a wonderful companion, encouraging Laila to be less serious, join in her jokes and some harmless mischief. They became great friends; their friendship lasted throughout Laila's life.

Having been so well cared for in Sweden, Juha, now without much supervision, was allowed to roam on the streets of Helsinki, getting into all kinds of mischief. One day Juha's picture was on the front page of *Helsingin Sanomat* (the main national paper). A reporter spotting President Paasikivi on his walk in the harbour area, had taken a snapshot. The President is pointing his finger at two small lads playing on the thin ice, and he was clearly issuing them stern words of warning, scolding them for their dangerous play.

Next morning, to our shock and horror, we discovered what Juha, one of the lads, had been up to. Juha, proud of having met the President, and the President addressing him, thought that going on the thin ice was worth the fame.

The beautiful, spacious apartment was filled with our furniture. Surprisingly, it looked amazingly elegant in their grand surroundings. The Kaihoniemi harmonium, a lovely memento from the summers in Karelia, housed by Aunt Laina, was now handed over to us; placed in the dining room. I was really pleased to be able to play every day. Even without tuition, I was progressing, able to accompany hymn singing in Mamma's religious gatherings.

Laila, the more musical one, had the privilege of carrying on with the violin lessons she had started years ago. She became proficient enough to join the Finnish Female Orchestra, where she was transferred to playing the viola. The orchestra, giving concerts, travelled to all the Scandinavian cities.

Mr Brummer agreed to some alterations that needed to be made for our use of the flat. The fine, huge parlour, with three large windows facing Aleksanterinkatu, was divided into two: a surgery and a waiting room for Mamma's dental practice; a part of the dining room was portioned off for a small room for our maid. The maid's room, next to the kitchen, was still occupied by the elderly housekeeper of the Brummer family; she also shared the used of the kitchen with us.

We had not been at Aleksanterinkatu for long before Mamma became concerned that anyone from the street could enter our home on the excuse of needing a dentist. One particular incident triggered her anxieties: Two Russian Officers came to the surgery requesting dental treatment. Mamma, having studied Russian for several years, was so shocked that she was unable to recollect a single Russian word.

As soon as these men left, she made her decision to give up her private practice. Instead, she began searching for dental work as a school dentist. It would be a relief for her to have a monthly salary, and no longer have fights with the Tax Office. They refused to believe that a dentist could earn as little as Mamma. They did not know her; if her patients gave honest reasons for their lack of funds, she would not demand payments, trusting that God would reward her in His way.

During the early part of the summer, she both completed the treatments of her dental patients, and managed to obtain a post as a school dentist covering several schools in the suburbs of Helsinki. The new job would commence in September 1945. She would have school holidays, a monthly salary, and no strangers walking into our flat. Our space would increase by the two rooms no longer needed for her dental practice. The rooms did not remain empty; in no time they were filled with a variety of relatives, staying with us for shorter or longer periods.

Mummi came back from Kuopio and came to live with us for the remaining years of her life. Our practical, hardworking, little Mummi became the manager of the household, deciding on the meals we would eat, doing the shopping, making and altering our clothes, supervising the often-changing maids, and teaching them, and us to cook and bake. Her room, a quiet room, with a window to the courtyard, and off the entrance hall, was separated from the rest of the flat, giving her privacy.

Verna

Before the war years Verna, Mummi's second daughter, had been a regular visitor to our home. Being her goddaughter, I had spent many lovely times with her. Verna was generous and showed her affection openly with warmth and cuddles. I sensed her being free from the pietistic rules of the Finnish society. She was my vivacious, sexy, seductive, sinful 'Red

Godmother'. For me she was the one person who loved me unconditionally. She was living with her partner Birger, a divorcee, a highly intelligent man, a Finnish Chess champion, a black-market dealer, and an alcoholic. Their relationship, initially passionate and an all- consuming love-affair, had degenerated slowly with Birger's heavy drinking. Verna, in order to be with Birger, joined him in his drinking. During the war years, Verna had qualified as a cosmetologist. She was given one room in our flat to use during the day as her beauty parlour.

An incident, affecting both my image of Verna and my relationship with her, was our swimming outing. She had invited me to go swimming with her to a beach on an island, just off the mainland. As soon as we left the flat, I knew something was wrong; Verna's speech was blurred, her eyes had a glassy look, her breath smelt of alcohol, and her walk was unsteady. She was drunk. I didn't want to miss the outing, nor had I the courage to say, 'I am not coming, you are drunk.'

Wobbling and trying to hold herself steady, she stepped into the tram. I saw critical eyes looking at us. I felt ashamed, wanted to disappear, and was anxious. I was angry with my godmother; I did not want to carry the responsibility for her drunken behaviour. What if Verna loses her balance when we are on the motorboat? I wondered. What if she keels over and falls into the sea?'

No major incident happened; we managed the boat journey. Little by little Verna sobered. I relaxed, left her on the beach, and had a good, long swim. The nightmarish beginning ended with both of us enjoying the outing, and each other's company. Our outing was my last swimming trip with Verna.

On our return to Helsinki at the end of August, we noticed that Verna no longer came regularly to her treatment room. Mummi told us that Birger hadleft Verna. She was unhappy, deeply depressed, unable to work; her drinking was increasing. She rarely came to see us. Mummi visited her regularly. Then one day, some months later, Mummi told us of Verna's serious illness: cirrhosis of the liver; she was no longer fit to live on her own. Mamma and Mummi managed to persuade her to come and live with us. By early spring 1946 Verna was unrecognisable: her skin was yellow, her face puffed up and blotchy, her eyes red-rimmed, sad and sunken. Neither Mummi's loving care nor Mamma's prayers were able to rescue her back to life. Verna, before she had reached her forty-fifth birthday, was going to die.

One day, she was rushed to hospital as an emergency, already unconscious. Mummi and Mamma went with her, sat by her bedside, and each in their own way, saying their farewells, Mamma became convinced of Verna's salvation. She had gained consciousness for a brief moment; smiled, opened her eyes, and Mamma had been able to announce to her dying sister, 'All your sins are forgiven. Jesus is receiving you to a new, better life in heaven.'

Mummi did not share her grief with us. Verna, her second child, had given her much joy with her sunny disposition, and had been her companion after her husband's death. After Verna met Birger, her life had worried and saddened Mummi; careful not to interfere; she had suffered in silence. Now, she grieved in silence.

Verna's death was my first experience of losing a much-loved person. She had been in my life since I was born. Her death left an enormous empty hole, a hole impossible to fill. My 'Red Godmother', with her free and 'sinful' lifestyle, had shown and offered an alternative, a contrast, to the puritan, life-limiting view of life, prevalent in the protestant Finnish society. Verna, warm and generous, had accepted me as I was, she had loved me, had awakened in me a curiosity about how I looked, and had taught me how to take care of my complexion. In my teenage years I would badly have needed Verna to give me confidence to be me.

How clearly I remember the day, when approaching fifteen, I looked in the mirror, studying the image confronting me as if seeing it for the first time: A petite young girl, large blue eyes, a snub nose, wrinkling when she smiled, the strong jaw made her face form a triangle, and was framed by long, wavy blonde hair. 'This is me, Arna.' I remember this moment still very clearly as a moment of separation from childhood, and being my parents' child, to a person in my own right.

Summer 1945 – Spring 1946

In early July 1945 Mamma, Laila, Juha and I went for our summer holiday to be with Isä in the province of Häme, for us an unknown part of South-West Finland. Isä had rented rooms from a local farmer for about a six week's holiday. During our time in Häme events took place that would affect Mamma's life, and mine, for years ahead.

The first one was Mamma's decision to take up drawing. In her youth she had wanted to study art professionally, if she wasn't talented enough to succeed as an artist, at least she would become an art teacher. Whilst recognising her drawing skills and admiring her aquarelles, her father, being a teacher, had been totally against her art studies or becoming a teacher in any subject. Instead, he was proud of his daughter's choice of going into the medical faculty. Unfortunately, he did not live long enough to see her qualify as one of the first female dentists in Finland.

Having, for the first time in her professional life a long, free summer, Mamma had the opportunity to return to her love of drawing and painting. She bought herself a sketch pad and pastel colours. Mamma's love of colour was obvious even in her dental work; she took great pain in making the right colour choice for her patients' dentures. This summer was the beginning of her serious desire to learn more, and the start of attending classes. She produced numerous pleasing and skilled artworks, and moved on to oil painting later.

Having encouraged me to join her in her sketching sessions, we sat together looking at subjects to draw, made pastel drawings of the grey, old timber outbuildings scattered around the farm, and we sketched the unfamiliar landscape around us: endless yellow grain fields, with a river cutting a blue band into the yellow pastures; there were no lakes, no hills or forest where we sat. I loved these sessions and learned a lot from her observations.

The second thing to happen was Mamma's serious illness. As long as I can remember Mamma had complained of feeling unwell or being tired. She was, in practice, a single, working parent, with Isä's work taking him away from home for several months. He, of course, contributing to parenting from a distance by his very frequent letters, giving detailed guidance to Mamma and each of us, but Mamma carried the day-to-day responsibility. As children we had no understanding of how hard her life was. She, even when physically present, was for me an absent mother: her thoughts somewhere else or she was working, tired, attending religious meetings, and unable to see to her children's needs. My longing for maternal care was brushed away by the comment, 'Arna can manage', and so I did, but feeling as a motherless child.

Mamma had been seriously ill for the first time in 1937, then diagnosed with pancreatitis. She had been given strict instructions about her diet, especially to avoid fried and fatty foods. After the anxieties, strains, and actual food shortages of the many war years, it was no wonder that Mamma's pancreatitis flared up in an alarming way. Her body had had enough. After suffering severe pains, and her complexion turning yellow, she was admitted to Turku General Hospital for observations and treatment. Visiting her with Isä, I saw her buried under the white sheets of the hospital bed, hardly recognizable, fragile, and shrunk. She had lost weight; her face was jaundiced. Her blue eyes, even bluer than before, in the yellow face, were focusing on me. Seeing my worried look, she picked up her Bible, opened it by random to find words of comfort, and read:

'God says: I have heard your prayer and seen your tears; I will heal you. I will add fifteen years to your life.' (Said to King Hezekiah, in 2 Kings 20)

What a relief! Mamma was not going to die, but the death sentence, colouring the next fifteen years ahead, was there. We, even Isä, took these words of God literally. How well I remember the constant, underlying anxiety about Mamma's sudden death: I panicked if she was late coming home; I panicked if she was resting, totally still and motionless; I panicked every time she was unwell.

'This will be my last coat, my last dress, my last pair of shoes,' these remarks of hers hurt, caused fear, were a knife stab in the heart. I sensed Mamma's longing to die, longing to be with her Healer, longing to be the bride of Jesus. The earthly life, we, her family, were too much for her.

The allocated time was up when she reached her sixtieth birthday. She had been absolutely and totally convinced of Jesus taking her, if not before, but certainly when fifteen years were up. Her birthday, 29th January 1960, arrived. Mamma did not die. A year later, at 61, she did nearly die of a serious brain haemorrhage. By then I was living in England, married, and had two small children. Mamma died in 1988, a month before her 89th birthday. Her funeral was a beautiful, joyous celebration; she was Christ's bride, He was receiving her into His arms.

The third event affecting my teenage years, and far beyond, was being sent, on Mamma's insistence and initiative, to a week-long Swedish YWCA summer camp, held in Houtskär, one of the outer islands of the Finnish archipelago of the Gulf of Bothnia. The camp's organisers, the Provost Une Gräsbeck and his wife Dagny, a loving, deeply Christian couple, were friends of Mamma. Letters had been exchanged; Dagny was pleased to welcome me. I was not keen to take part in a religious summer camp, particularly in one conducted in Swedish. There was no choice, the matter had been fixed.

Towards the end of August, I travelled by train to Turku harbour, found the right boat, and settled in a good place for the five hour's long boat journey. Still miserable and angry with Mamma, I began to observe the other girls, and listened to their Swedish natter, not wishing to join them. Looking at the glittering sea in the late afternoon sunshine, feeling the soft wind on my face, smelling the salty sea air, and watching the boat manoeuvring her way through the belt of islands, the smaller ones just cliffs, the larger ones filled with summer cottages, my mood changed, a sense of excitement and freedom filled me. As I turned around, my eyes were drawn to two girls, about my age and size, sitting separately from the group; one with almost black hair and unusually dark brown eyes, the other girl, with thick blonde hair, gathered into one braid. She had large, expressive hazel-coloured eyes. My ears pricked up: The girls were speaking Finnish.

The dark haired one said, *'Me ollaan varmasti ainoat suomea puhuvat'* (I bet, that we are the only two Finnish speakers in the whole group.')

I walked towards them, and responded in Finnish, *'Tässä on vielä yksi'* ('Here is one more'), and introduced myself as Arna.

The dark haired one said, 'I am Riitta, and this is my cousin Seija'.

I learned that that they both had a clergyman father, and that Seija's father and Riitta's mother were brother and sister.

The three of us bonded instantly, stuck together, remained detached observers of the group, and, when alone, carried on speaking Finnish. I was pleased to discover that Seija lived in the suburbs of Helsinki, making it possible for our friendship to continue, whilst Riitta came from a small town in Häme.

The days were filled with a programme of talks; we had free time to go swimming, play netball, and go for walks across wooden bridges to the other small islands forming Houtskär. In the evenings we gathered in the 300-year-old wooden church for prayers, talks, singing and music.

One girl, Yvonne, seventeen and older than most of us, was already a pianist of concert standard. She played solo pieces, and duets with the eighteen-year-old son of the Gräsbecks, he an already an accomplished violinist. We all watched with great interest and curiosity a romance, feeding our fantasies, growing under our eyes between these two talented musicians. It seemed obvious they were meant for each other. It was no surprise to discover their romance continued after the camp had finished, leading them to a professional partnership, and marriage. In London, only a few years ago, I had the chance to meet their son, an internationally known pianist Folke Gräsbeck. He was very interested to hear how I had come to witness the very beginning his parents' love story.

The purpose of this YWCA camp was to convert us to witness-bearing Christians, promising to follow Jesus, and professing our faith wherever or whenever there was an opportunity. Being over-saturated with Mamma's daily preaching, I had made a vow to myself not to be converted whatever pressure was put on me. I simply wanted to enjoy my little holiday, the invigorating seascape, the rocks, the vast open sea, the wind and waves, and make new friends.

On the last evening we walked together to the church. Many friendships had been made, such as my life-long friendship with Seija. On entering the church, we were greeted by soft organ music, candles lit at the end of each pew, and arrangements of wild flowers at the altar and on the windows. The festive atmosphere was promising an emotional farewell evening.

Mother Dagny, as we called her, stood up, spoke of the importance of having Jesus guide your life; ending by telling Une's and her love story. Une, aged twelve, had inherited a gold chain for a watch hanging around the neck. He decided to keep the chain for his future bride and buy her the watch. She, Dagne, age six, had inherited a golden watch, without the chain. The watch was put away into safe keeping, and Dagny made the decision that the chain should be her future husband's present to her. 'We were meant for each other long, long before we met,' she told us. 'Our love united the chain and the watch into one.' Then Mother Dagny added, 'Wait patiently, the right person will turn up. Love is precious, like a pearl necklace. Keep the necklace whole, ready to hand it over to your loved one. Do not scatter the pearls until you are sure of your love. Walk with Jesus. He will protect you from temptations.'

Then we were invited to stand up one by one, making our promise to follow Jesus. The first girl stood up, then one after another followed, committing themselves to Jesus. I remained seated, determined not to be forced to give a promise I may not be able to keep. Gradually, I felt more and more uncomfortable and guilty, particularly when Seija and Riitta stood up. Then one of the leaders rose from her seat, fixing her eyes on me, proclaimed, 'We still have amongst us one lost sheep. Jesus's open arms are here to receive you.'

The girls in the pews turned around and stared at me. I felt intense pressure, felt a traitor, and felt forced to stop resisting. I gave in. I shot up, my heart beating fast, my legs shaking, and with a trembling voice said, 'I too promise to follow Jesus.'

'Praise be to the Lord, the last lost sheep has found her way home,' the leaders said in chorus, all singing, 'How beautiful is the sound of Jesus's name....'

I was not proud of myself; the promise was made in weakness. It embarrassed me, it felt false, gave me no feeling of joy, instead a sense of serious responsibility to conduct myself according to what I had promised.

Returning home, there was Mamma eagerly waiting for me to tell her what happened. It took me a while to say aloud, 'I have been converted.'

Having heard my story and my promise, Mamma dismissed my confession.

'I don't think that you have received the Holy Ghost. Where is your joy, where is the wonder?'

According to her I should feel jubilant, and go around telling people, 'Your sins are forgiven, if you follow Jesus'.

Being converted became a real nightmare; something was demanded that I was not able to deliver. I was in an inner turmoil, hating the thought of becoming like Mamma, whose preaching had for years embarrassed me. I did have to witness my faith, and I solved it by having a golden cross on a chain round my neck and one on my blazer. My teenage years, conflicted, anxiety ridden, feeling both dangerous and exciting, had begun.

The autumn term began with the knowledge that this was going to be the last year for class A to be together. At the end of the spring term some of us would be leaving; the rest would be joining the class B, for another three years of studying towards the matriculation examinations.

One new girl, Eevi had joined us from far north, almost Lapland. Her parents, teachers in a small village with no grammar school, were keen to give their only daughter a chance for higher education. They had sent Eevi to stay with her Aunt, living on her own in the Olympic village, and attend the Käpylä Grammar School. Eevi, looking quite different from us fair skinned ones, was more like the Lapps with her almost black hair, dark brown complexion, and steel grey eyes. She was an excellent storyteller, entertaining us with tales from the north, told in her dialect, so different from the Helsinki slang. She and I quickly became good friends. On the days I was visiting Aunt Laina, we walked together to the Olympic village, and I learned much about her life.

The fifth-year pupils carried the responsibility for the choice and production of the annual Christmas play, chosen from one of the traditional fairy stories. Sakari Topelius, the most famous Finnish writer for children, had adapted many of these stories to plays in rhyme form. Our chosen play was going to be 'Prinsessa Ruusunen' (Sleeping Beauty), and Lukki had agreed to be the director.

We discussed who should take each role: Kyllikki would be the Queen, Reino, a sturdy blond boy, would be the King, Eevi was given the role of a pageboy. Smaller roles were found for all who wanted to act. The key roles were the Prince, the Princess and the Fairy Godmother. No discussion was needed for the role of the Prince; the only choice was Jaakko, the tallest boy, already seventeen, very handsome, looking like Clark Gable with darkish brown hair and speckled brown eyes, confident and relaxed in his way of moving.

There were several possibilities for the choice of the Princess; in the end it was narrowed down to Hilkka, a tall blonde girl, already looking like a model, and me. Lukki decided the final choice should be voted on, but anonymously. To my delight and surprise, I won the vote. I had had my fantasies, but to be actually chosen was just fantastic. Raija, another blonde, tallish girl, became the Fairy Godmother.

The cast now chosen, learning our parts, and the frequent rehearsals filled the autumn term. There were no funds for costumes; each performer was given the responsibility for their outfit. There was an acute shortage of new fabrics, so costumes had to be made from available old materials. Mummi confidently agreed to make the princess's dress from old lace curtains and worn-out cotton sheets, she being a real master in recycling, combining old materials, and redesigning something wearable from worn out fabrics. I was pleased with the astonishingly pretty dress she made for the princess.

The Christmas play, at the end of the term, was performed to the whole school, as well as for our families and our friends. In the rehearsals the scene of the kiss awakening the sleeping princess had been skipped over; Jaakko and I were too shy and embarrassed; Lukki did not insist.

The day arrived when Jaakko and I knew there was no opting out, the kiss had to be given. Nervous of acting in front of a big audience, we were ready. The hall was packed full, the stage setting looked great, the performance started well; everyone had learned their lines. The audience showed their appreciation at the end of the first act by both clapping hands and stamping their feet. In the second act the crucial moment had arrived: The prince walking slowly towards the sleeping princess, looking astonished by what he discovered, and stunned by her beauty, he stopped, bent down ready to give her a kiss, that life-giving kiss. Tensed up by Jaakko's slow-motion performance, waiting, I heard a child's voice, loud and clear, shouting, *'Nyt se pussaa Arnaa.'* ('Look, Jaakko is giving a kiss to Arna.')

I recognised the voice, Juha's. He knew the story by heart, and I knew he had been egged on by Rainer. The audience burst out laughing. The key moment was lost. I felt angry and embarrassed. Why had Rainer wanted to play such a mean trick? Why was he so cruel? As far as the audience was concerned, the play was a great success, in no way spoilt by Rainer's dirty trick.

After the performance we had a party with dancing. Dancing had been forbidden during the war years; school dances were again allowed. Having gone through my religious conversion, I was anxious to find out whether dancing was considered a sin. I turned for advice to my mentor Maria, a young, devoted Christian. She took my problem seriously, considered it, then came up with the suggestion, 'It is OK for you to dance, but avoid dancing a tango, dancing tango might awaken your passions.'

At the party Jaakko asked me time and again for a dance. We were both clumsy beginners, moving around with the music, Jaakko holding me firmly. Being so close, his warm hand holding mine, made a shiver go down my spine. Was this what Maria meant about passion awakening in me? Whatever it might be, it felt good and exciting. At the end of the evening, I was left happy and in anticipation of what might follow when we returned to school in January. We waved our goodbyes and parted for our Christmas holiday.

Our Christmas preparations were done as a real team effort: Isä was responsible for getting the ham from a local farmer, and making 'kalja' (mild beer), Mamma took charge of the sweets, such as making wafer-thin oat biscuits, and fudge, Mummi, Laila and I baked 'piparkakkuja' (gingerbread shapes), 'joulutorttuja' (prune tarts), and Karelian pasties. Rainer was sent to the local market to select a Christmas tree, taller than before, suitable for the grand living room, with its high ceiling. The Christmas tree was brought in early on Christmas Eve morning. Rainer, Laila, Juha and I were given the task of decorating it: a dozen or more real candles, in firm holders, tinsel, strings of flags, little tonttus, and sparkles hanging on the branches, ready to be lit when the time was right.

The room tidied, all the preparatory work done, by twelve noon the whole family, including Aunt Laina, gathered around the radio to hear President Paasikivi's declaration of 'Christmas Peace' for the following forty-eight hours, and his wishing the whole nation a Peaceful Christmas.

In the late afternoon we walked across the Senate Square to the Helsinki Cathedral for a short Christmas Eve service. The aroma of the spruce needles of the huge, candle-lit Christmas tree, and soft organ music greeted us. Time to be still before the service began, time to reflect on the Christmas message, and time to feel hope. The church was packed. This year the message of the service was special: 'Fighting had ended, Finland had peace.' The gratitude was heard in the massive sound of all joining in singing the familiar Christmas hymns, in the listening to the reading of the Christmas Gospel, and the choir's performance of traditional Finnish carols.

Back at home we carried on with a traditional, short programme: Laila playing a couple of violin pieces, Rainer reading the Christmas Gospel, and Isä, happy to show off his beautiful baritone voice, singing solo one or two Christmas carols, then we all joined, accompanied by me on the harmonium. Of course, Mamma preached of the miracle of Christ being born to save us.

Then it was time for the traditional Christmas meal. The dining table, decorated with candles and red tulips, ready to offer a 'Smörgårdsbord', with salads, liver pate', pickled herring, smoked fish, assortment of Karelian and other pasties, variety of bread, followed by 'Lipeäkala' (dried cod, soaked in lye, to soften it), served and made bearable with a delicious white sauce. The main course was ham, wrapped and baked in a rye dough, served with oven baked mashed potato, swede and carrot bakes, and peas. The meal was finished with rice pudding, an almond hidden in it. However full you might be, you just had to have some pudding in the hope of getting the lucky almond, and the luck for the whole next year. Laila was the lucky one. We would follow her year 1946 with interest.

Looking at the candlelit tree, we played a game of each choosing a candle, and seeing whose would last longest to burn out, and whose would die first, while we waited for the doorbell to ring, announcing the arrival of Father Christmas, the moment Juha had been waiting for the whole evening.

Father Christmas did arrive in person. Mamma had sneaked out, put on her fur coat inside out, wearing a mask with a long white beard, and Isä's walking stick to lean on. Juha was still fooled, he did not recognise Mamma, but was left wondering why Father Christmas left his walking stick behind. It was the first Christmas we, the Pelkonen family, had been together since 1941. Our hearts were filled with a deep sense of gratitude, and wonder: We had been spared. Once we were all in bed, feeling happy on so many accounts, I stayed awake a long while, my heart and mind too full of feelings, and dreaming about Jaakko, not only the prince in the play, but now my 'prince' I wanted to go out with.

How it happened, I do not know but after the Christmas break Jaakko and I started going out together, ignoring the teasing remarks, *'Pitkä ja Pätkä'* ('giant and stump'), Jaakko was 184 cm, and I, almost a foot shorter, at 158 cm. Trying to arrange our dates secretly was not difficult, as I now lived in the centre of Helsinki; none of our friends would see us there.

On winter nights we met at the harbour area, often just walking, looking at the frozen sea, and the cars driving on the road made on the ice, replacing the boat service, to the island of Suomenlinna, the 18th Century sea fortress, built by Swedes to protect the entry to Helsinki. As the spring, with its light nights arrived, we climbed up to the top of 'Observation Hill', sitting there on a bench, seeing the panorama of Helsinki in front of us, and sensing the world around us awakening from its frozen state, echoing what was happening within us. We were searching for ways of expressing, and understanding our tentative, tender new feelings of love. Hesitantly, Jaakko would take my hand, clasping it firmly in his big hand, or gently stroke my cheek, or his cheek would touch mine. I would lean closer towards him; he would put his arms around me, holding me tightly. Hardly any words were exchanged, they were not needed. There we sat, in the awakening of spring, my heart bursting with happiness. We did not kiss, we were too shy, and I too anxious to risk breaking my 'pearl necklace'. Before we knew it, the 31st May was there, the day the intermediate school ended, a day of celebrations for our achievements.

The tradition was to dress up in out-grown, too small and childish outfits, and bring our favourite dolls, teddies, and other soft toys to the school. It was a day of saying farewell to childhood, saying farewell to compulsory school attendance. The party atmosphere, the laughter, and the sense of freedom masked the sadness of saying our goodbyes to those friends who were not coming back to school in September. One of them was Jaakko.

When I left Helsinki in June to be a companion and a teacher of Finnish to the daughter of one of Mamma's friends, our farewells had been casual. We had assumed we would see each after the summer. A few letters were exchanged, no compensation for us being together. Then letters stopped. During the summer Jaakko's family moved north. Jaakko did not contact me to say 'Goodbye'. My first, sweet, unforgettable, but short-lived romance was over, leaving me with a puzzle: Why no goodbye?

Upper classes 1946-1948

The new term began with a sense of unfinished business, and sadness in my heart; Jaakko did not return to school in the autumn. The autumn term 1946 began with mixed feelings for many of us: excitement, curiosity, and apprehension. The two rival classes A and B had been combined, but never became one group; the rivalry remained. We were all missing those classmates who had left us after completing the middle school, amongst them, Jaakko. I felt let down by him, could not understand his behaviour. Our short, beautiful, so important romance had obviously meant far less to him than for me. I remembered every little detail of our time together.

My class was well aware of Jaakko and I going out together. Two boys offered to take Jaakko's place; one I simply ignored as a bad joke, the other one was Olli. He lived near my bus stop. He began waiting for me after school, walking with me, and seeing me off to the bus. I enjoyed his company; he was talkative and humorous. Olli was not a charmer to look at: average height, stocky, with a reddish, pimply face, deep set, small pig's eyes, and dark, thick and very straight hair, standing up like a hedgehog's spikes. He wasn't particularly clever; his greatest asset was his musicality, and his deep melodic baritone voice, even in speaking.

Olli introduced me to classical music. He took me to my first symphony concert. We heard Beethoven's 'Eroica' symphony, played by the Helsinki symphony orchestra.

I sat listening spellbound, emotions and feelings in my body stirred up as the orchestra blasted full force the jubilation of victory. A new world full of treasures had opened up, thanks to Olli. We enjoyed many concerts together; we remained good friends for many years, until he wanted more than a platonic friendship. As an undergraduate, Olli applied, and was accepted to become a member of the famous ***Ylioppilaskunnan Laulajat, YL*** (Male choir of the University Students), and for years he found deep satisfaction singing in this fine choir. The choir made many trips abroad.

I had moved away from my school friends to a different circle of friends, the Christian teenagers, meeting in the centre of Helsinki. A romantic dreamer, I was still searching for my new Prince Charming amongst like-minded boys, and rejected Olli.

Kyllikki and Eevi carried on in the upper classes. My friendship with Kyllikki had altered soon after starting the Grammar School. She was serious, not interested in skating or skiing, nor in boys or other girly things, whilst I was quite sporty, had a group of mixed friends, and was living in a romantic fantasy land. Kyllikki became infatuated with our new female teacher in History, and history became her key interest, and she still continued to be the highest-ranking student in our class. It was obvious that she was heading towards an academic career, entering the Helsinki University with History as her main subject, and gaining a MA (with the highest award, laudatur). After her degree she took a post as a History teacher in one of the Helsinki Grammar Schools, and, later, was appointed the Head Mistress of that same school and stayed in that position until she retired. She was highly regarded both by her colleagues as well her students. She never married. We remained friends, exchanged letters, e-mails, and meeting occasionally throughout the years. In 2015 I met her for the last time for lunch in Helsinki. By then her breast cancer had spread beyond further help. We remembered events from the many school years we had shared, reminiscing on the hard times during the war. Then we said our goodbyes. I was left with the memory of a fine, highly intelligent, thoughtful, deeply respected friend.

Eevi and I continued our friendship. On my regular visits to Aunt 'Law', before being scrutinised by her critical eyes, I stayed in Eevi's place. We had fun together; I liked her humour, her way of speaking, her accurate observations, and, importantly, the fact that she had not shot up in height during the summer months, as most of the other girls had. We were the two shortest in our class.

The autumn term had not been going for long when we all noticed that Eevi was coughing a lot, but we thought no more about it. She did not return to school after our Christmas break. The alarm bells started ringing. I was not surprised when a few days later Lukki informed us that Eevi would not be coming back, and continued, 'Eevi's parents have been told that her cough is due to Eevi suffering from tuberculosis. She needs plenty of rest and needs to be cared for at home.'

Before the half term skiing holiday, Eevi's mother wrote to me inviting me and two boys to travel up to their home

near Oulu to spend the holiday with Eevi. We accepted the invitation, and so Pertti, Eevi's special friend, Olli and I took the long train journey up north, looking forward to the fantastic chance to ski in the region with a chain of Arctic mountains. At the station Eevi's father, a small man, with a weatherworn darkish complexion and a welcoming smile greeted us, saying how much Eevi was looking forward to our visit. A horse and sledge were waiting outside the station. The snow was thick on the ground, the air crisp and clear, not too cold, a comfortable
-12C. The horse trotted along the snowy road towards a large wooden building. Eevi's father said, 'Welcome. This is our school, and the right wing is our home.'

The smell of newly baked bread greeted us as soon as the door was opened. Eevi, even smaller and thinner than when we last saw her, was standing next to her mother, a fair, roundish, homely woman, taller than her husband.

Eevi, beaming with happiness at seeing us, said, 'Great, you are here. I didn't believe that you would come.'

Eevi's mother joined her in welcoming us, expressing her gratitude to us for coming.

We were starving; this was understood. After unpacking, we settled down to a typical country meal of rye bread, butter, meat stew and mashed potatoes, followed by lingonberries with homemade ice cream. Eevi was keen to hear all the news from our school, and her various friends from our class. It hurt to see the sadness in her eyes as she listened to our tales with great interest.

Next morning, Eevi's father guided us, showing us the ski track to follow. We all set off, skiing up to the fells. When he turned to go back home, Eevi decided to join him, no longer strong enough to ski for several hours. The track took us first into a dense forest with tall, heavily snow laden spruces. Their majestic, serene beauty gave an overwhelming feeling of the sacredness of an ancient Holy Forest. We were criss-crossing through the forest to white, treeless spaces, either fields or forest lakes, and then began the climb up the fell; Olli and Pertti challenging each other to be first at the top. Olli won; he was good at all sports. A vast panorama of endless forests, white fields, frozen lakes, here and there scattered dots of red houses broke the monochrome scene and brought home the sparse population in this wilderness.

We had been skiing for almost three hours; it was time to turn back to be with Eevi. Pertti and Olli skied with ease down the long track from the top; not so easy for me. The initial exhilaration of the speed was fantastic, but as the speed going down increased, my excitement turned into fear. 'I'll hit a tree, help!' I cried. Braking did not work; my panic was increasing. The only way to stop the speed was to use my bottom, sitting on the skis. It did the trick. The hill in front of me was now manageable, but I could feel my ski-pants being torn when my bottom hit a broken tree branch sticking up on the track. I continued upright down the hill, with the torn cloth flapping like a flag in the wind. The boys found my poor effort highly amusing and were joking, 'Your underpants are showing.' I felt embarrassed and ashamed of my poor skiing skills. Eevi's mother mended my skiing pants, enabling me to join the boys with more success the following day. We made many lovely trips down the slopes, and spent plenty of time with Eevi, before the three of us took the long railway journey back to Helsinki.

Eevi and I carried on writing to each other during the spring term, then in the middle of June her letters stopped. I did worry even though during summer holidays schoolfriends were forgotten, and the holidays take over.

Summer 1947, Isä's 50th birthday on 21st June

Preparations had been going on for weeks and weeks for the celebrations of this important day. Mummi and our maid were responsible for the catering, available all day: fresh coffee, served with a savoury 'sandwich cake', homemade cookies, and, most importantly, a birthday cake, a sponge cake, moistened with alcohol spruced juice, filled and decorated with cream and the season's first strawberries. Our front door would be kept open; the celebrations started already at midnight. Isä's colleagues had planned a surprise visit then. During the day of his birthday people would be coming unannounced with their gifts.

Mamma had been told of Isä's colleagues' plan. She wanted to welcome them with a cocktail, but alcohol wasn't available, unless you had obtained a ration card. As a Christian, she wouldn't apply for one nor allow Isä to have one. Her solution was she would make her own delicious liqueur by using *lakka* berries (cloudberries), sugar, some spices, and 'Spiritus Forte' (70% pure alcohol). As a dentist she was able to write a prescription for *'Spiritus Forte, for external use only'*. I was sent to the Chemist with the prescription. This special, golden, and heavenly tasting lakka liqueur was going to be Mamma's gift to Isä on his special birthday as well as served to some chosen guests.

Midnight came. We heard male voices singing a serenade outside our door. Isä, having suspected something might happen, went down to meet his colleagues, and managed to look startled. He was delighted to lead his friends to our impressive living room. Mr Hyry, a close friend, spoke for all the colleagues, praising Isä for his modesty, his friendship, and his ability to work as an equal with men under him; then inviting the head of the department, Mr Bockström, to join him in handing over the present, a huge oil painting, depicting a scene from the Helsinki Harbour, painted by a well-known Finnish artist, Kalimo. Isä's thanks and response were genuine, amusing and witty. Mamma had meanwhile disappeared into the dining room, now she came to the doorway, carrying the beautiful Persian tray my Aunt Ester had given us, with glasses filled to the brim with lakka liqueur, just taking the small step up, leading to the living room. Shock and horror; there was an almighty crash; Mamma had stumbled. Broken glasses, sticky yellow liquid flying all over the floor. I rushed to clear the mess. Mamma did not apologise, instead she said, 'This was God's punishment for getting the alcohol on wrong pretence.' I could see how embarrassed, crestfallen, and upset she was.

This was by no means an end of Mamma's liqueur making; using lakka, black currants and *mesimarja* (artic raspberry, the literal translation is honey berry) she made many delicious liquors. The best one was her *mesimarja* liqueur, this berry, growing on the edges of ditches, is the most precious, rare, and sweet of all the berries. In Finnish folk poetry a lover uses *'mesimarja'* to address his beloved: 'My honey berry, my *mesimarja'*.

Isä, undisturbed, and determined not to have his celebration fail, came quickly to Mamma's rescue. He found new glasses, and decided to take care of handling the liqueur around to his colleagues. All ended well, mamma joined to be thanked for her liquor, better than what was commercially available.

All day guests came in a steady stream, they had to be happy with coffee and cakes. The festivities ended with those still with us joining in the thanksgiving hymn: 'Kiitos sulle Jumalani, armostasi kaikesta...' (Thank you my God for your grace, for all my experiences, good and bad...)

It was my turn to spend my holiday with the Dahlström family in their country place, Halmenjoki. The large log house on three floors had been in the Dahlström family for three generations. In the autumn of 1939, during the evacuation, we had spent some weeks living there. Now in the summer, the villa and especially the garden, looked totally different. The veranda had flowering plants and garden furniture, the garden was full of flowers, fruit trees, red and black currant bushes, and strawberry beds. Two enormous commercial greenhouses had been added, filling most of the area leading to the lake. Two of the four cousins, Piittu, seventeen and Hannu, a year younger than me, were the ones I spent time with.

Eevi's death

In late July my stay was interrupted by a phone call from Mamma. 'I have sad news to tell you,' she informed me.

'God has taken Eevi to heaven. So sad, but you should rejoice that her suffering has ended.' She insisted that I need to attend Eevi's funeral.

After Mamma's phone call, I was not able to think clearly; I was acting like a zombie, putting a few items in a bag, ready to take a train up north the next day. Sitting in the train, sad and lost, I had time to think. I need a floral tribute for Eevi. I have hardly any money, what shall I do? Perhaps I could make a spray of wild flowers? I remembered Eevi telling me about a forest lake close to her home, and how it was full of waterlilies each summer. What would be more appropriate than to make my floral tribute of waterlilies? I could use conifer sprigs as the base into which to fix the flowers. My decision was made.

Naturally, I wanted to bid my goodbyes to my close friend Eevi, but the journey terrified me. What could I say to Eevi's grieving parents? There was no way to comfort them or even attempt to understand the depth of their heart-breaking sorrow. Eevi was their only child. On arrival at Eevi's home, feeling awkward, not knowing what to do or say, I was rewarded by seeing how much Eevi's parents appreciated my coming. They were trying to make me comfortable in spite of their sorrow. Early on the day of the funeral, I sneaked out. It was a glorious summer morning; the sun was well above the horizon. Walking along the path to the lake, in the eerie beauty of the misty morning, a strong, almost medical smell of the white marshland flowers hit my nostrils. The world was soundless; the stillness of the lake only disturbed by rings made by fish jumping. Eevi was near me as I stepped through the soft marshland into the lake. Tears, held back until now, broke free, rolling down my face and naked body.

As I waded into the muddy water, the icy water hitmy legs before I started swimming towards the waterlilies. Keeping afloat by paddling with one hand, and pulling the flowers up with the other hand, was challenging. The effort was worth it, I had enough for a spray. The virginal, white spray looked stunningly beautiful.

The sun was by now well up in the sky, the air was warming rapidly, promising a hot summer's day. Walking briskly back to the house, I was shocked to see at the centre of the yard a large stand with the open coffin being placed on it. Wooden benches filled the yard behind the stand. Putting my spray on the ground, I tiptoed timidly towards the coffin: There was Eevi, dressed in white, lying with her fingers crossed; a New Testament resting on her chest as if she would be asleep, like Snow White, so lifelike, so beautiful. Bursting into uncontrollable sobs, my heart shouted,

Why you Eevi, my dear friend, why did you have to die? Please, let it be a dream. Please, walk with me again, laugh and tell jokes.

The courtyard was beginning to fill up with country people: women in long black skirts, men in dark suits, young people and children putting some colour onto the sombre scene. Only then did it dawn to me that the funeral was going to be held right here, in the open air. Leaving my spray behind, I ran in, quickly changed into my best summer dress, and joined the mourners. The vicar was standing behind the coffin. Crying silently, unable to take in the funeral service, unable to hear what the pastor said, and unable to join in singing the hymns, I sat on the wooden bench in a haze, waiting for my turn to step forward to the coffin. I had never seen a dead body before, nor had any of my contemporaries died. The ceremony felt unreal, as if I was watching a film. I saw the long line of mourners coming to the coffin, some standing still for a moment, some bringing a single flower. It was my turn to lay my spray amongst the many floral tributes. As I picked the spray up, to my horror, all I could see, was limp, wilted waterlilies; they had not survived in the hot sun. I felt so ashamed. I had tried so hard to give Eevi something special and beautiful, and had failed. Suddenly my anger turned towards Mamma. Why had she made me come? It was too much to ask; I wanted to run away to someone who would hold me, who would comfort me, and who would understand me.

The next morning what a relief it was to close the door of 'the house of death' and take the train back to Kuopio. On the four-hour journey there was time to go through the many memories I carried in my heart, time to say goodbye in private. How well I remembered Eevi's arrival into our class: A strange, small dark bird from the north flying into our well-established group. It didn't take long for her to join us in our pranks, have fun and be one of us. Then, as suddenly as she had arrived, she flew away, this time far, far away to an unknown world. Back in school, I would tell the class about the funeral, we would hold a memorial for Eevi. She had become a close school friend. The truth was, that my after-school life was no longer in Käpylä. I had now many new friends from different schools, and Seija had become my 'best friend'.

Back to Halmenjoki

The sun was shining brightly on my return to Halmenjoki, echoing my joy to be back in the carefree summer life. Piittu welcomed me with her news of us two going the same evening to '*lavatanssit*', (a dance held on an open-air platform) some five kilometres away. What welcome news. My first dance event outside school dances, would, for sure, bring me back to being a normal teenager; worried only how I looked and how I danced. My party frock was waiting. There would be time for me to wash my hair. Now would be the time to use the sachet of special shampoo from Sweden, saved for a special occasion.

Piittu, having attended many dances, was confident, relaxed and excited. I, a newcomer, was nervous, anxious, and scared, but at least confident with my blonde hair looking great and giving a slight scent of lily-of the valley. When we arrived, the dance was in full swing; we heard the music from a fair distance away. There was no fear of us being left standing as 'wallflowers'; young lads, farmers' sons and farm workers were waiting as we approached the area. Piittu had her favourites, I danced with anyone inviting me. During the evening, one lovely looking blond boy, Jukka, a son of a farmer, became my regular dance companion, rushing to ask me for the next dance as soon as the music stopped. Jukka offered to escort me home on his bike. Cycling in the white summer night, with me sitting on the bar, Jukka leaning close over me, burying his face into my hair, breathing in its fragrance, what could be more wonderful?' My precious shampoo had done its trick. The whole evening had been special, giving food for new fantasies: What would life be like as a farmer's wife? I did not have a chance to go to a dance again. My stay with the Dahlströms was over; the weeks with my cousins had been great.

Seija and her family

Back home in Helsinki, the summer holiday was nearly over, but there would still be time to be with Seija and her family, and join the activities arranged by the local parish on one of the islands nearby. Seija and I had initially met only now and again, but our friendship had strengthened, and she was now my closest friend. Her home was some distance from the centre, in Laajasalo, one of the islands linked to the city by a bridge. I visited the Vaalas family often, taking Juha with me on many occasions. Our parents had met and were happy on both sides that we came from 'good families'.

The Vaalas family lived in a large, detached house, with plenty of land, left in its natural state, around it. Seija's father was working as the Director of the Finnish Mission Society, under the Lutheran Church of Finland. He had not been a missionary, but had, when newly married, spent time in Canada, working with the Finns living there. Seija, the couple's first child, had been born in Canada. Seija's mother, Maija, belonged to the von Bell family, originating from Scotland, and one of the Swedish speaking noble families. Mamma soon discovered that she and Maija were related through a common ancestor; Mamma's paternal grandmother Matilda was a member of the noble Roschier family.

Pauli and Maija, the parents, were in their early forties. Pauli was a good-looking man, with good carriage, average height, dark hair and a stern expression in his steel-grey eyes. He was highly respected, even feared; his comments could be sharp, and at times cruel. He was a rational man, and did not tolerate stupidity or impulsive behaviour, but had a good sense of humour, of the sarcastic variety. His emotional side was expressed in his musicality, he was an excellent piano player, and had a deep bass voice. He and his wife Maija, a soprano, sang duets together at many functions. Two opposites, they gave an impression of working well as a couple. Maija was always warm, open and welcoming, but often unwell, and physically not robust. She was slightly overweight, shortish, attractive, with brown hair, light brown eyes, a large sensual mouth, and a tanned tone in her complexion. I sensed a well-hidden submission of her own spirit, an unlived life under the dominance of her strong husband.

They had five children. Fifteen months after Seija's birth, Jussi had been born. He was the apple of Maija's eye. Jussi, being close in age to Seija and me, was the only one I knew well as a teenager and young adult. The third child, Marjatta, was born four years after Jussi, and was seen as the 'problem child'. Maija found it hard to cope with her and had disciplinary problems with her; Pauli was of little help; his daughter's behaviour simply irritated him. I never came to know Marjatta. The next one was Anna- Maija, eleven years younger than Seija, the 'sunshine girl', always accommodating and easy to handle. She was very pretty with large dark brown eyes, perhaps in temperament most like her father. Coming frequently with me, Juha and Anna-Maija's became good playmates. The 'nest egg' Kari, was born in 1946. I still remember Seija's embarrassment about her mother's pregnancy, aged forty, so late in her life, and Seija's puzzlement about their lovemaking.

Pauli invested all the hopes that the other children had not fulfilled into Kari. Luckily Kari showed his musicality early; the violin became his instrument. His skills improved quickly, and he was encouraged to play at all possible gatherings. In the end he rebelled, giving up his violin playing for good, and concentrating on singing in a motet choir.

The Vaalas family offered me an old-fashioned, traditional model of a family: an authoritative father ruling the family, a kind, caring mother, softening his sternness, and the children, each quite different, but close together as siblings, and as adults making choices not always to Pauli's liking, thus showing their individuality and rebellious side. Pauli's attitude to sex certainly coloured Seija's life. He was watching over his attractive teenage daughter like a hawk, giving her a very strict code of behaviour. If she wanted to avoid open collisions with her father, Seija had no choice except to be a 'good girl'. She had to be satisfied with having fantasies of the perfect boyfriend somewhere. At our Christian gatherings we met many attractive, interesting students, but for her, it was the leaders, unavailable as they were, that were a safe focus for her dreams. She and I we were inseparable; perhaps we were protecting each other by substituting real boys with romantic fantasies. We were spring babies, born in March 1931, she on the 3rd March in the sign of Pisces. We both made a commitment in Hotskär to follow Jesus; she has continued on that path. This path took us to search for events catering for Christian teenagers, where we would meet like-minded young people. We joined a group run by the parish in the centre of Helsinki and made many good friends there. Seija fancied a sensitive, shy boy, giving him the nickname 'Runo' (poem), and filled her diary with fantasies about him. I doubt he was aware of her dreams; she certainly kept her feelings hidden. Looking at her, it was hard to understand her lack of confidence in herself and her attractiveness: medium height, good, shapely figure, large, brown eyes with green specks, soft, peachy complexion, aristocratic nose and thick fair hair. Our friendship has lasted, and as friendships go, ours has been special, a rich treasure, a lifeline in hard and sad times, and a rare gift for both of us.

Mummi

Towards Christmas we noticed a change in Mummi; she seemed tired, often withdrawing into her room to rest. She was losing weight, looking even smaller, and frequently complaining of stomach pains. Something was seriously wrong. In early January 1948 Mummi was admitted to the hospital for an exploratory operation. Our fears were confirmed: Mummi had stomach cancer, inoperable. Mummi took the news courageously, never complaining, and carrying on with her various tasks as before.

In early March I received confirmation that I had been selected as one of the five teenagers to take part in a Christian gathering in Norway. Mummi, as weak as she was, wanted to make me a practical outfit for the trip. She chose a blue and white checked cotton and made me a matching skirt and blouse. Combined, by mixing and matching, with other blouses and trousers, these two items would offer me a variety of choices. Her care for my outfits was her way of expressing love, and this meant a lot to me. Sadly, I did not have a chance to tell her the pleasure her parting gift had given me, and how practical it was going to be for the cycling trip, luggage limited to a small rucksack.

Anxiously, we observed Mummi becoming thinner and thinner; she was no longer able to hold her food down and took to her bed. My two aunts, Eva, crying inconsolable, and Ruth, contained and calm, arrived to sit at Mummi's bedside. Ruth, a fine artist, and Mamma would sit for hours with Mummi; making daily, new sketches, as if imprinting every detail of her face, once so beautiful, into their memory. Perhaps also wanting to push away the approaching death by immortalizing their brave mother, looking by now more like a skeleton.

The 31st May is a great day for all students everywhere in Finland who have passed their matriculation examinations. It is the day of the final goodbye to school, and, more importantly, the day you receive your white velvet cap with a golden lyre set in centre of a stiff black velvet band. The cap, worn every day of the summer, is a mark to outsiders of your success. Rainer was going to receive his white cap and his final school certificate on the 31st May in 1948.

The tradition is for parents and relatives to attend the ceremony in the school and give roses to these achievers. With my single pink rose, I went to school early, waiting excitedly for the ceremony to begin. No sign of my parents. Well, how typical, Mamma is always late, no need to be concerned, I thought. The ceremony had reached the point of the headmaster giving his address, and there was still no sign of my parents. Now I was anxious, my heart was throbbing, fear was building up, as I became certain that something had happened to Mummi. Ceremony over, I rushed to Rainer, gave him my rose, and ran to catch the bus. Opening the front door, I could hear Isä's voice, raising above Mamma's. They were singing the funeral hymn: *'Nyt ylös sieluni, nous' ylös mullast' tästä...'*('Arise, my soul, stretch for things eternal ... ') What I had feared, was there to be faced: Mummi's earthly life had ended, her pain had ceased, she had slipped away. I started to shake, my legs went to jelly, then slowly, slowly, stopping at each step, I climbed up the stairs to the hall. The door was open to Mummi's room. I saw my parents standing in attention next to Mummi's bed. Mamma was crying and praying, Isä was carrying on singing. I tiptoed to stand next to Isä; he put his arm round me. I saw my beloved Mummi lying there lifeless, painless and still. I stood there stunned, tears rolling down my cheeks, my heart aching, not believing that Mummi was dead.

The enormity of Mummi's departure from our lives took a while to sink in. She had been an essential part of our family as long as I could remember; she had lived with us since we moved to Aleksanterinkatu. She, in her unassuming way, had been the backbone of our family; backbone to a family with a mother working, tired, unwell, or attending religious meetings, and to a family with a father absent for months and months. She was our practical mother, she cooked, baked, shopped, she conjured new outfits from old ones, and made new dresses for Laila and me. Always busy and practical, she was capable of tackling any job. I have no recollection of her cuddling us, giving hugs or kisses. Laila remained Mummi's special grandchild, and Mummi was very important to Laila; she, having as a small child been frail and needing special care, had experienced the softer, loving side of Mummi. Their bond had remained.

I know very little of Mummi's childhood. She kept her feelings to herself, and never told us tales from her early years. This I know: Hilma Elin, nee Sjöblom, was born 15 August 1875, and she came from the costal town of Vaasa. We had no idea what her parents were like, except that her mother had been a very religious person, making Mummi sceptical of Mamma's religiousness. We did know that she had one sister, who married a Mr Etholen. They had two daughters, Ragnhild and Arna. Ragnhild had married a Norwegian and moved to Norway. We never saw her. Arna, my name sake, lived in Tampere with her Latin scholar husband Gunvar Ranke. They had no children, but later adopted a boy. Arna visited us often and was close to Mamma.

We knew that Mummi had continued her education after school in a commercial college in Vaasa, where her faith was sealed by her teacher Johan Herman Nylenius, ten years older, who fell head over heels in love with this petite, blue eyed, dark haired, attractive and clever student. He set out to charm her with his romantic wooing. How could she resist this charmer, addressing his letters to her with these words: *'Min innerligt älskade, ljuvliga Elin.'* (My most deeply beloved, sweet, adorable Elin)? He, a romantic, impractical scholar, buried in his study with books and cigar smoke, needed this efficient, practical, capable and beautiful woman as his life companion. They married in 1898. Their first child, Lilli Karin was born in January 1900, and their youngest daughter, Ruth, was born when Karin was only five. Mummi was forty-six years old when Herman died of leukaemia. By then both Karin, studying, and Verna, working, had left home, Eva, 17, and Ruth, 15, were still at home finishing their schooling.

Only three years after Herman's death, the first one of the four sisters, Eva, considered as the most beautiful one, married the wealthy businessman Kaarlo Dahlström. Verna, in my opinion, equally beautiful, was not in a hurry to marry. My mother, Karin, the eldest, and Ruth, the youngest, were married five years after their father's death. Mummi's new role had begun before she had had time to think of her own life. She sold the family home in Oulu, and bought a small two roomed flat in Helsinki, where she lived when she was not needed by her daughters. She was the always available grandmother, responding to the needs of her daughters, until Karin monopolised her mother's life by Mummi agreeing to be her receptionist in Käpylä, and she became part of the Pelkonen family.

The family history of Johan Herman Nylenius, our *morfar* (mother's father, in Swedish), was well known through the endless stories we heard. We met an infinite number of Nylenius family members throughout our childhood. Mamma idealised her father, describing him as an absentminded, highly intelligent, totally impractical, utterly romantic, warm and loving father and husband, demonstrating his love by bringing small gifts to his wife and his four daughters. Herman was the first born of two boys and three girls. Mamma never saw her *farfar* (grandfather in Swedish). *Farmor* Matilda's family history is well recorded, and Seija's and my family histories are linked by shared ancestors.

Mummi was the only grandparent we had; the three others had died before I was born and had become idealised, archetypal figures: Isä's father a saint, Mamma's father an absent-minded genius, Isä's mother a self-sacrificing, idealised, wonder woman; all, as far as I could see, unreal cardboard cut outs. How I longed to have known them as real people.

Seventeen

Tucked between starched, white hospital sheets, miserable and fed up, yellow, like a Chinaman, I am waiting for the ward round, for the tall, blonde female doctor, followed by the plump, round-faced ward sister, to sail in. They arrive; hardly giving me a glance, the doctor turns her attention to the flowers on my bedside table. She picks up one of the cards, sighs and hands it over to the ward sister, saying, 'Wouldn't it be wonderful to be sweet seventeen again, and to be receiving blue violets and red roses from your boyfriends?'

They both giggle; I feel pissed off. Never mind my flowers, what about me? All I want to know is, can I go home?

Coming back from her reveries, before I have time to voice my question, the doctor picks up my chart, looks at it, and remains silent for endless minutes. Then she announces her verdict. 'I am afraid you'll have to stay in hospital for at least two weeks for the infection to clear.'

This is the last thing I want to hear. They walk out, leaving me to deal with the verdict. Only few days ago my world was carefree, and I was well. Then suddenly, for no obvious reason, I was vomiting, had severe stomach pains, and my temperature climbed sky high. Mamma decided to call the duty doctor. Unable to make a diagnosis, he felt the symptoms were serious enough for a hospital admission. My symptoms continued in hospital, and were still a mystery to the experienced medics. Then, after a couple of days, my skin and the white in my eyes turned yellow. The diagnosis was clear: I had hepatitis, the infectious variety, originating, most likely, from an unsterilized knife. I could trace the culprit: an ear and nose specialist had lanced a boil in my throat some six months previously. Now, here I was, imprisoned in a hospital bed at the most critical time in my life, suffering from the consequences of someone else's lack of hygiene. How unfair. I should be at school. It is my final year. I should be busy studying. The all-important matriculation examinations are looming in a few months' time. Top grades are expected of me. I have been amongst the three top students every year, never ill, now feverish and too tired to even lift a book. Burying my head in the bedclothes, I let tears of frustration and helpless anger flow into that dark space.

Memories of my isolation in the Swedish hospital, nine years ago, flood again into my consciousness, filling me with same sense of being deserted, and being a victim to forces beyond my control. I calm down eventually. The doctor's flippant words are echoing in my ears: 'How wonderful to be seventeen.'

Much has indeed happened since my seventeenth birthday: There were the sad months of spring with Mummi's terminal illness, and her death on the last day of spring. At her funeral at the beginning of June, we were still in a state of shock and deeply bereft, but the funeral was a kind of closure; life forces took over for me. The planned cycling trip to Norway was due to start just after midsummer. That trip changed my life. I had a first taste of an exciting, expanding world, and new vistas, in every sense, opened up.

My eyes turn to the flowers on the bedside table. Never before have I received flowers from a boy; now boys have entered my life with a different interest than before. There had been short, childish infatuations, and temporary fallings in and out of love, there had been the tender, shy first romance with Jaakko, my Prince Charming; now a fond memory. After him only good friends as far as I am concerned. The red roses came from my special friend Olli, my faithful admirer. The deep blue violets came from Jussi, a boy from a different school, and a different story.

I had seen him at the skating rink during the winter months. We had only looked at each other without exchanging any words. Then, in the spring, he had been giving me friendly waves as he cycled past me on his way to his school. He looked smashing, tall and slim, with dark, wavy, unruly hair, and stunningly blue eyes, the colour of the violets on my bedside table. I used to think, I wish I could get to know Jussi better. Then the miracle happened. The planning meeting was arranged for those chosen to take part in the summer camp in Norway. The Christian Norwegian Association had invited five Christian teenagers from Helsinki Grammar Schools to attend their summer gathering in the very north of Norway, near Tromsö. The Norwegians would pay for all the expenses in Norway.

Imagine my surprise when I went to our first planning meeting and saw Jussi, one of the two boys taking part in the trip. Now I would have a chance to get to know him well during the cycling trip. As good looking as Jussi was, to my great disappointment, it did not take me long to find him dull and boring. As witnessed by the bunch of violets, he, on his side, became really interested in me, wanting us to carry on meeting and going out after the trip. Lasse, the other boy, quiet, wearing glasses, shy and reserved, hadn't made a special impression on me. The two girls: Tiina, small, plump, with curly blonde hair, and Raija, tallish, pimply-faced, with straight mousy coloured hair, came from the same school, and they were good friends already. During the trip they clung to each other; I had no need to be the third wheel.

Two undergraduates, Vilho and Eeva, had been elected by the Finnish organisers to be in charge of our little group. Vilho, a twenty-seven-year-old architecture student, tall, well built, fair, blue eyed, and serious, looked mature and older than most students. He gave an instant impression of reliability and kindness. Being old enough to have fought in the war, he had been forced to postpone his university studies. Returning to his studies after the war, and with his life-changing experience, made him different, wiser and more mature. In contrast, Eeva, looking younger than her age of twenty-one, was more like one of us. Blonde and pretty, she was studying to become a teacher. It was good to see that our leaders were working well together, and had already made our travelling plans: we would to take a night train to Rovaniemi (the most northern town in Finland, situated on the Arctic Circle).

Vilho explained, 'From there we'll continue on our bikes, cycle all the way to Tromsö. En route we'll be sleeping in tents, except for a stop at Kilpisjärvi.' (The border post on the Finnish side between Finland, Sweden and Norway). We had already been told that various host families would be offering accommodation in Tromsö. Vilho added, 'You'll be pleased to know that final bit of the journey to the camp is going to be by boat along a fjord, paid by the Norwegians.'

Our leaders then stressed the importance of making sure our bikes were in good order. Eeva gave this advice, 'You need to be aware that the arctic weather can be very hot at the end of June, but icy, arctic winds can play tricks, causing a big drop in the temperatures. Be prepared both ways. One certainty is, there is going to be swarms and swarms of mosquitoes, hungry to suck your blood. Finally, remember all your gear has to fit in a rucksack.'

I remember coming home from the meeting excited, the trip was really going to take place. Thanks to Mummi, I had had no worries about my wardrobe; in fact, Vilho had praised me for the practicality of my various clothes. But I was worried about my bike, an old, second-hand one Isä had bought as a bargain, so typical of all his purchases. It had been put together with some new bits. I knew my bike wouldn't last the trip, and I also knew there was no chance of getting money for a new bike. Rainer, understanding my dilemma, surprisingly, came to my rescue. He somehow persuaded his girlfriend, Anna-Liisa, to lend me her new bike. How generous of her and how good of Rainer. What a pleasure it was to cycle with a good bike.

On the day after midsummer celebrations, the night train to Rovaniemi pulled away from Helsinki station. How well I remember the nervous, excited chatting, giggling, and looking at each other, as we seven stood in the corridor of the sleeping apartment, wondering how we would get on, and how we would cope. None of us were experienced cyclists, except Vilho. It would be a miracle if we managed without major mishaps. None of us could speak Norwegian, all had school Swedish, though I had the advantage of speaking Swedish fluently. Our worries were minor and didn't matter. Our adventure had begun; we trusted our two excellent leaders.

Arriving at Rovaniemi about ten the following morning, we were faced with a scorching day, the temperature already 27C. Our leaders made a quick decision; to take the waiting post bus for the first part of our journey, while the sun was at its hottest. By the time the bus dropped us, we were more than ready to begin our cycling. The temperature had gone down, the sun still high; evening was approaching. The sun was not going to disappear; we were in Lapland, in the land of the midnight sun, further north than any of us had ever been.

Vilho suggested, 'Let's use the light night, and cycle for as long as possible in the cooler air; and pitch our tents later for a rest.'

We began cycling in a close line, and gradually the distances between us grew longer. It was as if each of us needed our private space to take in Lapland, its lightness, its eerie stillness, and its stunning scenery: majestic dark fells, no trees, only low undergrowth, and here and there small mountain lakes glittering like pale blue sapphires. The sun was playing its game of slowly going down, never disappearing behind the fells, and then at midnight, began its rise higher and higher.

By five in the morning, we were tired out; time to have a break. The boys helped Vilho in pitching the tents, whilst we, the girls, with Eeva's guidance, prepared porridge on a primus stove. It did not take long before the hungry mosquitoes discovered a good catch, and swarms, as thick as the porridge, were attacking us relentlessly. It was no longer possible to continue with our tasks without first dealing with the attackers. Two of us were delegated to make leafy whisks, and use them for whisking away the hostile mosquitoes, while the rest of us had our breakfast; one of us returning the service to the two starving good doers.

Exhausted by all the new experiences, our bodies aching, we were ready to hit the bed. The tents turned out to be of no use, too hot, and the irritating hum of mosquitoes, already occupying the tent, was too disturbing for going to sleep. The decision was made to take our sleeping bags out into a shady place in the open, and a rota of two taking their turn in whisking the mosquitoes away. This system worked; each of us managed to at least rest if not sleep. In this incredible lightness the time and the difference between day and night lost its meaning. We did not need much sleep before we were ready to pedal on. How well I remember the state of ecstasy at the first sight of the Norwegian snow-capped, sharply pointed, sunlit Alps, so different from the dark, rounded Finnish fells. A heavenly sight! In a trance, overwhelmed by the beauty, I slowed down and allowed everyone to pass me. I needed to be alone, undisturbed, and bask in this state of wonder.

The sight of the Alps meant that we were nearing Kilpisjärvi. In the distance was the recognisable shape of Saana, one of the highest arctic fells in Finland, still with snow on its Northern slopes. Below we could see a large mountain lake and some red, scattered wooden buildings in the valley. We were approaching the site where architecture students, Vilho's colleagues, were working on a project. They had agreed to put us up for an overnight stop. We were more than ready for a break: starving, needing a proper cooked meal, dripping with sweat, dirty with the dust from the sandy roads, limbs aching, bums soar, and so, so tired. As first aid we badly needed a swim and a sauna, then a hot meal. Once these needs were met, we longed to slump down into a proper bed, protected from being eaten up by mosquitoes. Leaving Vilho and Eeva to sort out the sleeping arrangements, the five of us ran to the lake. This was the end of June, but we were astonished to see patches of snow on the ground, and could not resist the temptation to make snowballs as we ran into the lake. Expecting the water in a lake to have been warmed by the twenty-four-hour sunshine, what a shock to our hot bodies to be hit by icy water, not all that comfortable to swim in, but certainly invigorating. We slept round the clock, felt refreshed, relaxed, and happy to listen to our leaders' plans for the day. Vilho and Eeva, both excellent singers, were keen to explore our musicality. They had thought we might form a little choir and surprise our hosts at the camp by giving them a performance. Vilho invited us to sing a few

Finnish hymns and folk songs. Having listened, Vilho thought we were good enough, and he decided who would sing in each voice, he himself had excellent bass voice. Turning towards me, he said, 'Arna, you have a beautiful voice. You would enjoy singing in a choir, why don't you find one? There are many students' choirs, I know you would be accepted as a member.'

I remember how surprised and pleased I was. Nobody had ever praised my voice, on the contrary Rainer had always teased me. Often, when I sang, he asked me to bring cotton wool swabs for his ears. Isä had labelled Laila the musical one, worth spending money on her violin lessons, but not on piano lessons for me. As this all was coming back to my mind, here in the hospital bed, I promised myself, that once back in the land of living, I would join a choir.

Vilho was wonderful in the way he found something to praise in each of us. I had told him during our cycling that Mamma and I had been drawing together. He remembered and suggested that the two of us would climb up the Saana mountain for a sketching session. He had brought a sketch pad and pastel crayons. Eager and excited, I took up his suggestion. We climbed up the mountain, found a spot, settled down, sitting close to each other. While he drew, he was teaching me, saying, 'Look at the scene, look carefully, select something that interests you before you start to draw.'

When we finished, he offered me the two sketches he had done: one a view from the mountain, the other a detailed drawing of the flora around us. I loved them. I had them framed immediately on my return home and hung them in my room as a memory of the trip and of Vilho.

I think of Vilho as one of the special people in my life; far more mature than any young man I have known. Warm-hearted, strong, honest, and gifted, he gave me confidence and encouraged me to trust myself. In his eyes, most likely, I was just a little teenager, almost like a daughter, and one needing love and fatherly guidance. Maybe, he saw my insecurity, saw my need to be seen with understanding and acceptance.

I met my hero Vilho a couple of times during the winter months of 1949. His studies came to an end, and soon after that he got married. He had been married only for couple of years when I heard that he was seriously ill, suffering from an incurable cancer. I had a chance to go and see him in hospital some weeks before he died, and had a chance to thank him for what he meant to me. He took my hand and said, 'Arna, trust yourself, and never forget who you are.'

The next morning our journey continued to the border post, and we entered Norway, a foreign land. There, waiting for us was our guide, a Viking Prince Hans-Ludvig, smiling, revealing perfect white teeth, tanned, slender and tallish, and oozing charm and health. His blonde, almost white hair was blowing in the wind as he greeted us. 'So good to see you, welcome, I'll be your guide and assisting you with your queries.'

Hans-Ludvig's first task was to see us safely down from the heights of mountain level to the sea level. Cycling downhill was tricky, the sandy road was easy to skid on, and the speed easily accelerated beyond safety; we had the wall of the mountain on one side and on the other a steep drop down to the valley and fjord, so absolute concentration was needed. As Tiina took a sharpish bend, her front wheel started wobbling, came off, and started rolling towards the slope, Vilho caught it in time. Hans-Ludvig discovered that a nut had come lose and had fallen off somewhere. What now? The only way for us to continue was a temporary remedy of attempting to combine two bikes into some kind of a tandem. Vilho's bike was the strongest, and he, as the leader, had to make the decision whether this would be feasible. Somehow, he and Hans-Ludvig managed to make a bike for two. The journey down to Skibotn, and then to Tromsö was painfully slow, we arrived in one piece and exhausted. Hans-Ludvig assured Tiina that a new wheel could be fitted in time for our return journey.

Many happy memories float back from the summer camp. I made new friends, including Åse, the girl whose parents put me up in Tromsö. Åse was one of the small group of Norwegians who came in August this summer to a similar meeting in Finland. Åse and I decided to start corresponding after the group left from Helsinki. We carried on writing to each other for years and years.

Another new friend was Gunhild. We too decided to correspond, she writing in 'Ny norsk', the second official language, and I in Swedish. Gunhild's home was even further north than Tromsö, where her father works as a teacher. (We are still exchanging emails, Gunhild, a year older than I, is living in Denmark with her second Danish husband.)

Reliving the trip, I am back in the summer life of Lapland: so free and easy. Time didn't matter, people were happy and open, and making full use of the miracle of the round-the-clock sun.

One warm evening, on the spur of the moment, our Norwegian friends suggested, 'Let's climb up the mountain behind our camp. We'll take a picnic basket.' The climb up was fascinating. I noticed the change in the vegetation as we ascended: the first part was a gentle climb through forest, then no tall trees, moving to heathland with low-growing alpine birches. We could see masses of cloudberries, ready for picking in a month's time. The further we climbed the more barren the landscape became. Reindeers were wandering in small groups searching for something to eat, and were satisfied with lichen, covering the stony ground. The vistas were stunning. We could see miles and miles in all directions; looking north the vast Arctic ocean, and beyond the ocean, there would be the North Cap, otherwise fells, fjords and wilderness. Far removed from everyday life, we were on top of the world. The Norwegians made a campfire, while we, the Finns, soaked in the extraordinary experience. Hunger soon brought us back to earth. Each of us was given a sausage to cook on the fire. Joking, telling tales, laughing and singing, the late evening changed to a new day without us noticing. What fun it was, how relaxed and easy going the Norwegians were, hugging us, giving us compliments, such as, 'You are fantastic. Thank you for coming.' How lovely it was to know that we would soon meet again, as a return visit by a small group of our Norwegians friends had already been arranged.

Six weeks later, eight of our Norwegian friends came to Mikkeli, a small town in the centre of the Lakeland, joining a gathering arranged by the Finnish Christian Students Union. I was disappointed not to have much chance to be with them at the convention, as their programme had been pre-arranged by the Finnish organisers. I had my chance to be with the group of eight, as they had decided to come to Helsinki and accepted my offer to put them all up in my home. The flat was empty; the family members were spending their summer away from Helsinki. The Norwegians were astonished to see the grand apartment, and to have the freedom, with no grown-ups interfering in how we arranged our eating and sleeping. There were enough sleeping places. The girls made the beds, while the boys went to the market to buy food.

There had been the instant spark between Hans-Ludvig and me the moment we met. During the camp we had stolen time to be together, and we had looked forward to meeting again in Finland. The most intimate time had been in Helsinki. As we were getting ready for the evening meal, Hans-Ludvig took hold of my hand, announcing, ‘Let me have the honour of washing the hair of my Finnish maiden.’ I remember the gentleness of his fingers massaging my scalp, and his caressing way of drying my hair. It felt so good and told me all I needed to know.

Clean, happy, hungry, and the meal cooked, we settled around our large dining table, Hans-Ludvig next to me, squeezing my hand under the table. Inspired by the harmonium in the dining room, the Norwegians arranged an impromptu musical show. Sverre, the musical leader, had a guitar and began by playing solo pieces, and then he and Lotte, a skilled pianist, played duets; surprisingly, the guitar and the harmonium sounded fine together. We loved singing together, we made a lot of noise, we shared jokes, we laughed and had fun.

Soon after the Norwegians went home, Hans-Ludvig and I continued our friendship by writing a couple of letters to each other. Then, out of the blue, I received a 'thank you' present of Norwegian songs from him. As no more letters have arrived since, I think, his present was both a 'thank you' and 'goodbye'. Our 'midsummer dream' had ended, leaving an unforgettable, happy memory.

Now, in my hospital bed, I have been reliving the trip again: the many happy, unexpected experiences, the wonderful Norwegians we met, the new friends I made. I agree, wholeheartedly, with the doctor: 'It's fantastic to be seventeen.'

The cycling trip had opened vistas, had shown me a wonderful, exciting and beautiful world worth exploring. I had felt so at home with the Norwegians, felt more a Scandinavian than a Finn. My name Arna is an old Scandinavian word, meaning eagle. 'Nomen est Omen'. Where will the eagle wings take me?

Enough of dreaming. Once I am back home from this hospital bed, I'll need to be seriously catching up with my studies, and need to find out how much I have missed in these weeks. We'll carry on with our usual lessons until 28th of February. On that day we'll be marking the end of normal school days, forever. A period of independent study will follow, until in the end of April. Then the matriculation examinations are taking place at the same time in all grammar schools in Finland.

The last day, February 28th, arrived, and, as the tradition was, we were, again, dressed up as young children, most of the outfits looked comical and ill-fitting. Each of us carried our favourite toy from childhood. We looked at each other, bursting into laughter. We were already in a party mood. A lorry had been hired for us to join in a cavalcade of lorries from all the Grammar Schools in Helsinki, heading to *Esplanaadi,* a wide street with a park on one side, and shops selling luxury items on the other, in the centre of Helsinki, and leading to the harbour. Large crowds of onlookers had gathered to cheer us on. Waving, swinging our toys and making as much noise as we could, we were jubilant and shouting, 'Goodbye school for EVER!' A great day of freedom, fun, and celebration. We carried on parting until late at night.

Then the hard slog began, on our own, studying for the examinations looming ahead. My subjects were: Finnish, Swedish, German and General Knowledge (History, Geography, Biology, and Religion; History was my strongest subject in this section). Curling up in my great grandfather's chair, with music in the background, I settled down for hours of reading. I can well remember the occasion, when stunned by the beauty of the music I was hearing: Sibelius's Violin concerto, for the first time, played by Anja Ignatius. I stopped my reading, just let the music take me far away to a world of beauty and dreams.

To improve my understanding of spoken German, I had begun attending services at *Die Deutsche Kirche*, a small German church within a walking distance from my home; the church where my parents were married in 1926. Pastor Schwenke, a tall, thin, middle-aged man with almost black hair and a piercing look in his grey eyes, spoke each word distinctly and clearly. To my surprise, I had no difficulties in understanding him. His sermons were quite short, his message meant to be remembered. The sermons were always constructed with three main points, and at the end of the sermon, raising his long finger, he reiterated the three main points: *'Punkt ein, Punkt zwei und Punkt drei'.*

As important as it was to hear good German spoken clearly, the main reason for attending these services was meeting other students outside the church afterwards. Going to church was a welcome break from studying on my own. I missed my friends in my class. We came together again to face the examination papers in the large assembly hall. I felt quite confident, if anything, over-confident, expecting 'laudatur' both in Swedish and General Knowledge. My German was also improving; the only slight concern was writing an essay on the Finnish test. We were given three subjects to choose from. I had luck. One was: 'My most memorable hymn'. I wrote about the hymn Isä was singing when Mummi died, a year ago. I had been celebrating Rainer's success, when I entered our flat just as Mummi had taken her last breath. That hymn and that moment has stayed in my mind as a drama of the joy of life and the sorrow of death crossed, arousing contrasting, unforgettable and powerful emotions. Perhaps I succeeded in portraying my feelings. I received high marks for my essay. Unfortunately, in my Swedish test I made one stupid, but cardinal mistake; that mistake cost me the expected laudatur. My laudatur in general knowledge was secure; I was pleased with the overall results.

Our headmaster handed us the white velvet student cap with a black band and a golden lyre with the final school certificate on 31st May in a festive ceremony. All the pupils of the whole school were present as well as closest relatives with their bunches of roses.

On that occasion the boys wore suits and the girls tailored costumes with white or light-coloured blouses. In 1949 it was almost impossible to obtain new cloth. My 'white' godmother May solved the dilemma by offering me her light brown, hardly worn costume of the finest wool, re-made to fit me, and Aunt Ester had managed to obtain very light grey silk for the blouse. One more item was required, a party dress for the celebration dinner for the new Helsinki students at the best restaurant Kalastajatorppa.

Aunt Laina offered to take me shopping and surprise, surprise, we found a light-blue fabric in silk with a faint white pattern. She had a professional seamstress friend, who equipped me for the great day. Mamma took no part in these matters. She did not even pay for the material for my dress. The only thing she had a strong view about was the shape of my white cap, and the size of its golden lyre, insisting I choose the middle way between the Finnish cap with a small lyre, and the Swedish-Finnish one with a large lyre and more generous cap. I made the required compromise.

The tradition of students wearing a white velvet cap goes back to 1865. On May Day the students began using their caps to celebrate the end of the academic year and the approaching summer. The cap was the students' common headgear over the summer months. The Finnish students wanted to separate themselves from the Swedish speaking students during the language conflicts by designing a slightly different version of the cap, not quite as high and the lyre smaller. In 1949 all new students wore their cap with great pride, but by the beginning of 1960 its use had decreased. The one day in the year, when all, young and old, dig up their cap, often yellowed, and wear it, is first of May, Vappu.

After the festivities at our schools, all the new Helsinki students marched together to the Hietaniemi cemetery to place a rose at the foot of the monument commemorating the losses of the Finnish soldiers in the wars of 1939-1945. Many of us had suffered personal losses, all of us were deeply moved, some openly crying. In front of us we saw endless rows of marble plaques, each carrying a name of a soldier who had sacrificed his life for Finland's Independence. In the silence remembering, grieving and thanking.

One more task before we dispersed was to go and be photographed. As I was walking towards the photographer, proud and happy, announcing to onlookers my achievement with my whiter than white cap, an elderly, white haired, smartly dressed gentleman, swinging his walking stick, and smiling benevolently, stopped me and said,

'Congratulations, young lady. And remember, this day is one of the happiest days of your life. Make sure you enjoy it.'

I thanked him. We parted, him first giving me a fatherly pat on my arm. I continued my journey, pondering over what he had said, thinking, OK, for sure this a fantastically happy day, but there must be much more. This is just the beginning.

The photographer took a few shots, working out the best pose, then he said, 'Look straight into the camera.'

Doing as I was told, I decided to make an experiment, and said silently, 'I love you my unknown Prince.' I was curious to see would my declaration of love show on the photo; for sure, there is a wistful look in my eyes on that particular shot.

Seija failed in one of her subjects, thus having to retake it in the autumn. She missed the ceremonies and the joyous celebrations. I was conscious of her sadness, her disappointment and her angry frustration with herself. Her father was not too pleased either. Seija's failure somewhat marred my pleasure of using the white cap, if she was present. Naturally, I wanted to walk around Helsinki, showing off, seeing people smiling, looking at me, not believing I could be old enough to be a student.

Lukki invited us all to her home for a final get-together. Our class, the first one she had been a form teacher to, had been special to her. During the years we had learned to appreciate her and her care. As we sat on the floor in a circle, sharing memories of the school years, Lukki stood up, giving each of us a piece of writing paper and a pen, asking us to be fortune-tellers and imagine what our life would be like in ten years' time. What we wrote, remained a secret, sealed in an envelope for Lukki's safe keeping. The envelopes would be opened on our 10th anniversary dinner.I wrote: *In front of my eyes I have two different scenes, the first is an idyllic, peaceful rural scene, a Parish with an old church, and next to it a vicarage, where I would be living with my humble country pastor.* In the second scene: *I am a missionary in Tanzania. I see a simple building, high in the mountainous area, overlooking Mount*

Kilimanjaro. I am surrounded by black children, teaching them to read. If I am not a missionary, I'll be the wife of one.'

Lukki kept our letters, addressed to ourselves. Our class had annual reunion gatherings each year, Lukki always joining in. Once I had moved to England, it was seldom possible for me to be present, and I missed the 10th reunion gathering when these letters were read and handed over, but I received a card and photo of all present. After Lukki's death, a girl from my class contacted me, and, to my utter surprise, gave me back my letter, together with Lukki's a pencil drawing of me, at the age of fourteen. I was deeply touched. In May 1999, it was our 50th anniversary gathering. As a special celebration, an all-day boat trip had been arranged. My husband had died in March of that year; the class was aware of my bereavement. As we stood on the deck, they locked their arms, forming a circle around me. Standing next to me was Osmo; he had become a vicar. He put his arms around me and read a short prayer. There I was in a circle of love and safety, in a circle of longstanding, true friends. It was a home coming, an unforgettable, consoling experience.

Summer of Dreams

The celebrations and the goodbyes were over. No need to make decisions about what next. I would have the long summer weeks to think, make plans, and seriously consider the suggestions Isä and Mamma had made regarding my further studies. This summer promised to be quite different from any of the previous summers, after the loss of Kaihoniemi. Something important and exciting had happened: During the autumn months the Finnish Government had been paying compensation for properties and land lost in Karelia. Joint owners of Kaihoniemi: Isä, Ester, Laina and Jaakko, had received their compensation money. Isä's three siblings decided to use their share to buy a new summer place together, close to the new border with Russia, whilst Isä took his share separately. As soon as the money came through, he was eagerly searching for a summer place for us. His long-term plan was to find land in the Sotkamo area, and have a house built near where he worked each summer. One day, during the winter months, he announced, 'I have found a small one roomed cottage with a spacious loft on an island.' He added, 'I'll have a smoke sauna built as soon as I find a builder; a rowing boat has already been ordered. It'll be ready early in June.'

We were stunned into silence, then getting excited, asking hundreds of questions about the island. Isä spread a map of Finland on the dining room table and showed us the exact spot; a tiny island on the northern end of a big lake Vuohijärvi. We could see that the train line Helsinki-Kajaani had a station, Voikoski, not far from our island. Isä explained, 'The train journey will take about five hours from Helsinki, and about the same time for me from Kajaani. Next to the station is a village shop, selling almost everything. The station is five kilometres from the farmer, who owns the island. We'll get milk, butter, bread, eggs and potatoes from his farm.'

Looking excited and really pleased with himself, our usually reserved and cautious Isä was changed to an animated, lively, and almost manic man, as he continued. 'The farm is close to the lake; the island is only a short distance from the mainland. At the centre there is a high hill, our cottage is on the other side, so the best way to reach it is to row round, about 2 kilometres. Think, we'll be the only family living on this island. It'll be all yours to explore, to climb to the top of the hill, and to make exciting discoveries.'

Now it was our turn to be excited. Enthusiastically planning our 'Robinson Crusoe' adventure, we had many discussions around the dining table, each of us putting forward our thoughts and ideas. Rainer would not be joining us; his summers were already fully occupied with training and running in competitions, involving trips to different parts of Finland and even Sweden. He was becoming famous. All his free time from running he spent with his girlfriend Anna-Liisa at her parents' summer place, close to Helsinki.

As a new welcomed member of the family, we now had a young bitch, Taru, thanks to Laila's insistence to rescue the dog whom Mamma's friend was no longer able to keep. Taru was a cross between a Karelian bear dog and Finnish Spitz. We could already imagine how happy she would be roaming around the island, and what a lovely companion she was going to be on our explorations.

Just before midsummer we set off to our adventure. Isä was able to take a few days off to help with the packing of the essentials we would need, such as bedlinen, pots, pans, crockery, all too heavy items for us to take with us, and to be sent by train to Voikoski. The farmer, Toivola, had agreed to fetch the loads from the station and transfer them to the cottage on the island. Isä had visited the island, brought fishing nets and fishing rods ready for us. Unfortunately, he had to return to Sotkamo before Mamma, Laila, Juha, Taru and I were ready to set off on the train journey with our suitcases, personal belongings, some food such as a whole smoked ham, and a round of Edam cheese; Laila happily travelling in the goods carriage with Taru.

The farmer, Toivola, with his horse and cart, met us at Voikoski station. After loading our luggage onto the cart, we crammed in, Mamma sitting next to him. Trotting along the country lane brought back the memory of our sad, hasty, final departure from Kaihoniemi in June 1944. The longing for and the memories of those innocent childhood summers, soon switched to an eager anticipation of what Isä had managed to conjure up for us.

The new rowing boat was waiting to take us to the cottage. The lake was calm, and the boat had no problems coping with our weight and luggage. I can remember well our landing on this uninhabited island. I, a romantic girl, just eighteen years old, felt that I was coming to a paradise, a magic place for my fantasies to flourish. There, not more than thirty metres from the shore, in front of us stood the little red cottage waiting and welcoming. Taru and Laila were the first ones to jump on land. I just stood still, taking in the scene in front of me: on the left a birch wood, its white stemmed trees looking like young virgins. Turning right I saw an inviting sandy beach and opposite it, within an easy swimming distance, two small islands with smooth cliffs, with some vegetation, but no trees. Looking beyond them, quite far away, I saw the shoreline of the other side of the lake. Behind the cottage stood the high imposing hill issuing an inviting to climb to its top. Could it be true that we had a whole island just for us to explore?

The cottage had a small entrance veranda, with one door leading to a minute kitchen, another door to the only room, a room big enough to hold a table and four chairs and a wooden settee, that could be pulled out as a double bed for Mamma and Isä. On one side of the veranda stood a sturdy, wooden ladder, leading to an opening into the loft. The loft would become Laila's, Juha's and my sleeping area, and a place to escape to on rainy days. Peeping into the loft all I saw was a large open space with three mattresses, filled with straw, on the floor, no other furniture.

In front of the cottage there was a small patio with a low stone wall separating it from the surrounding land, with a wooden table in the centre. Using the wall as our seats, as often as the weather permitted, that's where we ate, played games or just sat admiring the idyll in front of us. The small, new log building, the smoke sauna, Isä's pride, was even closer to the lake than the cottage. The sauna, with no chimneys, was like the original ancient saunas. There was just a fireplace built from stones, and benches to sit on. The sauna was heated with birch logs, the door kept closed so smoke filled the room. When the room was hot enough the fire was allowed die down, and the door was opened to ventilate the room, and ready for the first *'löyly'* (water thrown on the hot stones). Isä was right, we could all agree that we got the best 'löyly' we'd ever had – and also a black bottom!

The island, Palosaari, was about two kilometres long and one kilometre wide. Our cottage was on the west side, facing the setting sun. Each evening Mamma would burst out in wonderment, *'Titta på den härliga belyssningen,'* (Look at the fantastic lighting), urging us to admire the always new and unique sunset, its changing colours and patterns reflected on the water. Mamma's love of painting was greatly inspired by what was around her; she sketched the trees in the birch wood, the wild flowers, the panoramas from the hilltop, and of course the sunsets needed to be immortalised evening after evening. This kept her in a world of her own for hours and hours.

Milk had to be fetched each day; Laila and I took it in turns to row to the farm. Juha, now eight, was able make the trip on calm days, accompanied by Taru. Isä had fixed a mast for sails onto the rowing boat, even though it had no keel. Isä, a good sailor himself, had given us strict instructions only to put the sails up when the wind was light, and to take the sails down if the wind was increasing and the waves became higher. Sailing was fun and made the daily journey of fetching the milk a pleasure. We had brought with us a good supply of food, but surprisingly quickly a trip to the village shop in Voikoski was needed. These trips took most of the day: first, rowing to the mainland, then, cycling the five kilometres, getting the shopping done, cycling back, and picking up our milk and bread before rowing back.

To my great delight Seija's parents agreed to let her come for a fortnight. We two had a marvellous time exploring Palosaari. We walked and talked, sharing our romantic dreams. Each of us had fantasies of a mysterious Prince, who would appear, and who, with his love, would be hacking his way through warnings and prohibitions. Seija's father, far stricter than my parents, was watching his beautiful daughter like a hawk. His authoritative attitude had made Seija frightened to explore real relationships with boys; she lived with her fantasies much more than I.

On the south side of the island, we discovered a fantastic, sandy and totally unspoilt beach, stretching over a couple of hundred metres. We took our clothes off to sunbathe and ran into the water for a cooling swim. After sun had dried our bodies and with dresses on, we were keen to carry on our explorations through the woods, clambering between rocks, towards the top of the mountain. There, at its highest point, was a massive rock, challenging us to scramble up its vertical façade to see the best panorama of the lake, its many islands, and the forests beyond. Spontaneously, we burst into a song: '*Mä oksallla ylimmällä oon Harjulan seljänteen* .....' (a most beloved song, praising a lake view from a top of a tree, words written by Topelius). Taru was always keen to join us on our explorations, and filled her mouth with bilberries, whilst Seija and I were busy picking enough berries for all of us to enjoy with sugar and milk for our supper. Having Seija with us was fun also for Laila and Juha. The four of us spent hours sitting on the stone wall, playing card games, using the innocent 'Snow White' or 'Olympic Game' cards, cleverly designed with 52 cards in four suites, making it possible to play most card games. In my home, as well as in many Finnish homes, playing card games was considered a sin. Mamma often repeated the story of her mother-in-law's first visit to the newlywed's home. She spotted the cards on a table, picked the pack up, threw it into the air, the cards scattered all over the floor.

Clearly very angry, she turned to Mamma and said, 'God's blessing will never be in a home with playing cards.'

Mamma burnt the cards. We were lucky that she was not interested enough in the cards meant for children to question our games.

It had been lovely for me to have my best friend sharing life on our Paradise Island. The day of Seija's return to Helsinki, and her studies, came too quickly. We all, especially I, missed her. Mamma was very happy that I had a friend from such a good family.

Rainer and Anna-Liisa came for a brief stay. They were very much in love, using the freedom of the island for their loving, soon discovering the sandy beach on the south side. There they were spending hours, safely hidden away from onlookers. Sleeping arrangements in the loft had been already changed for Seija's visit, so Anna-Liisa joined Laila and me in the large open space, whilst Rainer had to cram in with Juha in the small space above the kitchen.

We adjusted quite quickly to our uncomplicated life on our island, and each of us found a way of using the uniqueness of our location in an enjoyable way. Our daily life was simple, our food basic. Under the kitchen there was a dugout cellar; it kept the perishable food cold amazingly well. The lake had plenty of fish; Juha enjoyed fishing for perch from the pier and was happy to stand there for hours trying to catch fish with his new rod, often succeeding in bringing small perch for Mamma to clean for our supper. On calm evenings we would lay the nets, Laila rowing, and I standing at the rear of the boat, Mamma, Juha and Taru coming just for the boat ride. Of course, when Isä came, he was in charge, and we fished and laid the nets every evening.

Wild mushrooms and berries were plentiful on the island, and on our trips to the shop we bought minced meat, pasta and other cold meats. Of course, 'sauna sausage' was always on the shopping list to be cooked on an open fire. The farm provided us with bread, eggs, butter and milk.

Swimming, reading, playing games, and exploring the island gave us enough to fill our days and to not feel bored. I did most of the simple cooking with Laila's help. We had no radio, but there was a permanent invitation for Mamma to join the farmer and his wife in listening to the Sunday service. She was happy to row to the mainland even on her own, though often one of us accompanied her. Mamma, if not painting, often felt unwell and tired, spending time resting or just reading her Bible, leaving us to manage.

Isä, as often as he could, spent short breaks with us from his work in Sotkamo. He had the habit of surprising us with his unexpected arrivals. (No phone, slow post.) In the early hours of the morning, we could hear his way of announcing his arrival by the whistling of the war time song: *'Auf der Heide blumt ein kleines Blumelein und das heisst: Erika...'* (On the heath, there blooms a little flower and it's called Erika). Mamma's name Karin is Erika in German. Isä had taken the night train from Kajaani, arriving at Voikoski at 3 am, then he walked 5 km to the farm, borrowed Toivola's rowing boat to row cross to the island, and finally walking over the mountain to our side. His arrival was a celebration; it allowed Mamma to admit her anxieties, and for us children to feel secure. He brought little presents, sweets and special delicatessen. He made simple stools and shelves, he fished with Juha, and, of course, heated the sauna every day.

My day started with a swim, I loved swimming across to the two little islands, staying there for sunbathing or just being alone, dreaming. Our breakfast, consisted of coffee or tea, bread, butter, cheese, and some cold meat. Lunchtime, we made porridge or had 'viili' (whole milk soured in a special way) and berries, afternoon coffee with 'pulla' (buns) was a must. Mamma loved baking and delicious oat biscuits were her speciality. For our main meal we had potatoes or pasta with ham, minced meat or fish, cheese and eggs.

The memories that have stayed with me are of joy, happiness and freedom, and no interference from grown-ups. There were dramatic moments: thunderstorms were really frightening, waves too high, making it too dangerous to row to the mainland.

My most frightening memory from our first summer was being left in charge of Juha and Laila for a couple of weeks. Mamma had joined Isä in Sotkamo, and she also stayed with her sister in Kuopio. One beautiful summer day, Juha volunteered to go and fetch the milk, providing he was allowed to take Taru with him as his companion, and to have the sails up. Juha was by then used to handling the rowing boat, also sailing with it. The sun was shining, the lake looked relatively calm, enough of a wind to be able to sail. I was not particularly worried, and so Juha and Taru set off.

After an hour or more I saw dark clouds gathering in the sky, the waves were getting higher and a storm was brewing. I was beginning to get anxious, and ran to the eastern end of island, hoping to see the boat coming around the corner. There was no sign of the boat. By the time three hours had gone my heart was beating faster, and my anxiety had increased to a panic level. What if something has happened to Juha? Perhaps the wind was even stronger on the other side of the island? What should I do, what could I do? There were no mobiles or telephones. The only thing I could do was to pray, 'Please, God look after Juha and Taru,' and, 'Please, God let them return safely back.' Well, God heard my prayers; the wind began to calm down. Another half an hour went. Finally, the boat became visible, still with its sails up. Juha and Taru next to each other at the rear, relaxed, totally unaware of the panic I had gone through.

In questioning Juha why they had been so long, the explanation he offered was that the wind had died down completely on the side facing the mainland, and he was too scared to stand up in the boat to take the sails down, so they just waited. I had my suspicion that they had lingered on the farm. Maja, the farmer's wife was very fond of Juha, she might well have fed him. I praised Juha for his sensibility, and said to the Lord, 'Thank you for looking after my little brother, and thank you for forgiving me my irresponsibility.' Naturally, my parents would have blamed me if something had happened to Juha. At no point then or later, did it occur to me to be angry with my parents for leaving us three, aged 18, 14 and 8 on our own for weeks with no way of checking if we were OK. Mamma trusted God, and my parents simply assumed that I would manage.

We had our Paradise Island for three more summers, but for me the first summer in 1949, was the magic one, my last long, carefree summer, and the only one when we were the sole occupiers of the island. The following summer Mr Saari, a man who worked on the railways, bought, very cheaply, a small plot of land close to the top of the mountain and built his family a log cabin up there. To Juha's delight, they had two sons of his age.

Summer 1952 was special, as it was the summer of Helsinki Olympics, and Rainer had been chosen to represent Finland in the 400m hurdles. For the family it was our last summer on the island. Isä had, by then, managed to obtain land from a Karelian farmer in Vuokatti for our permanent summerhouse as a replacement for Kaihoniemi.

I was in no way ready to leave our wilderness cottage and was there on my holiday at the end of July, including Helena Day. On the morning of Helena day, Mamma wrote to Isä:

'It's early morning, just after five, the lake is calm, it's warm, but cloudy. I popped out to pick a bouquet of flowers for Arna on Helena's Day. I have already prepared for her a little, modest name-day table: fudges made by me, one orange and a book I brought from Helsinki. In the afternoon we'll drink coffee with a cake, and we'll also remember your mother.'

The bouquet of wildflowers (harebells, clover, wild chervil, etc) was so beautiful, that I asked Mamma to make me a pastel drawing of it. I still have it, framed and hanging in my bedroom, a lovely memory of this special time. The summers on the Paradise Island had been enchanting, magic, filling me, a young girl, with romantic dreams and fantasies.

The last summer that we still had the cottage, Isä gave me the task of renting it out. A lovely young couple responded to my advert in the Helsinki paper, rented the cottage, and fell in love with the Paradise Island, like we had done, returning there the two following summers, until our cottage was sold.

Matriculation photos:
Arna 1949, Seija 1949,

Skiing holiday: Seija, Minnami, Kaaki, Kaaki's sister, and Arna (1951)

Graduation photo:
State Registered Nurse
1953

Chapter Six
The years of study 1949-1953

Life as an Undergraduate

During the summer weeks after my matriculation examinations there had been many discussions with Mamma and Isä about what studies I should embark on. Isä's suggestion was teaching.

'Think, how wonderful to have three months summer holidays,' he said to me.

Mamma, now a school dentist, suggested, 'Why don't you study medicine, and become a dentist? All my dental instruments are unused, and you would save a lot of money not having to buy new ones.'

I had much more altruistic ideas, such as of being the head of a children's institute, looking after orphaned children or working as a missionary in Africa. For either of these choices, I would need two separate professional qualifications: firstly, in nursing, and secondly, a Masters' Degree in Psychology. In my thinking, it would be best to undertake the nursing training first, as I might not be too happy emptying bed pans or scrubbing floors with a degree in Psychology. Determined to follow my plan, there was now a gap year to fill, as the Nursing College did not accept students younger than nineteen.

In September I enrolled myself at Helsinki University, just across the Senate Square, easy to get to and easy to run home, if there were gaps between lectures. I decided to put my main effort in studying Latin, and to pass the 'pro exercutio' examination in Latin, the compulsory requirement for studying in the faculty of Philosophy and Languages, would be done. I was aiming to cover the three-year course in a year by taking lessons every day. I passed my Latin examination. Now there were no obstacles to taking any Degree in that faculty later. In addition, I joined classes in English, and took up a course in Art History, covering the Flemish Art from 1500-1600.

As a student at Helsinki University, I became automatically a member of the students' union, and was able to take part in the various pursuits available for students. Remembering Vilho's praise of my singing voice and his encouragement to join a student choir, I took the challenge, went for an audition for one of the best choirs, and was accepted as a mezzo soprano. How rewarding and different it was to be singing in a 'proper' choir. Initially, I felt nervous, self-conscious and scared to use my voice, but as soon as I began to master the pieces, my confidence grew. I felt elated, excited, and singing was a joy.

The performance, with the Helsinki Symphony Orchestra, of 'The Captive Queen', a choral composition by Sibelius, was the first work I sang with the choir. We, the sopranos and altos, were required to wear long white dresses. Luckily, I had been allowed to keep Eevi's confirmation dress; that would do for now.

On the morning of the performance, I went to have my hair done. To boost my confidence, I decided to have a colour rinse. What a mistake, what a shock! My hair was as bright orange as a carrot. I could not face the choir with this hair, so I rushed home, washed my hair time and again, but the colour hardly shifted. Mamma would say, 'Your vanity has played a trick.' A lesson learned, no more colour rinses. I had to carry the consequences of my vanity.

By the time we were walking onto the stage, my hair had no importance, instead the collective excitement and nervous anticipation was there to be felt. The choirmaster had told us of him having sung 'The Captive Queen' in this, now packed concert hall in 1935, at a concert celebrating the 70th birthday of Sibelius. Sibelius with his wife Aino, sat next to Marshall Mannerheim, on the front row. Perhaps this memory spurred him on; we performed well. The relief afterwards was great. I was in a state of ecstasy, so happy to be a choir member.

After couple of years our choir was combined with another student choir to become a new, much larger, and more demanding choir, 'Akateeminen Laulu' (Academic Singers). Our repertoire included such challenging choral works as Mozart's Requiem, Mendelson's 'Elijah' and Verdi's Requiem. I carried on singing in this choir right up until I left Finland.

At the university I met Seija's good friend and classmate Minnami Herlin, the daughter of the owner of the universally well-known Lift company Kone. She and I used to stand in the university corridors and chat for hours. Minnami, the tallest woman I had ever seen, at about 184 centimetres, stately, beautiful, and highly original, became easily excited during our conversations, gesticulating her points of view with her long arms, going on and on. Standing next to her I felt embarrassed for both of us, feeling that we were looked at as a very unlikely pair. Minnami also decided to apply for the nursing training, we became close friends, and our friendship lasted until Minnami died, aged 73.

During the winter months Seija, Minnami and I applied for places at the Helsinki Nursing College. After the war years, our choice seemed right to us. What could possibly be better than caring for the ill and vulnerable?

In order to be accepted for the three-year course, we had to go through interviews, testing our motivation, and practical tests, showing our ability to think logically. One task was: '*What would you pack in a suitcase, and in what order, if you were travelling with a small baby?*' This had to be done in under ten minutes. Many of the questions seemed almost silly, like: '*What should you do before you remove the patient's shirt?*' Answer: '*You open the shirt button.*' Or: '*Why is it better for a baby to suck the thumb than a teat?*' Answer: '*The thumb doesn't fall on the floor.*'

It did not take many weeks before a letter, signed by Aino Durchman, the Principal of the Helsinki Nursing College, arrived, informing me that I had been accepted as a student nurse, so had Seija and Minnami. The three-year training course, the last six months spent in specialising in the branch of nursing we chose, was to commence on the third of August 1950.

August arrived and a new world with new challenges was waiting. Having recently returned from a scholarship trip to America, and having been deeply influenced by the nursing training in USA, the Principal of the Helsinki Nursing College, Miss Aino Durchman, wanted to make major changes in the nursing training in Finland. Miss Durchman, approaching her sixties, a pale-faced, tight-lipped, grey-haired, tiny, and totally sexless spinster, had high ambitions for the future of the nursing profession. The Helsinki Nursing College was going to be the one to lead the way.

Her aim was to make the nursing qualification comparable to a university BA degree. She had already begun taking the initial steps in this upgrading process. Firstly, she had decided that applicants needed to have passed their matriculation examinations to be accepted for training in nursing, and secondly, she planned to change the position of student nurses on the hospital wards; they would no longer be auxiliary nurses, treated as part of the workforce on the wards. From now on the training was going to be college based, and students would be on the wards to learn particular skills in each of their placements. They would receive no salary, and they would work the hours decided by the college. These quite radical changes were impossible to implement straight away, but some changes had been made. Sister tutors had been appointed to all the major teaching hospitals in Helsinki; they, not the ward Sisters, were in charge of the practical tuition on the wards, and of the theoretical studies at the college.

The Helsinki Nursing College, offering accommodation for several hundred students, was a purpose-built modern building. Even we, the handful of us who came from the Helsinki area, were obliged to live in the college. The rooms, with two students sharing, were allocated in alphabetical order with no right to express any preferences regarding with whom you shared. That right came later in the training. My initial room companion was Ellen Pekki, a sensitive, attractive, albino-blonde, and an ultra-feminine girl. We got on all right, but when, a year later, we were allowed to change, Seija and I chose to share, using the opportunity to bring items, such as rugs and pictures, from our homes to make an attractive, welcoming room.

The first four months of our training, both practical and theoretical, was college-based. We made several short visits to various hospitals with our Sister tutors. Aino-*äiti* (mother), as we called Miss Durchman, had not only come back from America with her transformative ideas for upgrading the status of the nursing profession, she had also been deeply influenced by the new psychoanalytical ideas and thinking. She was determined to make her students familiar with the revolution happening in psychiatry. She managed to persuade one of the leading psychoanalysts and psychiatrists, Martti Paloheimo, to teach us psychology for the first term. We had only been attending these classes for a couple of weeks, when Aino-äiti called me into her office, wanting to know how the course was going.

She asked, 'Miss Pelkonen, tell me what is the 'red thread' of nursing?'

Having not the faintest idea what she was talking about, I stood in front of her silent, nervous and puzzled.

Miss Durchman looked at me sternly, and said, 'Miss Pelkonen, you need to know and remember, in all nursing the red thread is psychology.'

After four months in 'the preparatory school', and having, as observers, made our visits to the main hospitals, we moved to work on the wards. I was sent to a male urological ward in the Surgical Hospital, one of the oldest hospitals in Helsinki.

The large wooden building had eight wards, each with a large dormitory and, for seriously ill patients, two side rooms. The hospital had a very busy Out Patients' Clinic and an Accidents and Emergencies Unit.

On the wards, each student was allocated one patient to observe and care for. At the end of this first placement, we had to write a report on the patient, and our first experiences of working with real patients. The ward Sister, Miss Räikkönen, was a woman in her late forties, average height, slim, her dark hair pulled into a tight bun. She had a reputation of being strict. Looking at me from behind her dark-rimmed glasses, I saw her piercing brown eyes, and felt nervous and scared that I might not meet her approval. Indeed, Miss Räikköen was strict, requiring high standards, but fair. We got on well.

She invited me to follow her into one of the side rooms to introduce my patient Mr Heino to me. He was lying on his back, showing no physical movement, very still, looking at me with curiosity from under his sheet. The little I could see, was a good-looking, youngish man, and sadness in his grey eyes.

'Mr Heino, meet Miss Pelkonen, she is a student nurse who will be your special nurse while she is on placement with us,' said Miss Räikkönen.

Mr. Heino greeted me without a smile on his face. Looking into my eyes, he replied, 'I would not want your job; it's not going to be a pleasant one.'

Feeling uncomfortable, I simply smiled, and said, 'I look forward to being your special nurse.' What should or could I say?

Back in the Sister's office, I was told Mr. Heino's history. He was a lorry driver, working for a quarrying firm, taking slates from the quarry to building sites. He had done this job for some years; then came the day that changed his life forever. Unloading the stones, he stumbled and fell. Unable to stop the full load falling on top of him, he was crushed. He was trapped, screaming with pain, then went into a shock. His workmates removed the stones carefully, without daring to touch him. An ambulance arrived within minutes, driving him full speed and with the shrill sound of sirens to the Accident and Emergency department of this hospital. After the assessment he was moved to a ward, where I met him. The examination had confirmed his worst fears; his spinal cord had been permanently damaged, resulting in a paralysis of his body down from his neck. Nothing could be done; he was forced to face the full, cruel truth about his injuries, and his future. He would never be able to stand or walk on his own legs, he would not even have enough strength in his arms to eat, he would have to be fed, washed, and have a catheter inserted to urinate. He, a father of two young children, would not be able to pick up his children, play with them or share with his wife their day-to-day care. Instead, he would be an extra child, or much worse, a lump of a human being in a bed, from which he would never be able to get up unaided. He was totally useless as a husband, father, and a man. Was there any point in staying alive? These thoughts he gradually shared with me, thoughts that were his morbid companions persecuting him day after day, as he lay immobile in his hospital bed.

In order to ease the pressure on the same part of his body, and to prevent bed sores, I needed to turn Mr. Heino every four hours. The nurse showed me how to do it and what my job was. What I saw to my horror, was a gaping bed sore with pus oozing from it, in the centre of his back. The sight of the sore, and the smell made me want run away, to vomit. All the romantic ideas about being a 'healing angel' disappeared. Straight away, in nursing my first patient Mr Heino, I was forced to face the reality of a nursing career. My 'romantic' job was going to be: turn Mr Heino every four hours, clean and take care of his bedsores, clear his shit, wash and feed him, and, after being taught, insert a catheter into his penis to help him urinate. I had never touched a man's penis, never really looked at one. Oh, my GOD, there it was automatically erected, swollen and big. I learned that the vegetative system isn't affected by the paralysis, it works independently.

Overcoming the initial shocks, I made a good relationship with Mr Heino, and looked forward to nursing him. He began to trust me, sharing his thoughts, admitting being deeply depressed about his future.

'If I'm honest, I feel hopeless, I want to end my life. What use am I to anybody?'

I had no words of comfort, there were none to be given, inwardly I cried; my heart was aching.

As weeks went by, I discovered an intelligent man, who struggled to make sense of his life as it now was. Accepting his fate, Mr Heino's life force began to return slowly. He even began to make jokes of his condition. Enough power had returned to his arms, so once I had chopped his food up, he was able to feed himself.

In four months, Mr Heino gave me, a naïve girl, the shock treatment I needed to be able to carry on in my chosen profession. I came to understand, waiting for me in the hospital world would be more pain, suffering, even death to be faced. Was I up to it? I was sad to leave Mr

Heino, and I knew he had grown fond of me. We would miss our special relationship.

Being on a urological male ward, I had no option but to get used to looking at penises. The men needed their bottles to urinate into; some needing a catheter inserted or changed. One youngish man became infatuated with me. There was his penis wiggling, issuing an invitation to touch him each time I was taking the bottle to him. Luckily for me, he was too ill to be allowed up from his bed, otherwise he might have followed me around. As his discharge day approached, he begged and begged me to come and see him off at the station on his return to his home town. I felt sorry for him, gave in, and agreed. Standing there at the station, in his civilian clothes, was this small, much older looking man, in shabby, civilian clothes. A huge shock. Both of us embarrassed, looking awkward, and not knowing how to handle this civilian situation. I knew I had made a massive error in judgement in promising to meet him outside the hospital ward. We had a quick coffee at the station, and we parted never to meet again. I learned my lesson: Do not mix your work with your private life.

Rainer and Anna-Liisa

I had been living at the Helsinki Nursing College for only a few weeks, when I heard someone in the communal kitchen shouting, 'Arna, come quick; this phone call is for you.'

Usually, the calls were from anxious parents of those students coming from long distances away from Helsinki, and the phone ringing was just a background noise of no interest to me. Running to the kitchen, I was thinking, who and why would anyone phone me?'

The call was from Mamma. She was upset, that I could hear from her voice; she refused to discuss in detail why she had called; simply insisting, 'Arna, please come home as quickly as you can; it's important,' then adding, 'Nobody is ill, but something has happened, and I need to talk with you face to face about this matter.'

Luckily, I was free, and set off immediately. My head was spinning with guesses about what could have happened, and what was so urgent for me to have to rush home. When I arrived, Mamma led me to the dining room, closing the door behind us.

'Let's drink a cup of coffee first; more relaxing to talk,' she said.

We settled to enjoy our coffee. I sensed Mamma's hesitation, and her search for the right words, then she began. 'I have some shocking news to share with you.'

Looking at me, as if she wanted to read my thoughts from my expression, she continued, 'Rainer came home yesterday telling of his and Anna-Liisa's visit to the doctor. What they had feared was confirmed: Anna-Liisa is pregnant. The baby will be born at the end of February.' Mamma, now looking extremely upset, continued,

'As you can guess I'm deeply shocked. I trusted Rainer, I warned him not to fall for the temptations of his bodily desires. He did not listen.' Then, gesticulating with her arms, and her voice raising, she added, 'What will people say?'

Of course, I understood perfectly well Mamma's upset, but decided to keep my mouth shut and just listen, though

I was thinking that nobody should be shocked or surprised. We had all been aware of the seriousness of Rainer's and Anna-Liisa's relationship. They had been together for about five years.

I remembered that it was in the autumn of 1944, when Anna-Liisa, a new girl, arrived at our school, joining the students in Raikku's class. (Rainer was called Raikku by all his contemporaries in school, and by Laila, Juha and me). Anna-Liisa looked different, older than the awkward, self-conscious, pimply faced teenaged girls in her class; she caused curiosity. Clearly, she had left her puberty behind, and had reached her adult height of 167 cm. Her curvy, sexy, and shapely figure had not gone unnoticed by the boys, Raikku amongst them.

Having already had his first teenage romances, Raikku was confident of beating the competitors, and he set out to win the new girl for himself. At sixteen he had gone through puberty and become a handsome 'Viking' charmer; tall, slim as a bean pole, and admired for his increasing success as a sportsman. As could be expected, he succeeded in conquering Anna-Liisa. They became a steady couple almost immediately, Anna-Liisa never looking at another boy, whilst Rainer had a couple of little side hops.

I did not get to know Anna-Liisa in our shared time at school. Three years older, and, initially, in a class two years above me, she was, in my opinion, quite dim. We did not share friends, or have common interests, other than sharing our affection for Raikku. I was neither interested in nor paid much attention to her looks. Yes, she had a good figure, thick auburn hair, and dark blue eyes. What spoilt the beauty of her face, was what Mamma called 'the third-degree bite', the lower jaw protruding in front of the upper jaw; this affecting the bite and spoiling her looks.

Both Anna-Liisa and Raikku had to repeat a year, and were then just one year above me. After having to repeat yet another year, Anna-Liisa ended in the same class as me in the sixth form. She left school the following year without taking the matriculation examinations.

I did not express my thoughts to Mamma, but having witnessed them together, seeing them so obviously in love during their holiday on our Paradise Island, and knowing them having the freedom to be alone for long periods at Anna-Liisa's parents' summer place, what else could we expect? In fact, in my opinion, it had been a wonder that the pregnancy hadn't happened long before.

Anna-Liisa and Raikku had on New Year's Day announced their engagement, both twenty-one years old. They wanted everybody to know of their commitment to each other. Isä was not happy about their engagement, and had expressed his concern about Rainer tying himself down before completing his University studies; his authority was limited to voicing his objections. Isä had been so right with his concerns. Anna-Liisa's pregnancy came at a most inconvenient moment for Rainer. Firstly, he had only started his three year degree course in Physical Education at the Helsinki University the previous autumn. Secondly, having already competed at an international level in athletics matches between Finland and other Scandinavian countries, Rainer was being trained for the Helsinki Olympics in 1952, and he had a brilliant running career in front of him. Thirdly, Rainer had to do the eleven months' long, compulsory military service. The sudden responsibility for a child and wife was certainly not on his agenda, nor did he have the required financial resources to take this on. I felt really sorry for my brother.

We drank our coffee in silence; each in our thoughts. Then Mamma picked up two letters she and Rainer had been writing to Isä, still up in Sotkamo. She wanted me to read them before Juha would post them. Rainer wrote:

'Isä, I never wanted to write to you this kind of letter. I have always known that I had the best parents in the world, and for that reason this task is even harder, as I am going to distress and hurt you. My wish is to speak to you as a man to a man; if you can, try to understand me. I have betrayed yours and Mamma's trust in me. Isä, something unfortunate and wrong has happened to me. Anna-Liisa saw the doctor today, and he confirmed that Anna-Liisa is expecting a baby. If you can, please forgive me, if not now, then, even after years. Isä, remember that Anna-Liisa is innocent, do not think badly of her. I hope you'll like her; she loves you already. Isä, even if you reject me, please, be not angry with her. I don't know why this should happen to me, to us, perhaps there is a reason. Perhaps I needed to be humiliated, for sure, that I will be.

You, my beloved parents, have to discover that your own child is no better than anyone else, in this case worse. I know, I have been a bad young man, lazy and without stamina. What is now happening, I'll learn from it, I am sure. There is a saying that a young person needs a 'knock' from God before he matures. I would have given you anything, even my sport, rather than cause you to feel ashamed of me.

I love Anna-Liisa, and think, Isä, how lucky I am to marry my beloved one, and don't have to take any odd 'shoddy stranger'. I want to look forward bravely. It may not be easy; people so easily judge mistakes. Isä, when we are over this most difficult year, perhaps you also may have become reconciled, though I can't believe in my heart that you are truly angered. Do not feel hurt, encourage us. I see you sitting with 'little Raikku' on your knee. He will be a better boy than your own son. I should have written to you much earlier. I have been anxious; I haven't been able to sleep. My running in competitions has not worked as well as I had wished. It is not possible to succeed with a heavy mind.

We have discussed this matter with Anna-Liisa's parents. After the first shock, they have been very supportive. A grandchild will be very special to Anna-Liisa's mother, as she never had a child of her own. (Anna-Liisa was adopted by Aino and Jarl Stenholm when she was three years old, her birth mother was unable to keep her child.) *Yes, Isä, now we have a wedding in front of us, a quiet, unassuming, and simple one. I do hope that the pastor will be a real man, not one who judges us. As a man I want to stand behind my deeds and take care of the consequences. Isä, I hope you still hold me as your son, even though I do not deserve it.' Love from, Rainer*

Mamma included her letter with Rainer's:

Dear Yrjö, I have just been allowed to read Rainer's letter. What a shock. I have been so proud of my son, and have held him above boys of his age, so moral and irreproachable. I should have understood without Jesus one is not able to repress one's desires when passions are aroused. I don't condemn. Rainer has condemned himself, God does not condemn him, neither have we the right to do so. Yrjö, remember your own youth. Have you been absolutely clean? I have the feeling, even though you have never spoken about it, that you have had erotic adventures, adventures void of any real love. They are far more shameful.

Rainer fell down with his loved one, that is human. Let's forgive and understand them. Rainer is so mortified. This morning when I was listening to the morning prayers, I could hear his quiet sobbing. God is seeking Rainer, and us all, through this misfortune. Are we able to take the right attitude? Have we warned the young ones enough, have we talked of the dangers? I feel guilty. Dear Yrjö, don't you think we have reason to turn to God? May He forgive our mistakes, also in this matter. Before you reply to Rainer, I beg you to turn to God. Karin

Isä made both Rainer and Mamma wait. Then, finally, after a week, Rainer received Isä's response:

Dear Rainer, I thank you for your letter, the most dismal one I ever have had to read. You had to force yourself to write it. It hasn't been your habit to write however desirable it would have been to receive letters when you have been away from home. I read your letter yesterday on my return to Sotkamo. I have to admit, it's hard for me to comprehend what has happened. I am sure you understand that your letter 'knocked me out', and I have not recovered yet. Your deed is punishable, and that punishment is already being carried out. I feel sorry for you having to swallow this bitter pill. We, your parents, also carry part of that punishment.

You may recollect, I was not pleased with you and Anna-Liisa getting engaged. In my opinion it was too early for you to make such a permanent commitment; your adult life was only just beginning. You have never understood what it has meant to live under a stranger's roof, eat in the cheapest place, and to study by taking a loan. These circumstances force you to put all your effort in reaching your goal. The only bright side I can see, is your need to draw out all your inner strength in your struggle to achieve your life goals, and for you to be able to take care of your family. You have paid a heavy price for having your eyes opened.

Time moves on, and is a leveller. I have been fearing that something like this might happen. You have had far too much freedom in your courting. I trusted your common sense. What has happened is human, and your circumstances gave an excellent opportunity. You are now crestfallen and humiliated. I have no wish to add to your burden by refusing to give you my forgiveness. That I will give you, and you remain my beloved son. You have received such a knock, that it might make you see your strivings in a completely new light, supporting you in the new phase that is about unfold. In spite of all the difficulties you might face, the future is as open for you as before. Do you have the strength to make the decisions that are now needed? I believe you'll succeed. Loving greetings,

Raikku shared with me the content of Isä's letter, pointing out sentences Isä had crossed out, and he had even 'forgotten' to sign it. We knew it had been a difficult letter for him to write. I was not too surprised by its harsh tone, having myself come across Isä's sanctimonious attitude. I was in my early teens when he said very firmly, in the middle of our family meal, 'Get up, go and wash all that makeup off your face.'

Well, he was a clergyman's son, and his mother, I understand, was a highly moral, puritan Christian. Mamma, though endlessly preaching and trying to convert us, was not narrow minded, she was surprisingly tolerant and understanding, often blaming herself for having been a bad mother rather than criticising her children. To me, this fuss about Anna-Liisa's pregnancy seemed 'Much Ado about Nothing'.

It was decided that the wedding would be held in Anna-Liisa's home, after Mamma and Rainer had discussed with the Stenholms. They had a large detached house in Käpylä and were well off. The date chosen was Monday September 18th. Why that date? There were two main reasons. Firstly, the preceding weekend Rainer was competing in the athletics championship between Finland and Norway, running for the first time in the 400 metres hurdles. Secondly, on 18th September in 1926, Karin Nylenius and Yrjö Pelkonen had been married. Why not share the anniversary date?

Rainer was eager to get the wedding over, as his University term was commencing at the beginning of October, and in addition he was in a hurry to start his military service as soon as possible, aiming to have served a few months before the baby's birth. He had put in an application to do his military service at the coastal artillery division on the island of Suomenlinna, close to Helsinki. The fortress Viapori had been built there during the Swedish rule as a defence against attacks from Russia, and it continued in the same role also under Russian rule, now, as a defence against attacks from the west. Once Finland became independent, the fortress was renamed Suomenlinna (Castle of Finland), housing various Defence Force units, and was a Finnish garrison until the early 1960s.

Then, only the Naval Academy remained there; otherwise the island was housing a civilian population.

Raikku's plan worked: He was accepted to the artillery unit in Suomenlinna, his military service commencing almost immediately after the wedding. Secondly, having applied, he had been given a year's leave of absence from his university studies. Suomenlinna, being so close to Helsinki, made it easy for Raikku to carry on with his athletic training under the guidance of his coach.

I could see my brother changing almost overnight from a boy to a man. I sensed his determination to make a success of his life, and to accept his new responsibilities. That single-minded determination to succeed has been Raikku's driving force not only in running but also in the way he has conducted his life.

September 18th turned out to be a warm, beautiful, and sunny autumn day. Isä had informed us that he was not able to attend. His stated reason was, 'unalterable work commitments'. No work commitment, in my opinion, could be that important; he was sulking, unable to put his son's needs above his own pious feelings. I was angry and deeply disappointed in Isä. How could he be so cruel and horrible towards Raikku, his first-born son? Having never had a father to guide him, perhaps he was unable to see how much Rainer, his son, would have needed a father next to him on this important day? I had no way of understanding then what it had meant to Isä to be a fatherless son, and of being deprived of a father's support and guidance in growing up. To me, he was simply unable to see the importance of his presence for Rainer.

Used to arranging parties and dinners, Anna-Liisa's mother had succeeded in making their home welcoming and festive for the simple ceremony. Chairs had been arranged around the bay window with a view of the garden. A table, with a white lace cloth, two candlesticks, a Bible, a bouquet of flowers, and a silver bowl, filled with water, had been placed in front of the window to function as an altar. There were enough matching seats for our small gathering: Anna-Liisa's parents, our family members, and my cousin Kaarina, who had come to stay with us for a while.

Near the stairs, leading upstairs, was the piano. Rainer had asked me to play the Wedding March, composed by the Finnish composer Erkki Melartin. (In Finland this march is used far more frequently than Mendelssohn's one). Even with my limited skills, I agreed, as the tune was quite simple, and the audience wasn't critical. Moving towards the piano, I glanced up, and saw Anna-Liisa stepping slowly down the stairs towards the living room where her father was waiting to escort her towards the 'altar'. I could sense her nervousness as she stepped forward, wearing a dove blue long dress, the little bump hardly noticeable, and carried a bouquet of lily of the valleys. The sun made her thick, auburn hair glitter like copper, her violet blue eyes were filled with tears, and a smile of happiness lingered on her face. She was looking stunningly radiant. Whatever I had thought of her and her looks, today, on her wedding day, she looked lovely. I freely admitted that the two of them, Anna-Liisa and my brother Rainer, were an extremely handsome pair.

Mamma's second cousin, Pastor Rainer Lautsiala, still a bachelor, performed the short wedding service. The ceremony ended with us singing a thanksgiving hymn: *'Kiitos sulle Jumalani armostasi, kaikesta...* (Thank you, Lord for your grace, and all I have received....), a hymn sung at all our family festive occasions. On Anna-Liisa's mother's invitation, we then moved to their spacious dining room for an excellent wedding meal. Anna-Liisa's father said a few loving words, first to his daughter, then to them both as a couple. Rainer said words of thanks to Anna-Liisa's parents, promising to take good care of their daughter. Mamma, true to form, emphasized the importance of following in the footsteps of Jesus, ending with these words, (repeated seven years later at my wedding): *'Onnelaan on kaksi avainta: Kiitos ja Anteeksi'* (The keys to your happiness are these four words 'Thank **you'** and 'Forgive **me**').

Quietly, the now officially married couple slipped away. Mr Stenholm had booked them a room in the best hotel of Helsinki for their wedding night; the rest of their honeymoon they would spend at the Stenholm's summer place. The newlyweds had a very short period of living together in Anna-Liisa's home before Rainer began his military service in Suomenlinna, joining the costal artillery unit. In January 1951, for the remaining period of his service, Rainer was transferred to the Naval Academy, and he was seriously considering a military career, but gave up the idea, as Anna-Liisa was totally against Rainer changing his career plans.

Marshall Carl Gustav Mannerheim, the great Finnish hero, and the sixth President of Finland died on the 27th of January. The nation was in a state of mourning. His funeral, a bitterly cold day, about minus 25C, took place on the 4th of February in Helsinki Cathedral. Rainer, training to become an Officer, was one of the naval cadets chosen to carry the official floral tributes to the cemetery and lay them on the grave.

The funeral procession proceeded from the Helsinki cathedral along the streets of Helsinki all the way to Hietaniemi Cemetery. The five kilometre long route was lined with university students; I was one of them. We were ordered to be in the position at least an hour before hand, wear our thin white caps, and to stand to attention for the length of the endlessly long procession. It did not take long before my feet were freezing, my toes going numb, and every part of my body was icy cold. Finally, when we were allowed to disperse, I ran home, filled a bowl with hot water to soak my feet. The pain of the gradual thawing was excruciating, but a pain worth suffering for Marshall Mannerheim.

On the 26th of February, Anna-Liisa's and Rainer's son was born. Rainer wrote to Isä, beginning his letter with: '*Dear grandad*', and ending with these words:

'I am so happy that all went well, and Anna-Liisa coped with the difficult, frightening moments. We are so grateful that we now have a family, and now have a totally new life in front of us. Isä, I am hoping that your harsh thoughts have melted away, and that with us, you, with gratitude, are going to take this little new-born into your shared protection. Loving greetings, Rainer.

Naturally, Isä was proud and happy to be a grandad, but it was Anna-Liisa's mother who became the key grandparent. She adored this little baby. He remained the special one, even after having three more grandchildren. The christening took place in Anna-Liisa's home; this time

Isä was present. The baby was named: Aarno Rainer; he became my first godchild.

There was the opportunity to rearrange the use of the various rooms in our flat after Mummi's death and my nursing training. My parents made the decision to offer the young family a space of their own in our flat once Rainer had completed his military service, late in September 1951. Rainer, seeing it as a sign of reconciliation from Isä, and having no income, was more than pleased to accept this generosity. He wanted to be there supporting his son in his new role as father.

Organising a couple of his military colleagues to assist him, Raikku undertook the task of re-decorating the two joining rooms in the front of the house. Anna-Liisa was especially pleased to have their own place, looking forward to being left in charge of Aarno's care without her mother fussing over him. Mamma had no difficulties in handing over some responsibilities in the household to her capable daughter-in-law.

The University Hospital for Internal Medicine

In early March 1951, I began a four months' placement at the University Hospital for Internal Medicine. The hospital, like the Helsinki University, was one of the neo-classical buildings, around the Senate Square, designed by the German architect Carl Ludvig Engel in the early 19th century.

Working irregular hours and split shifts, I asked for permission to live at my home, and, surprisingly, obtained this. I have to admit that I had become used to the busyness and fun of communal living at the college; my home felt quiet and empty, Mamma, Laila and Juha, each finding something to do away from the home. Perhaps they, like me, felt that the home was soulless. Mummi, our little hardworking Mummi, was missing. Three years had gone since her death, we should have got used to her absence, but no, we missed her, especially Mamma did. As a tiny, tiny consolation there was Taru, always waiting, always pleased to see you, and always hoping to be taken out for a walk. There were maids taking care of the household; often staying only for short periods, before moving to new jobs and giving Mamma the problem of finding a replacement.

I noticed how tired Mamma looked. After her long hours of standing, she came home from work needing to rest, but in spite of her tiredness she was attending religious meetings most evenings, leaving Laila and Juha to take care of themselves. Since Mamma's serious illness in 1945, I had lived in fear of her death. Now, when at home in the mornings, I observed Mamma, always late, running full speed across the Senate Square, hurrying to catch her train. On days I was doing a shift, I often sat near the window, waiting to see Mamma coming across the square. If she was late, those feelings of fear returned with full force; my heart began to beat faster, my anxiety levels increased, and in no time, I began imagining that Mamma had had a heart attack and died. Enforcing my fears, was Mamma's openly expressed longing to be united with her Saviour, and her readiness to give up the struggle of the earthly life. Mamma admitted that she was missing me. I had been of practical help in running the household, someone she was able to talk to, and someone to share her concerns with, mainly about Juha. He was just ten, and was left, far too often and for far too long, to manage on his own. No wonder he was getting into all kind of troubles. Mamma wrote about her worries to Isä:

'Today I had a serious encounter with Juha. We discovered that he had taken money from Arna's 'Mission Box', at least 100 mk. It was difficult to speak with him about this. I tried to make him understand that he has stolen from God. I am punishing him by us going together to see the Mission Pastor. We'll confess our sins together: I, as a bad mother and educator, Juha, as a thief. We are returning the raided mission box. I am worried about Juha's honesty. If God does not take hold of him, I do not know what will happen to Juha. This boy would need a praying father, a father striving with him, and a father reading the Bible with him etc. We, as parents are responsible for our children's souls. Does this not bother you? It bothers me.'

Juha, by stealing from me, might have indicated how let down and abandoned he felt now that both Raikku and I were no longer at home. We, each in our own way, had looked after him from his birth. I was concerned for him, and when there was an opportunity, took him with me to visit Seija's family. Juha was most welcomed there, almost a family member. He was even included in a family portrait, sitting on Seija's mother's knee. Juha and Anna-Maija, Seija's younger sister, aged nine, were great friends for many years.

Laila and Juha had a close sister/ brother relationship, enforced by their stay with the Hallander family in Sweden. Laila was now a teenager and had her own interest; horses were her passion. She had begged and begged to have riding lessons, but had reluctantly accepted that there was no spare money. She had found her own solution: working at the stables. She spent hours after school brushing and cleaning the horses, being rewarded with free riding lessons.

Laila had found a new friend in Matti, a boy who lived diagonally across the courtyard, where his father had a repair shop for antique furniture on the ground floor. Laila and Matti had been friends since we moved to Aleksanterinkatu. The friendship with Matti had become much more important, as Laila, in an all-girls school, had little opportunity to meet boys. Matti, in his teens, had grown to a fine young man. Both of them were very capable of doing practical tasks. Together they redecorated Mummi's old room for Laila's use. For the first time in her life, she had a room of her own with no interference from her bossy sister.

Being the second girl, Laila felt that she was in the worst position within her siblings, seeing herself as 'the black sheep'. Mamma, thoughtlessly and insensitively, had told the six-year-old Laila that her pregnancy with her had not been welcome, due to their financial difficulties. Laila had never forgotten or forgiven Mamma or Isä for being unwanted. Using Mamma's guilt, she was able to get what she wanted. I felt both envious and annoyed when she showed me her new, leather briefcase that Mamma had bought.

Having enjoyed the freedom without my interference, Laila was not too pleased to see me back home. She knew that Mamma would ask my advice before agreeing to her wishes. As an adult, Laila still remembered, having wanted a new coat, and Mamma asking my opinion. Nastily, I had said, 'Laila does not need one.' Mamma took my advice; Laila was left without a new coat. Laila did not want my interference. I do admit that, at times, I was not a kind older sister. The loveliest and happiest childhood memories of us together were from the summers spent on our Paradise Island. We grew to know each other really well late in our lives, when we spent summers together in Vuokatti, and shared our childhood memories. I admitted how horrible I had been on various occasions.

It was a joy on light spring mornings to walk across the Senate Square, past the university buildings, and enter the two-storey, historical hospital building, housing only four wards. Once again, I was going to be working on a male ward. I was met by the sister-in-charge, Maija Miettinen, who welcomed me, and showed me around. The large dormitory, with its high windows, was sunlit and light, instantly making me feel that I was going to enjoy this period. The sister then introduced the patients to me: a mixture of men in all age groups; suffering from illnesses such as diabetes, ulcers, kidney problems and other internal medical problems. The atmosphere felt relaxed. I heard joking comments, men promising to be an easy patient, and making encouraging remarks. As we left the dormitory, the sister pointed out the two empty side rooms and said, 'These are reserved for seriously ill or dying patients.'

On the way to her office, I looked at the sister-in-charge, estimating that she might be in her late thirties, average height, curly dark-blonde hair, green eyes, slightly overweight, looking pretty and cuddly, no wedding ring. Why not? Maybe she was one of the thousands of women who had lost their husbands or sweethearts in the war.

Sitting opposite her in the small office, I carried on making my observations: a flowering pot plant on the windowsill, a couple of small prints on the walls, and her large desk full of papers, and an opened box of chocolates, presumably a gift from a grateful patient. I was told what my duties were going to be, and that I would be expected to do night duty for the first time. Sister Miettinen noticed my worried expression, and said, 'No need to be worried, a qualified nurse, covering all the four wards will be in charge, and available to offer help.'

The memories that have stayed with me from this period were of Sister Miettinen's interest in the astrological chart, and her knowledge of the characteristics of each sign in the zodiac. She firmly believed that the horoscope sign under which you were born colours your character, determines your life path, and is vitally important in choosing your life partner. This was all new to me; I listened with great interest. She went on to explain the four elements: fire, earth, air and water, and their characteristics. 'Your horoscope sign of Aries belongs to the Fire element. It is important that your life partner should be in the same element: Aries, Leo, Sagittarius,' she added. Believing in her theory with conviction, she would speak of her patients more in terms of their horoscope signs than in referring to their illnesses. One day she announced jubilantly, 'An unmarried Libra (air element) has been admitted to the ward.'

After I had left this placement, I heard that Sister Miettinen, a Gemini, fellow in the air element, and the unmarried Libra had become a pair; they married a year later. The Libra was lucky to find his lovely Gemini woman.

I have not forgotten the report I received at the end of this placement, indicating how well I had performed. This was sent to the Nursing College. On the report what a student was good in was underlined in blue, and what she needed to improve on, was underlined in red. In my report there were a number of points underlined in blue, and just one in red: patience.

Handing me the report, Sister Miettinen said, 'I haven't an example to give you of your impatience, but because you are an Aries you must be impatient.'

I thought that, without evidence, this was hardly a professional judgement. But in my heart, I knew she was right; I am impatient.

I still remember quite clearly my first week on night duty. We were already in early May, enjoying the 'white' nights, spring was in the air, life felt good. In this happy mood I walked in to take over from the day staff, and was told that there was a new admission in the single room, a fourteen-year-old boy, Timo, suffering from lung cancer. His illness had reached a stage where nothing could be done, he needed constant care. He had been admitted to be cared for in the safety of a hospital for the final weeks of his life. Hospice care did not yet exist. My task would be to stay close to him, administer morphine injections at regular intervals as pain relief, and give him a feeling of security and trust in the strange surroundings. First, I checked that other patients were all right. 'What about a good night kiss?' I heard an old man calling to me, I blew a kiss in the air, and carried on with the ward round. By then I was used to hearing all kinds of remarks and invitations. The patients well settled; it was time to meet Timo. As I entered his room, Timo opened his eyes, turned towards me, and I told him, 'I am Miss Pelkonen, I'll be your night nurse.' I took his cold hand, and asked, 'Do you need anything right now?' He looked at me with his big hazel-coloured eyes and just smiled, but did not reply.

Timo's bed was next to the open window. Looking out, he could see the courtyard with its linden trees, just bursting into leaf, smell the blossom, and hear to the dawn chorus as the sun was rising. It was a quiet, still room.

Sitting with Timo night after night, seeing him getting weaker, and obviously in more pain, was so unbearably hard, everything in me was rebelling. Some nights he talked of his life, what he would miss most: his mother, his family and his friends. He had ambitions to become a scientist, wanting to work in the field of medicine. At times he cried, buried his head, but gave his hand for me to hold. I cried, not with him, but on walking home in the early mornings, then my tears ran freely. I could not bear the thought of Timo, such a bright, lovely young boy going towards his death. How could life be so cruel?

Another evening a new patient had been admitted just before I arrived. He was a big, heavy man in his late fifties, a diabetic, his insulin intake needed checking, but the main problem was his addiction to morphine. He was a pharmacist, and with easy access to morphine he had become an addict. An important part of the treatment plan was to wean him off his morphine by gradually reducing the dose.

In the handing over report by the staff nurse, I was given a strict instruction not to give him another injection until six in the morning. Soon after 2 am, just as the sky started lightening, he rang his bell. I hurried to him, wondering what was the matter. 'Good morning, Miss, it's a lovely morning,' I heard him shouting from the end of the dormitory. It took a while to convince him that it was still night. An hour later his bell rang again, and as I approached his bed I was met by the same cheerful greeting, 'Good morning, Miss, it must be morning now.' My patient, desperate to have his fix, called me to his bedside at shorter and shorter intervals. After consulting the charge nurse, I was given permission to bring forward the time of his injection. 'Thank you, little Miss,' he said with a blissful smile.

Finally, all was quiet, and peace reigned on the ward, but the world outside was waking up to a new morning: the dawn chorus was drowned by the less musical sounds of early trams on the move.

We were now in June; my placement was coming to an end, and my first year as a student nurse over. The year as a student nurse had been exhausting; too many new experiences, too much new learning, and too much suffering to witness. My romantic dreams of being a nurse, and the naïve innocence of relieving suffering, had been replaced by the reality of seeing patients in pain, anxious and frightened, and having to accept that, at times, all I was able to offer was the best possible care. The reality of my nursing practise was the day-to-day routine of taking temperatures, making beds, giving bed baths to patients too ill to wash themselves, and feeding those unable to feed themselves. What was required of me was to do these tasks with thought and compassion.

Helplessly watching as Mr Heino struggled to gain some inner strength in his attempts to rebuild his shattered and broken life, or night by night, seeing the life force draining from Timo, and him facing his untimely death with dignity and courage, these had been experiences nobody could have prepared me for, experiences that had taught me about the unpredictability of life. I did want to become a good nurse. Now I needed time to reflect, make a separation between the world of hospitals and the world of a twenty-year old, in her own state of turmoil, not physical but emotional.

The year had not been only about the serious side of nursing; it had also been about life in the college, learning to live together, and sharing what was happening on the wards, and in our lives with each other. We had become a friendship group, we had had enormous fun, and had laughed a lot; perhaps as a way of coping with the daily suffering facing us on the wards.

One girl, Kaarina Simojoki, or Kaaki as we called her, was exceptionally good at making us laugh. She was a master at imitating different voices, telling jokes, and playing pranks. One evening, quite late, the doorbell rang. Utterly surprised and perplexed by the arrival of an unexpected visitor, one of us rushed to open the door. There was an old, stooped woman, dressed in a long black skirt, and wrapped up in a big, dark shawl covering her head, and almost hiding her face. Her eyes disappeared behind old-fashioned, darkly rimmed glasses. The only thing to do was to usher her into our visitors' room. Leaning heavily on her walking stick, the old woman limped in, and, without hesitation, she sat down. The first thing she said was, ‘Please, give me a cup of coffee,’ and adding almost immediately, ’Please help me, I have no money, and nowhere to go, please, let me sleep here.’

There was something really odd about her. Yes, she was obviously old, but her face had no wrinkles. Destitute? Maybe, but she had clean, good clothes, typical for country women. How had she entered the building? Why had she chosen our floor? We were puzzled, but not able to put our finger on it. One of the girls brewed a cup of coffee. I noticed that our strange visitor had difficulties in drinking her coffee, and wouldn’t accept a biscuit. Those of us gathered around her needed to find out who she was, why she had come to the nurses’ college, and why to our floor. As she settled, we encouraged her to tell something about herself. Speaking in a strong Savo dialect, I thought her voice sounded faintly familiar. She began telling us that she had arrived by train that same morning from Savo, and added, ‘I do not know Helsinki, it’s far too big and frightening for a somebody like me. I got lost as soon as I came out from the railway station. I have been walking around, and then saw the name ‘Helsingin Sairaanhoitajaopisto’ (Helsinki Nursing College), and thought the people in there will help me.’

As the story proceeded, we were finding holes in it, and started bombarding her with new questions. Her answers became more and more vague; the story didn’t sound true. After a while we noticed that our visitor had difficulties in keeping a stern face. In an attempt to hide her smile, she turned around to face the wall. Then, quite suddenly, she burst out in a loud giggle. That giggle gave her away; we shouted in unison, ‘Kaaki!’ Sure, enough the old woman was Kaaki. Putting her coffee cup down on the floor, still laughing, she turned around to face us. In one hand she held a set of false teeth, in the other the dark-rimmed glasses. We were speechless and astonished for a couple of seconds, and then we all burst out laughing. How could we have been fooled so easily? How could a set of false teeth alter and make a face so unrecognisable?

Kaaki explained, 'Shortly before my grandmother died, she had this set of false teeth made. She never had a chance to wear them, and they were just left in a drawer. One day I experimented: I put the false teeth on top of my own, looked at myself in the mirror, and couldn't believe the massive change to my looks; I was unrecognisable.' She added, 'I was sure that with a bit of acting, and suitable props, I would get away with acting an old woman.'

In spite of having been fooled, and knowing Kaaki's prank, we still asked her from time to time to dress up, and play her role as the old woman just to have a laugh.

Kaaki joined our little friendship group of Seija, Minnami and me. Coming from Savo, in middle of Finland, she was the only one not from Helsinki. Her father was a clergyman in charge of a large parish, and her parents were members of the revivalist, pietistic, Lutheran movement, '*Heränneet*' (the Awakened). The movement had been started by a crofter, Paavo Ruotsalainen, in the 1850s. Paavo's simple message, emphasising the worthlessness of us human beings, contrasting it with the greatness of God, had an immediate appeal for country people, feeling themselves to be insignificant beings against the greatness of God. He encouraged us, the sinners, to wait patiently for God's grace and His rewards after death. Modesty and humility were seen as core values. Women pulled their hair tightly into buns, and used grey, black or blue in their clothing; red was the colour of sinfulness, and forbidden. The movement, 'Herännäisyys', spread rapidly across middle and northern Finland, and was accepted within the Lutheran church. In addition to worshipping in the church, the members gathered in their homes to sing hymns, listen to short talks, and share their concerns. The Summer Festival, lasting several days, is still an annual event, drawing 30,000 or more participants.

Already by 1928 'The Herättäjä Yhdistys' (the Association of the Awakening) had opened students' houses for students of theology; a great gift for many poor students. The association had thought that the best way to guarantee the continuation of followers was through education, and bringing like-minded people together while they were studying. After the war the movement went through a drastic modernisation, changing some of the strictest rules to more liberal ones.

When I told Mamma about my new friend Kaaki, she soon worked out that she knew Kaaki's father. Arvi Simojoki had been a young, newly qualified clergyman in the Kuopio parish when my parents lived there at the time when I was a baby. 'It's a small world,' said Mamma, telling me that Kaaki's father had been the pastor who christened me. She remembered him as a dashing young man with almost black, curly, thick hair. Kaaki had inherited this dark, curly, thick and beautiful hair, showing off her enviable locks in her free time. As a student nurse, she had to keep her hair tightly tied away under her nurse's headgear. Kaaki's brother Jussi, two years older than she, studied theology, and lived in a pietistic student house with many other young theology students known to Kaaki from the Summer Festivals.

Being far freer from sexual inhibitions than Seija and me, Kaaki soon picked up admirers. Thanks to her, we came to know many of these young men. They, equally shy as we two, were scared to take any initiative. Jussi was Seija's secret love. It took a year of secret admiration before Jussi, finally, had the courage to invite Seija out for a date.

It was a different story with Kaaki. It did not take long before she had made her conquest, no surprise to us. She had found her ideal man in Raimo Pihkala, a tall, blond, theology student, nine years older than her. He had taken part in the war, and this had delayed the start of his studies. Their passionate love affair flared up quickly. From the very start they both knew that this was it, and there was no need to search any further. All they had to do was to wait patiently for each of them to complete their studies. Raimo's studies were coming to an end in about a year's time.

As soon as he was qualified, he was appointed as an assistant pastor in a parish in a small costal town. Kaaki was left behind, eagerly waiting to join him, but first waiting for the day she would become a fully trained nurse, in August 1953. A year later Kaaki and Raimo married. During their engagement she worked, but never after their marriage. Kaaki concentrated on being an exceptionally good wife to a parson, and a wonderful mother to her four children. Their first child Hanna-Leena was born in the autumn 1955. Seeing Kaaki's happiness, and the ease with which many of my student colleagues picked up and dropped admirers, made me look again at my attitude to boys. Two things had been instilled in me: Firstly, the importance of having a career, and to become financially independent, before even thinking about marriage. Secondly, to have boys as friends, but not get involved with one boy in a close way before marriage. 'At all cost avoid temptations.' 'You can be admired but not touched.' 'Your chastity will be rewarded, and marriage will happen when the time is right, and 'Mr Right' will appear, you needn't worry.' These attitudes and instructions were the norm in the Christian circles, but 'flesh is weak', so many rules were broken. Having attended a mixed school with plenty of boys available as friends, and in addition, having a teasing older brother, I had not been particularly worried by the fact that I hadn't fixed myself up with a special boyfriend.

In the nursing college, I now met a different breed of young women, freer, openly both showing and using their sexiness. Some of the students had no intention of working as qualified nurses. Instead, these attractive, self-confident young women saw their nursing training, and their placements in teaching hospitals, as excellent opportunities for making a good catch of a young medical student. Being a doctor's wife would be far more desirable than just being a nurse. In my year of student nurses, an unusually high number met their doctor husbands on the hospital wards. Other good hunting grounds were the dances arranged by the Student Union. I did not attend the dances, as dancing was considered a sin for Christian students.

I had no experience of 'girly' tricks, I did not know how to flirt or to make a catch, nor was I interested. Comparing myself with these self-confident young women in my group, I felt inferior, still more a girl than a woman. I might have been told that I was pretty with beautiful eyes, lovely blonde hair, and had shapely legs, but who would be interested in a naïve, petite, small breasted girl?

Olli was still there in the background and there were other young men, mainly the ones I met at the Christian Student Union's meetings, but no romances at this stage nor a 'Prince Charming' among them. I would instantly recognise him; most likely he would be a theolog. I lived in a state of denial. My fantasy world compensated for the reality, and saved me from the danger of doing something forbidden. Of course, these questions troubled me. There were times when I felt sexually aroused; this might happen when I looked at my own image in the big mirror. Was it the devil, leading me to sin? The sexual excitement in my body was dangerous, and felt frightening. I was living in a cage, my head full of warnings about the dangers of passion and lust; I was very confused, wanting to break free, wanting to experiment, wanting to rebel, and face danger, but not knowing how.

As often as I had time, I attended the meetings of the Christian Students' Union, held on Sunday evenings, and found them spiritually enriching. A good place to meet Christian students from all over Finland. I had already made friends with Esko, a dark haired, green-eyed, sturdy, and shortish medic from Turku and his theolog friend Paavo, quite tall, slim, attractive, softly spoken, and with a benign, humorous look in his grey eyes. In my opinion, he was the most attractive of the many theologues around, and Paavo became my secret love. Paavo and Esko were always together; this gave me an opportunity to enjoy Paavo's company without revealing my interest. Perhaps he, on the other hand knowing Esko's interest in me, stayed loyal to his friend. Both of them moved later back to Turku to continue their studies. Paavo became a bishop, and I met him in that capacity some years later at the Finnish Church in London. We had a chance to reminiscence, laugh at our inhibitions, and Paavo admitted that his friendship with Esko prevented him from asking me out. He was impressed with my liberation, and added that, his wife, in her position, would never dare to wear make-up. I would have been a bad wife to a bishop!

The Sunday evening meetings were quite informal. We explored what it meant to be a Christian in the modern, post-war world. I soon discovered that a much more liberal attitude was creeping in, mainly coming from America. The Finnish Lutheran church had very good connections with the Lutherans there, and the church had been receiving financial donations from the American Lutheran church. Finnish students of theology were being offered scholarships to study in America. These students, returning back home, were full of fresh ideas, wanting to share them, and put them into practise. One big new idea was the introduction of Confirmation Camps.

In a Lutheran country, like Finland, confirmation classes were compulsory for young people between 14-16 years of age, and each parish held them within their premises. The culmination of these studies was the confirmation ceremony. The participants reaffirmed their Christian faith, and their part in the Christian community to which they had been baptised. Almost all young people attended these classes; the main reason for the high attendance wasn't a religious one; you had to be confirmed to be allowed to have a church wedding.

Having discussed with the church authorities the idea of running one of the first Confirmation Camps in Finland, the Christian Students' Union received the full backing from the church and was ready to organise one. The one-week long confirmation camp, in early July, would be for girls only. A student pastor and a female theolog were chosen as the leaders; in addition, there would be two 'big sisters' as assistants. The chosen site was Punkaharju, one of the world's oldest nature reserves, an area of outstanding beauty, and a famous camping area, near Savonlinna. The amazing, seven kilometres long ridge, with majestic pine trees and an undergrowth of blueberries and lingonberries, was a remnant from the ice age. This green, narrow band, cutting across the blue waters, had been created by the power of the thawing ice pressing landmasses from two sides.

Having been asked to be one of the 'big sisters', I was flattered, excited, and jumped at the opportunity. This suited my holiday plans extremely well, as I was going to spend the first part of my six weeks' holiday on the 'Paradise Island', joining Mamma, Laila, Juha and Taru. The travel from Voikoski to Punkaharju would be easy, only about three hours by train.

I looked forward to being on our island. Just the right place for me to digest in peace and tranquillity what had happened in the year, what had changed within me and where I was I now. In the birch woods, some distance from the cottage, I found a big, quite flat stone, like an altar. This became my secret, holy place. God would speak to me here in the silence of the woods. He would give me a deeper understanding to the questions bothering me. Changes were taking place in Finnish society. After the isolation and austerity of the war years, there was now a different mood of freedom. What had been instilled in me no longer seemed important or relevant. Who could I discuss these questions with? Perhaps, the discussions at the Confirmation Camp would give some answers.

I had been asked to arrive a day before the participants. At Punkaharju station I was met by Erkki, the student pastor, whom I already knew well and liked. The short journey from the station along the ridge on a country road put me straight into the mood of a unique experience. The scene was breathtakingly beautiful. Through the pine-lined road, I could see water on both sides, as if being driven along a never-ending bridge. Leading where? I was ready to let the road take me on a journey.

Two massive army tents had been erected in the forest. These were going to accommodate the girls, each tent having beds for twelve, including one for the 'big sister'. Irja, the female theology, and Erkki had proper rooms in a building next to the church. I was given time to settle in before the evening meal, and time to go for quick swim in the lake. Feeling totally free and relaxed, almost as if some chains had already been removed, I dived into the crystal-clear water, and then just let it caress me.

The camp day was structured to facilitate Christian living: morning prayers before breakfast, then Bible studies, and lunch. After lunch there was no formal programme, we could swim, play games (netball was particularly popular) or just go for walks in the forest. Walking on the ridge, between the tall pine trees, standing there firmly like rods, each making a connection between earth and heaven, and the sparkling blue waters on both sides, was a spiritual experience not to be forgotten.

To end the day, we gathered around a log fire in the forest, singing, talking, raising and answering questions. These informal gatherings were, to me, the most valuable part of the camping experience. The young girls opened up with questions about their faith, their beliefs, their doubts, their life. Being one of them, I was learning with and from them.

Music played an important part in these evening gatherings; a couple of girls had brought their recorders with them, and we all were keen to sing. The light lingered on almost to midnight. We watched the gentle sunsets, the colours in the sky changing, and the lake becoming still, reflecting the sky and the trees. The magic of those evenings made God's presence real and tangible.

I was so lucky to have had the opportunity to be part of this first Confirmation Camp experience. We had gelled as a group, and many of the young girls had made use of us 'big sisters' in wanting to have private chats about their personal problems and difficulties. It had been for us all a unique, life-changing experience, a spiritual transformation, aided by the exceptionally beautiful setting. We had had a wonderful opportunity to live, eat, learn and play together. The Christian values had been re- enforced through our study sessions; there had been an opportunity to share thoughts and worries, and seek answers to the many small and big questions troubling young teenagers.

Confirmation Camps, with boys and girls attending the same camp, are now the norm. Interestingly, their popularity has increased to such an extent that teenagers who do not belong to the church, are coming along to enjoy the experience.

I returned to Voikoski enriched by the experience, with a feeling that I was looking for something more than nursing as a career, but happy to continue with my studies to get my qualification, and then think about what was next.

January 1952- August 1952

Before describing my hospital placement in the spring term of 1952, I'll first share with you the Helsinki Olympics. I remember so well the excitement and anticipation when we heard that Helsinki would be hosting the 1952 Summer Olympics. A wonderful compensation for the cancellation of the 1940 Games, as well as the world's recognition of our bravery in fighting for our independence in the war. By the time midnight on last day of 1951 had passed, the Olympic fever had spread like measles; every Finn was 'spotty' with excitement, and the long dormant 'infection' was now allowed to spread unhindered. We were ready to show the world a recovered, modern, and proud Finland: 'Come, see, and admire what has been achieved in the seven years of peace'.

There was an urgency to be ready in time. Some facilities built for 1940 had been put to different use. During the war years the Swimming Stadium had been used to store root vegetables, and the Olympic Village, ready and waiting for competitors in 1940, had been needed and used to house the dislocated Karelians. Luckily, Helsinki already had the most beautiful Olympic Stadium, built in 1936, with its seventy-two-metre-tall white tower, and the imposing statue of Paavo Nurmi, 'the Flying Finn', the world's fastest long-distance runner, at the centre of the entrance area. In a minor way the Helsinki Nursing College became part of the Olympic scene. The modern building, with good bedrooms and facilities, was chosen to house the female athletes. Vacating the building for their use was relatively easy by simply moving our annual leave around the dates of the Olympics.

Early in the spring a photographer came to take pictures of the communal spaces, the lecture halls, the classrooms and the bedrooms. A few weeks later a pile of brochures arrived, showing us the information that was going to be sent to the participating countries. There, on the centre page, was a large photo of two nursing students sitting reading in one of the bedrooms: Seija and I in our room. Fame at last!

The already manic mood was hyped up by something totally divorced from the Olympics. During the spring months, for the first time since the war, a Maid of Finland competition had been held. Armi Kuusela, the winner, was as perfect a Maid of Finland as one could wish for: blonde hair, large blue eyes, peach-like complexion, slim, shapely figure, 167 cm tall, and only seventeen. She was going to represent Finland in the brand new Miss Universe competition to be held in California in June; the first Miss Universe to be revealed just three weeks before the opening ceremony of the Olympics.

Identifying ourselves with Armi, we, the nursing students, had fantasies of something similar happening in our lives. We had followed every tiny step of her climb from obscurity to become the most talked about young Finn. She, a modern Cinderella, came from a humble background, one of seven children, and from an unknown small village in the north of Finland. Devouring her romantic story, we wanted to know every detail about her. Who had discovered this stunningly beautiful young girl, and who had thought of putting her name forward for the Maid of Finland contest?

By the 28th June, Armi, already in California, had passed the eliminating rounds, and was one of the twelve finalists. With our cups of coffee, we gathered together into one bedroom, sitting on the beds and on the floor, glued to the radio, listening all night to the live broadcast from America. The sound was distorted, hard to hear, and the monotonous male voice almost lulling us to sleep, then suddenly, the pitch and tone of the reporter's voice changed. We, now fully awake and alert; obviously, something exciting was happening. First, all we could hear was lots of background noises. Minutes went by. We held our breath, not even daring to speak. Finally, the announcement came loud and clear in English: 'The winner of this very first Miss Universe competition is - a long pause - Miss FINLAND, Armi Kuusela.' The Finnish reporter was too excited to be able to make a proper sentence, just screamed into the radio, *'Armi voitti!'* And a second time even louder. *'Armi voitti.'* (Armi won.) We jumped for joy, hugged each other, and shouted, 'Fantastic, wonderful, incredible. Can you believe it? Armi Kuusela from FINLAND, an unknown country, is MISS UNIVERSE!'

Now people all over the world would want to find out, where is this unknown place? Are there more such stunning girls to be discovered?

Armi became instantly, and at that very moment the most famous Finn in the world, our country's Ambassador to the Universe. This fantastic publicity just days before the opening of the Helsinki Olympic Games! What a gift from God.

Armi's story continued in the same fairy-story manner as it had begun. As Miss Universe she took a world tour, and after few months of traveling she arrived in the Philippines. There, in Manilla, at a dance, her 'Prince Charming' was waiting and ready to win her heart. He succeeded. As a result, Armi choose to give up her crown less than a year after having been crowned, and married her Prince, the Filipino businessman, Virgilio Hilario. Armi left Finland for good, but did return for a visit with her new husband. She set a trend of Finnish girls going abroad, mainly to work but in their hearts, hoping for a similar romance. Widowed in 1975, Armi, aged forty, carried on living in Manila with her five children. Some years later she met an American businessman, married again, and moved to America. Her story was followed for years and years in the Finnish women's magazines.

XV Olympic Games in Helsinki, 19th July – 3rd August 1952

Wherever you walked in Helsinki there were signs of hectic improvement work and building programmes. Parks were cleaned up, benches added, flowers planted, and roads repaired. A new airport was under construction close to Helsinki. Time was short, extra workforce was needed, but from where? Well, prisons had plenty of unemployed men. These men were used as extra labour, and with their great contribution, the brand new Seutula airport was ready on time for the incoming visitors and flights. The official opening ceremony was on the eve of the Olympics. On my walks around the harbour area, I watched the rapid rising of the five-star luxury Palace Hotel, a top-grade international hotel, offering 'fine dining' services, conference facilities, and in addition, the most stunning views over the harbour, and the passage past Suomenlinna to the open sea. A new, sprawling Olympic village, not far from the old one, was waiting for the athletes. Opposite was a new outdoor swimming pool, erected as a practice pool for the competitors, but also open to all Helsinki residents; a wonderful recreational facility, which would remain there long after the Games were over.

The large Olympic Park had an eating area with a restaurant tent, serving international food, such as curries, paellas and pastas, food we Finns had never eaten or food such as frankfurters and beef burgers that we hadn't seen for a dozen years. The aromas were wafting around, teasing the taste buds; the abundance of food, and the colourful displays of foreign dishes was a treat for us, still living with food shortages and rationing. How well I recollect tasting 'the heavenly drink', Coca Cola for the first time. We mingled among the tourists in the parks or cafés, joining them in drinking Coca Cola, feeling part of the international world, and ready to experience the new opportunities and new freedom.

This freedom was not available for all. The competitors from Russia and other Communist countries were competing for the first time after the war, and their movements were under strictest control. They weren't allowed to mix with other competitors, nor walk freely in Helsinki or in the Olympic Village. They were provided with special, guarded accommodation outside Helsinki.

In Helsinki a metamorphosis was taking place. Our quiet, provincial capital was going through a transformation into a cosmopolitan, colourful and lively city. The buildings were sporting flags from different countries, little street cafés had popped up like mushrooms after rain, and streets were filled with foreign visitors, colourful, both in skin and dress, and speaking a multitude of languages. My eyes were drawn to the many dark skinned, dashing looking young men, and I was dying to find an excuse to start a conversation, but never quite dared.

Walking along our familiar streets, and suddenly coming face to face with the first black men I had seen in my life, blacker than I ever imagined, was exciting, but also somewhat bewildering. My image of black people was still from my childhood, from the stories told by missionaries, of half-naked pagans. Africa and African people had fascinated me for as long as I could remember. I had had fantasies of becoming a missionary working in Tanganyika. Seeing these tall, handsome athletes, smartly dressed in Western clothes, moving in a relaxed manner, smiling broadly, showing their splendid white teeth, and undisturbed by being stared at by the inquisitive, ignorant Finns, I felt thoroughly ashamed of my lack of knowledge and my naive thoughts.

Not far from the Olympic Stadium, linked to the city by two wooden bridges, was the leafy island of Seurasaari, with its Open-Air Museum. The Museum consisted of a collection of authentic, ancient, wooden buildings that had been transported from various parts of the country, and scattered around this island. The idea was to give a demonstration of traditional, simple lifestyles of Finnish country dwellers. These ancient crofters' cottages had been collected over many, many years, and old, unique buildings were still being discovered and brought to the museum.

During the Olympics Seurasaari was used as one of the camp sites for tourists; an ideal site to pitch a tent in the woodlands amongst these wooden buildings, and at the sea shore with a long sandy beach, the only one in Helsinki where swimming in the nude was permitted.

One evening Seija and I decided to head towards Seurasaari, keen to see what the tourists were up to. We were pleased that our foreign guests had been given such a delightful place to camp in, and that there they would get an authentic feel for the Finnish summer life. Usually, as soon as one crossed one of the wooden bridges, one would enter into a separate, quiet world, expecting to see people strolling in silence along the waterside, brown squirrels jumping from tree to tree, and guides in national costumes inviting visitors to come inside the Museum dwellings.

Now, as soon as we crossed the bridge, we were greeted by loud music, lots of noise, laughter, and the babble of many foreign tongues. I recognised some Italian, French, and Spanish words. We could smell the grilling of sausages, and see people milling around on the beach, some dancing around the campfires, swigging from bottles of beer in their hands, and some swimming, even naked in the sea.

By the look of it, they were having such enviable fun. We moved closer, hoping for an invitation to join one or another of the gatherings. Almost as soon as we had voiced our wish, we spotted a shirtless, brown skinned young man walking towards us gesticulating with his arms, clearly giving signs for us to come and join in their fun. He introduced himself. 'I am Ricardo, I come from Italy.' Speaking in broken English, he added, 'We are so happy to meet Finnish girls, please, please, come and join our group.' Seija and I were ready to let our reservations go, ready to have some fun, and happy to follow Ricardo towards the group of Italians. We felt warmly welcomed. We tried to tell them something about us, and find out more about them. Our attempts to communicate were hampered by limited language skills on both sides, but using hand gestures we did quite well. We sat round the campfire drinking Italian beer, grilling Finnish *'saunamakkara'* (special grilling sausage for campfires), and joining in laughing at their jokes, without understanding the words. We heard German being spoken, and saw a group of German youngsters going for a swim, shouting, *'Wunderbar, das Wasser ist sehr warm,'* amazed at how warm the water was.

The sun was going down, but there was no sign of the campers going to sleep, the beach was still full of life: singing, dancing, and laughing. The foreigners had never experienced 'white nights.' We heard utterances of astonishment: 'Incredible, wonderful.' 'Look at how light the sky is, and it's already eleven o'clock.'

By the time Seija and I left, the sky was getting lighter, a new day was dawning. Ricardo and his friend Carlos decided to walk us across the bridge. We had enjoyed our evening enormously, and said our heartfelt thanks, knowing that we were unlikely to meet again. There was no sign of Helsinki sleeping; the city was celebrating, and we were so happy to be part of it, and, with foreigners' eyes taking in the miracle of 'white nights.'

The Games and the various sporting events were in full swing. I had not been able to obtain tickets to any of the main track events, but Raikku managed to get me passes to watch some of the eliminating heats at the Stadium. Seeing these fantastic athletes competing for a place in the next heat was a totally mind-blowing sight; nearly as good as seeing the finals.

For years I had been Raikku's faithful fan. I had sat through endless competitions in all kinds of weather. Tense, excited, and always hoping to see him win. More often than not he did. The most exciting were the annual athletics matches between Finland and Sweden. The points between the two countries were on several occasions so even that the last event, the final 4 x 400 metres relay, decided the winning country. Imagine the highly charged atmosphere in the Stadium; everyone on edge, praying and hoping that Finland would pull through as the winner. There is my brother Raikku running, either the first or the last leg, and the whole audience standing up and shouting, 'Raikku, *Kiri, kiri.'* ('Raikku, spurt, spurt.') I was so proud of my brother.

Naturally, the highlight of Raikku's sporting career was representing Finland in the Olympic Games. Anna-Liisa was the only member of our family who was at the Stadium seeing him run. The rest of us had to be satisfied with watching him on film. We, who could not be physically present, were able to see film releases almost immediately. Of course, we followed the radio broadcast word by word.

I can remember very well one detail from the opening ceremony, perhaps more dramatic on film than for those present. Just as the last athletes had entered the Stadium, we saw a woman in a long, white dress, holding one hand up as a greeting, and gathering the hem with her other, as she ran full speed towards the podium and managed to climb onto it, ready to address the crowd. As she opened her mouth to speak, she, 'the Angel of Peace', with her message of unity and love, was removed. Order was restored, the rain stopped, and the sun came out. The Games could begin.

I will now add extracts from Rainer's own account of the Helsinki Olympics, written in spring 2012. Then, on the eve of the London Games, the Finnish Ambassador had invited a couple of still living Finnish sportsmen from the 1952 Olympics to a reception in London to recall their memories from the Helsinki Games. I quote from Rainer's text:

'For an athlete, to participate in the Olympics has always been the highest and most esteemed goal. All nations have the right to participate in the Games. The representatives of each country are selected through strict qualification trials. In Finland these took place at the end of June. You had only this one chance to be included in the Finnish team. I competed in two events: 400 metres hurdles (came first) and 800 metres (came second), and I was chosen for both events.

On the opening day the sky was cloudy and grey. It started to rain hard, but in spite of the rain the spirit was high. Every seat was sold out. The colourful uniforms and dresses of various nations made an unforgettable impression, even in the rain.

First, as always, the Greek athletes marched in, and last the host country's group. All were greeted with thunderous applause. This moment was one of the highlights of my life.

The president of the Republic of Finland, Juho Kusti Paasikivi, opened the Games, then the Mayor of Helsinki bid the guests welcome, and 6000 white doves were released.

It was announced that the Olympic Torch was on its way to the Stadium. The bearer of the torch had been kept secret. Finally, the runner carrying the torch appeared. It was 'the Flying Finn', the greatest long-distance runner in the world, Paavo Nurmi, then 55 years old. He lit the Olympic Cauldron. The flame was then taken by four athletes to the top of the 72 m high tower. There, the first of the Finnish world-famous long-distance runners, Hannes Kolehmainen, was waiting to light the flame for the duration of the games. Hannes Kolehmainen had run Finland onto the map of the world at Stockholm Olympic Games in 1912 with his three gold medals.

Next day the Games started in earnest. There was no doubt about who the greatest runner was. It was the Czech, Emil Zatopek. He did not only win, as expected, the 10,000 metres and 5,000 metres races, but also his first Marathon, establishing himself as an Olympic legend.

There was a surprising incident in the 5000 metres run involving the redhaired, British runner Christopher Chataway. He was in the lead on the final stretch, and was known to have a good spurt. Zatopek was running tightly on his heels, followed by France's whirlwind Alain Minmoun, and Germany's Herbert Schade. All of them ready for the final stretch, and had calculated their individual spurt. Then, only about 100 metres from the goal, the hope of England, perhaps the fastest runner of them all, fell to the ground. Why? Was he pushed? As a true English gentleman Chataway denied the pushing after the run, but left the world of sports a mystery to be pondered over. Could he have beaten Zatopek, the Czech human locomotive, if he hadn't fallen?

In the Helsinki Olympics I chose to run the 400 metres hurdles, even though a year before I had competed in 800 metres with the world-famous British miler Roger Bannister, and lost with a very narrow margin. Bannister was the first man to run the so-called dream mile in under four minutes. You can imagine how very excited I was as I stepped on the start line in front of a fully booked stadium to compete in the 400 metres hurdles among the world's best champions.

In the first heat I was competing with Lituev from Russia, Bart from France, Yoma from Chile, and Ferrer from Venezuela. I had a good run, and came second. After one hour's rest, the next heat was against new champions. But even though I ran my personal record, and the best time in Finland that summer, I was left fifth, after Russia, USA, Sweden and Scott of England. Still, I was happy having run my own best time in front of 70,000 spectators.

The number of medals for the Finnish team was a disappointment. One gold medal, really warming our hearts was the Gold for the way the Games had been arranged.

This medal was jointly given by all countries for the excellent organization, the fine sports arenas, the general ambiance, and the genuine hospitality, experienced by everyone, coming from the host country's heart.'

Finland, the land of thousands of lakes, did get four gold medals, all in canoeing, perhaps no surprise; one by a female competitor Sylvi Saino. She won the 500 metres single canoeing race. The Games had given a fantastic boost to Finland; the international window, which had been shut by the war years, had opened up in a big way. Finland was firmly on the world map as a modern, democratic, and high-achieving nation.

New experiences and challenges were waiting outside Finland, especially for the young. I knew that, once qualified in a year's time, I would be looking for opportunities to work abroad.

Lastenlinna (Children's Palace)

In the new year my first placement was to Lastenlinna (the Children's Palace), a placement I had been waiting for, and one of the happiest times in my training. The whole building was brimming with hope and light. Every detail had been planned with children in mind. The rooms were light, the furniture bright, specially designed for small people, pictures on the walls, and toys scattered around. I would be working with children who were not physically ill, but had educational and social problems.

The story of the origins of Lastenlinna goes back to 1918, to the aftermath of the Civil War, and to the two exceptional siblings, Marshall Carl Gustav Mannerheim and his sister Baroness Sofia Mannerheim, founder of professional nursing training in Finland. The War left many homeless mothers and children, and these helpless war victims were the deep concern of both the Mannerheims. Using their status, hearts, and combined knowledge, they founded 'The Mannerheims's League for Child Welfare', stating the following aims of the League to the public:

- To promote the wellbeing of children and families
- To increase respect for childhood
- To act as an attorney, making sure that children's views are taken into account in public decision making.

In inviting all citizens to join in the league's work, Marshall Mannerheim declared, 'Every child is entitled to a good and happy childhood.'

Funds started pouring in. Baroness Mannerheim used the funds and her own wealth to purchase a building in Helsinki to provide a home for the destitute mothers and children where they would feel safe, hence the name Lastenlinna. (Linna has two meanings in Finnish: castle and palace.) Dr Arvo Ylppö, Finland's internationally most famous paediatrician, was appointed the Chief Physician of Lastenlinna in 1920. He stayed in that position until his retirement in 1963.

Already by 1925, the premises were inadequant. In order to build a new, better equipped Lastenlinna a nationwide fundraising campaign was launched with a concert, with Marshall Mannerheim and Sibelius present, and a first performance of his composition 'Moroceau Romantics'. The manuscript was then auctioned at a Gala Dinner, arranged by the League. The Mannerheim League is still the largest child welfare organisation in Finland, with local associations throughout the country. Funds increased daily, and a plot for building was obtained. Building work began in the late 1930s, but was interrupted by the war years, until 1945.

The inauguration of the twelve-storey Lastenlinna, the highest building in Helsinki then, was in 1948. The building incorporated a special unit for premature babies, wards for children with neurological needs, and wards for children whose educational and social needs were assessed. The staff looked content, and felt privileged to work in this modern hospital. Professor Ylppö, in his white, too big coat was to be seen daily, wandering around, stopping to talk to his little patients, and joking with the members of the staff, including us, in his jolly exchanges.

His special interest was taking care of the premature babies, and also other infants too weak to be allowed home, and needing to stay in the special care unit. Mothers with breast milk to spare were invited to the hospital to donate their milk. One of these mothers was Ylppö's wife, Lea, a paediatrician. She had recently given birth to their second baby. I saw her coming to Lastenlinna daily to donate breast milk, and then walk around the wards with Professor Ylppö.

Being with the children was a delight, I feltrelaxed and confident. One little girl Maiju, aged 6, suffering from Downs syndrome, instantly attached herself to me. She followed me wherever I went. Maiju was a happy little girl, with the typical look of a Downs syndrome child - then called mongoloid. She had almond-shaped, upward slanting, pale blue eyes, a small, flat nose, her tongue was often sticking out in her round face, and her, almost white, blonde hair standing up. Every day, as soon as I arrived on the ward, there she was broadly smiling, taking hold of my hand with her tiny hand and chubby fingers, leading me to the play area.

Maiju came from a large farming family. Being a mongoloid child, she had simply been ignored as simple minded and stupid. She was not able to speak, she knew just a few words; her communication was done with sounds and gestures. Maiju had been admitted for a period of tests and assessments to find out what her potential was. Could she be taught to speak properly with individual attention? What was her intelligence level? In a year's time Maiju would be seven (the age at which obligatory education commences in Finland). Her educational needs had to be worked out, and a decision made whether she would need a special school or could she cope in a local elementary school, helped by an individually planned programme, just for her?

Professor Ylppö took a personal interest in each child. Seeing Maiju's attachment to me, he suggested that I would be her special nurse during my placement. My task would be to spend as much time as possible with Maiju, get to know her well, play with her, observe her, and use every opportunity to teach her words and skills. I was asked to write down my observations, and give a report each day to the ward doctor.

Maiju was ready to learn; we established a good relationship in no time. It was easy to teach her new words by pointing to objects around her. She clapped her little hands every time when she got the words right. I made short sentences from the words she had learned, and was amazed how quickly she progressed. Maiju was happy to join the other children in their activities; they sang and danced together. I noticed that she could sing in tune, and had a good sense of rhythm. She became easily excited, bursting out in loud laughs, and was pleased when she was praised for any little achievement.

My assessment was that she would be able to cope for the first couple of years, in her own village school, and living at home. Work needed to be done with her parents to help them see her as she was, and how much she would be able to learn, with their help. Maiju craved approval and love. I had a chance to meet her parents, a pleasant country couple, with a big family and a farm to run. It was easy to understand why Maiju, a happy, compliant child, had been ignored. They were utterly amazed to see the difference in their child, and hear her greeting them, *'Mulla on ollut ikävä'* (I have missed you). She then wanted to know how Pyry, the farm dog, was.

Far too soon the day arrived when I would be leaving. The assessment had not been completed, and I never found out what the outcome was. It was time to say goodbye to Maiju.

She, with tears in her eyes, clinging to me, said, 'Can I come with you?'

What could I say? I gave give her a hug, and said, 'You are a very special little girl, I will miss you.' Adding, 'You'll be going home soon, and see your Mum and Dad, your brothers and sisters. Pyry will be there waiting for you.'

The day I left, Maiju stood in the window, waving. Waving back, I tried to smile even though tears filled my eyes; I had become very fond of Maiju. With her happy disposition, she left me convinced of how much can be done with Downs syndrome children, once the out-of-date prejudices had been overcome.

'Every child is entitled to a good and happy childhood.' This was the message going back thirty years when Marshall Carl Gustav Mannerheim and his sister Baroness Sofia Mannerheim launched 'The Mannerheim League for Child Welfare'. Thanks to the original trio of Marshall Mannerheim, Baroness Sofia Mannerheim, and Professor Arvo Ylppö, with his passion and devotion, the service offered to every child in Finland was and is the envy of the world.

Lastenklinikka, the Children's Hospital

From Lastenlinna I moved on to the Children's Hospital, the second new hospital built after the war, on the opposite side of the road. The three-storey building, beautifully designed, and with its curved façade, represented the finest of modern Finnish architecture, and offered the best facilities for caring for the young ill patients. Lastenklinikka was one of the Helsinki University teaching hospitals, and had a different function to Lastenlinna, but in many ways these two hospitals were like twins, sharing the same Chief Physician in Arvo Ylppö, and both driven by the same passion of setting children's welfare, and their care as top priority.

My main memories are the pleasure of working in the light, modern, well-equipped hospital, and in an atmosphere where every single person was part of the team, and responsible for providing the best possible care to these sick children. Professor Ylppö had the exceptional ability to build good personal relationships with a wide variety of people, and in all their various positions across the hospital hierarchy. He enhanced the team spirit by arranging sporting activities and summer trips to the staff.

Looking after seriously ill little children was a new challenge. I could see that a child was in pain, but felt helpless to offer real relief from their distress. I suffered, with the child, and found it difficult to be detached. During the day life on the ward was busy. There were qualified nurses around, and it seemed as if the little patients sensed this.

On night duty I felt out of my depth. I was alone on the ward, being in charge of these seriously ill small infants and children was frightening. Often, a child was crying, unable to communicate what was wrong. How was I supposed to guess where the pain was or what the remedy would be? I picked the child up, tried to console him or her, and ask, 'Show me where it hurts?' Frequently, the crying stopped for a while, only to start again louder, and with more persistence as soon as I put the child back into his or her cot. I was desperately looking for some support and advice from a nurse, but was not certain when the right moment to call the nurse in charge of several wards was. Coming to the end of my second year as a student, I was expected to know what to do, and was afraid of being told, 'You should have been able to deal with this on your own at this stage in your training.' It had been instilled in me since I was a small child that 'Arna can manage'. This time it was not about managing myself, there were helpless little creatures, dependent on my decisions. In the stillness of the night, I felt something within me had changed. The 'managing Arna' had been broken down, her false confidence and self-assurance had gone. Still fresh in my memory was the serious mistake I had made in removing the empty saline bottle without clamping the tube. Would the children pick up that I was feeling anxious and scared and alone on the ward?

I felt a deep sigh of relief when the week on nights was over. Though, now in retrospect, I see I made no mistakes and nothing went wrong. The night nurse was gentle and kind; she was able to calm a child. With the same friendly kindness, she responded to me, encouraging me to call her any time during the night.

Most nights the majority of the children were sound asleep. Once the ward was quiet, I brewed myself a cup of coffee, opened the balcony doors, watched the rising sun, and was greeted with the wonderful sound of the dawn chorus of birds, sounding more like angels from heaven coming to wish me joy.

Before the summer break I spent eight weeks in Lapinlahti Psychiatric Hospital, but before describing that experience, I'll end this chapter with my last visit to Paradise Island.

Last visit to Paradise Island

Helsinki basked in the sun, with the vitality of foreign visitors filling its streets. The final ceremony of the Olympic Games was scheduled to take place on the 3rd of August. With a week left of my holiday, at the end of July I took the train to Voikoski to be with Mamma, Laila, Juha, and Taru on the Paradise Island.

To my pleasant surprise Juha, having shot up some five centimetres in the summer weeks, looking tanned and fit, meet me at Voikoski station. Our few kilometres walk gave me an excellent opportunity to hear the family news. We popped into the village shop to pick up some items for Mamma, and I bought, as presents, a couple of chocolate bars and a bag of Fazer's liquorice, Mamma's favourites.

Leisurely walking along the forest road, Juha told me, 'Isä is coming soon after you have left to discuss the sale of the cottage with Toivola.'

'How do you feel about the sale?' I asked.

'To be honest this summer has been a bit disappointing as far as weather is concerned, too many rainy and windy days. I am more than ready to give up our Robinson Crusoe life and return to Helsinki. Luckily, the two Saari boys have been here, and we've had lots of fun together, fishing and playing ball and card games, Laila always joining us in the card games. I think she has felt quite lonely without you. Of course, it's sad to leave our magic island, but I'll be pleased to be on the mainland. I have had enough of the daily rowing to pick up milk. I can't understand why Isä hasn't bought a small motor, it would be easy to fit into the rowing boat.'

We walked in silence for a while, each in our own thoughts. I took in a few deep breaths, smelling the freshness of the air and the fragrance of the forest.

Juha continued. 'Right now, it's been fun. The boys and I have been helping Mr Saari with his sauna building. Stupid idea, if you ask me, to build a sauna into the forest, far from the lake.'

I asked, 'What about Mamma?'

Juha replied, 'Now, that *mustikkas* (bilberries) are ripe, Mamma disappears into the forest for hours and hours. You know how she loves berry-picking. She brings back enough mustikkas every day for us to enjoy with sugar and milk, and we save berries for our breakfast to have with '*viili*' (home-made yogurt). Laila gets really worried if Mamma is too long in the forest, and goes off searching for her with Taru. Did you know that Taru loves mustikkas, and, by the way, eats them from the bushes?'

Juha didn't seem interested in my life, so I carried on asking him to tell me more about this summer on the island. 'The weather has been lousy: rainy, windy and quite chilly, but most evenings the sky has cleared, promising, in vain, a better day, and making Mamma rush down to the pier, shouting, "Come and look at the glorious lighting." Yes, we have had brilliant evening skies and sunsets. Mamma has been busy painting, and cooking has been forgotten. Laila and I are learning to make something to eat, otherwise we would starve. As you know, Mamma could survive with puddings, and now with bilberries.'

Juha added, 'Laila's friend Helena came and stayed with us for a week. She is a fantastic cook; we ate well that week. She and Laila, with Taru following, spent time exploring the island, and rowing to the small islands. Helena joined Laila and me in laying nets. During the weeks we have been catching enough for our needs.'

I asked, 'What about the Olympic Games? Have you been able to follow the Games?'

'We have been welcomed at the Toivolas to listen to the radio broadcasts as often as we have wanted. Laila and I use the milk picking trips to sit with them and were able to follow Zatopek's fantastic runs. Mamma came with us when Raikku was running. Wasn't it great? You can guess how we cheered. The Marathon is this Sunday, I'll go and listen to the broadcast. Would you like to come?'

'Yes, of course, I'll still be here.'

It was late afternoon by the time we reached the lake shore. Juha pushed the boat out and took hold of the oars. With his strong strokes the boat was gliding effortlessly, almost soundlessly, leaving behind a rippled groove on the lake's mirror-calm surface. Enjoying the luxury of being rowed, I was very conscious that this was my farewell visit to Paradise Island. I wanted to relive and imprint into my mind memories of the past summers, be back as the innocent young girl, just stepping into adulthood, and use the stillness to gather my thoughts. In March I had had my twenty-first birthday and was now legally responsible for myself; there was still a year ahead before I'd start earning and become financially independent.

Mamma and Laila were pleased to see me, waiting to hear my news from Helsinki. Laila had made a pasta bake for our dinner, with Mamma's mustikka to follow. There we sat for our meal on the wall, the stones nicely warmed by the sun. How lovely it was to sit with my family on this warm summer evening, listen to the nature's sounds. The sun slowly going down, colours changing, fish jumping; each splash leaving increasing circles on the water's surface. I had not seen my family since early June, and not very often during the spring term. I realised how much I had missed them. I was overwhelmed by a feeling of belonging, and felt like a small child, wrapped in a soft, protecting blanket.

We celebrated Helena Day together, on 31st July, before my return to Helsinki.

A feeling of sadness took over; our primitive 'Robinson Crusoe' summer life was nearing its end, for me in a few days, and for the rest of the family in a couple of weeks.

The final chance to visit Paradise Island had given me time to say goodbye to something precious, I had had time to focus on my future plans. Next summer, the new, purpose-built summerhouse would be waiting in Vuokatti.

Lapinlahti - the Oldest Psychiatric Hospital in Finland

During my weeks working with the children, and especially during my placement at Lastenlinna, I had gained new insight into the causes of children's pain and distress. I had seen how important the family and the social environment were in understanding a child's behavioural difficulties. Before the summer break I had spent eight weeks in the Lapinlahti Psychiatric Hospital. In anticipation of the weeks there, I had mixed feelings, both of curiosity and of trepidation. So many tales, based on superstitions and fears, were circulating about 'mad' people'. Lunatics needed to be locked away, they were dangerous. The common belief was that 'going mad' was God's punishment for having lived in sin, or that the mentally ill person was possessed by the Devil. In our psychology lectures we had gained some idea of Freud's theories, and I knew that these traditional explanations of mental illness no longer made sense.

'The key to nursing is psychology,' Miss Durchman had pronounced early on in our training. I had no idea what she meant; I'd simply been puzzled. Perhaps now I'd get an answer? I was hoping to gain new insights during the weeks in Lapinlahti. My only personal experience of mental illness had been witnessing Mamma's sister Eva being forcibly removed from our home to a private psychiatric unit. Following her serious illness, a long hospitalisation, and having been given morphine as pain relief, Aunt Eva had become a morphine addict. I understood that things had escalated out of control in no time, making her unfit to take care of her family. Drastic action was required. According to her physician, weaning Aunt Eva from her drug dependency needed in-patient treatment in a psychiatric hospital. Kuopio, where she and her family lived, was a small town, and they were well known, so her husband Kaarlo and Mummi decided together that admission to a private psychiatric hospital near Helsinki would preserve Eva's anonymity. Eva had agreed to the plan. Mummi travelled to Kuopio and brought Aunt Eva to our home. I can well remember how restless she was, walking back and forth in the flat.

The following day two male nurses arrived. Aunt Eva became hysterical, she was screaming, and using all the force she could manage in resisting being manhandled. The two nurses gripping her with force, ushered her into the waiting ambulance. I remembered how shocked I was, and how I hated seeing the cruelty with which my aunt was treated.

The previous summer, at the age of sixteen, I had stayed some weeks with the Dahlströms in their hug dacha, and had a great time with my cousins. I hadn't noticed much difference in Aunt Eva. She had always seemed totally self-centred, hyper-sensitive, and taking offence easily. Mamma, telling stories of her childhood, had described her sister as 'hysterical', over-reacting to the smallest things. I had seen Aunt Eva's reactions to Kaarlo's jokes and humour; she simply could not cope with his sense of humour. During my stay, my cousins had not told me anything of their mother's addiction. Later, once I knew the truth, my cousin Piittu told me of the hell they had been living in for a long time. Their mother Eva had forced the two sisters, she and Kaarina, to give her morphine injections several times a day. Aunt Eva's four children were scarred for life. She was weaned from her addiction but remained 'hysterical' and over-sensitive. I think, somewhere in my unconscious mind, I knew, already then, that becoming an abuser of morphine, like Aunt Eva or of alcohol like Aunt Verna, must reflect their personal unhappiness, and the drug was an attempt to drown it away.

****

Located on a peninsula between the old Hietaniemi cemetery and the sea, Lapinlahti Psychiatric hospital was surrounded by a vast land area. Some was left as parkland, some was cultivated, growing both grains and vegetables, and the area closest to the main building had been designed as an extensive garden, open for the general public to stroll in.

I loved my daily walk from the tram stop to the hospital. Leaving the residential area behind, I passed some old gravestones, noticing some famous names, all having had an important role in working towards Finland's independence, and identity. There they were, one after another: architect Carl Ludvig Engel, artists Gallen-Kallela, Albert Edelfelt, and Helene Schjerfbeck, and their contemporary politician and philosopher J.V. Snellman, one of the great Finnish men who had a towering importance to the Finnish identity, and to Finland's own currency, the mark. I also discovered the grave of Sophia Mannerheim, important to us nurses.

Looking left, behind a row of trees, there were the blue waters of the Bay of Finland and the expansive beach, the largest public beach for Helsinki residents to use.

By the time I reached the parkland, my pace slowed. I was entering an area of calm and quiet, a sanctuary. I could smell the resin of the pine and spruce trees, feel the wind from the sea, and watch squirrels chasing each other in joyous play. Plenty of birds were flying around, but no longer so much birdsong; they had built their nests, were busy feeding the young ones, and teaching them to fly. Ahead of them, quite soon, was the long flight to warmer places.

The final joy was the pleasure of seeing the rich variety of colourful plants and taking in the sweet fragrance hovering above the gardens around the main building. The kind head gardener, a nature loving man, took the mentally ill patients under his wing; over the years the healing power of nature had been proven. He noticed the changes in the patients, he saw them calming down, becoming more at peace with themselves. Working closely with the psychiatrists and ward sisters, he reported his observations back to the medical staff. Patients loved working in the gardens, enjoying the beauty of the flowers, and spending time in the open air.

Lapinlahti was one of the Helsinki University teaching hospitals, taking patients for short-term treatment from all over Finland. Behind the imposing gate was the two-storey, elegant, classical building. You could never have guessed that it was a psychiatric hospital. The same architect, Carl Ludvig Engel, who had been responsible for designing the neo classical buildings around Senate Square, and other important buildings, had designed Lapinlahti. Built in 1841, it was not only the oldest mental hospital in Finland but one of the oldest in Europe.

It had three male and three female wards; in addition, a children's ward. The two neurological wards and the children's ward were on the first floor. On the ground floor there were two locked wards for psychotic patients, and two open ones for depressed and neurotic patients. The student nurses were placed only on the ground floor wards. My placement was on the open female ward with patients suffering from depression, hysteria and various neurotic symptoms, but there were no psychotic patients on that ward.

Since the 1920s, when Sigmund Freud and Carl Gustav Jung began their pioneering work in understanding mental illness, there had been revolutionary developments in psychiatric treatments. Freud, the founder of psychoanalysis, had introduced the concept of an unconscious mind. He developed psychoanalysis, 'the talking cure' as a tool for investigating the unconscious mind. As a result, an entirely new approach to mental illnesses and treatments was gaining hold in the Western world. Before, madness had been an incurable illness, and those mentally ill doomed to be locked away into institutions. This no longer applied; thinking and treatments were changing rapidly.

The war years had left Finland behind in these new developments in psychiatry. There were no qualified psychoanalysts, nor was there any training available in psychotherapy. There were important developments in drugs to treat mental illness. Recently Largactil had become available for treating schizophrenia, reducing the need to keep patients on locked wards.

Outside Finland, mainly in the USA or in Switzerland, psychoanalysis had gained a foothold. These countries offered training opportunities in psychoanalysis to young Finnish physicians. A very important part of their training was their own personal analysis; this increased both the length and the cost of their training. Having experienced the benefits from the deeper understanding of their own psyche, the young psychiatrists were ready and excited to take on the task of revolutionizing the outdated mental health system in Finland.

The Head Psychiatrist of this Helsinki University teaching was Martti Kaila, an open-minded scientist, personally interested in seeing psychoanalytic theories being put into practise. He offered these young, returning physicians opportunities to put their new learning into practise. Lapinlahti became the first Finnish mental hospital experimenting with new drugs, and offering psychotherapy as a treatment to a selected number of neurotic patients.

Many physicians and psychiatrists refused to believe in these psychological explanations and treatments. For them there was not enough scientific proof available, nor were they able to give up their belief that organic causes would be found sooner or later for schizophrenia, and other mental disorders. There was a great resistance towards everything that psychoanalysis stood for; psychiatrist and psychoanalysts were in two different camps for years. Ongoing, quite recent, research has gradually drawn both sides of the debate closer to each other. They now work together, learning from each other.

Thanks to Liisa Ollikainen, the recently appointed Sister Tutor of psychiatric nursing, we were lucky to be part of the revolution in psychiatric care. Smitten by these new ideas, she was bursting with excitement and energy. Only a few years older than her students, clever, pretty and totally different from the other 'old maid' tutors, she was inspirational and very approachable. Unheard of in the hierarchy of nursing, we were allowed to call her by her first name Liisa. She was responsible for our theoretical training, both in engaging psychiatrists, neurologists, and psychoanalysts for the formal lectures, and giving seminars herself. The lecture series offered us the latest insights into the causes of mental disturbances as well as the more traditional views.

On the wards, the sisters had had longstanding domain as the practical teachers, now Liisa supervised our practical training. In spite of having the gift of the gab, she knew when to keep her mouth shut, and managed to avoid being a threat to the sisters. Smiling beautifully, praising, and flattering, she avoided conflicts and disagreements; but she talked and talked. Who could resist her? Soon she became accepted, even welcomed in her teaching role. With her personal enthusiasm, Liisa was both inflaming and feeding my interest in mental health. She and I gelled immediately; a life-long bond was born between us. No wonder, I discovered that she was an Aries, and only six years older, sharing even the date of our birthday, 31st March.

So, the 1950s was a time of radical rethinking of mental illness, its causes, and its treatments. Patients were no longer simply lumbered together under one label 'mad'. Careful physical investigations were made to eliminate possible organic causes for mental difficulties. If no organic cause was found for their insanity, then a psychological assessment and appropriate treatment would follow.

In the 1920s an accidental discovery was made: People suffering from epilepsy felt mentally less depressed after they had had a seizure. This led to producing seizures artificially, initially a chemical Metrazol was used to treat symptoms of depression, anxiety, and hallucinations. The after effect was a feeling of terror.

In the 1930 an Italian neuropsychiatrist discovered that seizures could be produced by giving electric shocks. This replaced the use of Metrazol and led to the wide use of Electroconvulsive Therapy (ECT) as a treatment for depression. Seeing ECT administered for the first time was frightening, ugly, and, in my opinion, barbarous. I had witnessed my school friend's sister having an epileptic fit. I could recall how utterly shocked I was to see her sudden fall to the ground, followed by her uncontrollable convulsions, the frothing of the mouth, and animal-like sounds. This memory was now uppermost in my mind. I did not want to be an observer of ECT treatment, but had no choice.

The patient was ushered into the treatment room. She was physically held down on a wooden bench. I could see the fear in her eyes, no-one spoke to her or calmed her down. No pre-medication was given. A device with electric wires was placed on her temporal bone, this led an electric current to the frontal lobes of her brain, causing her to have an epileptic fit. The powerful convulsions were so strong that they risked serious fractures of the back. Patients hated and feared the ECT treatment. As an observer, so did I.

This treatment suited depressed patients, often suffering from irrational guilt feelings for sins they believed they had committed. They saw it as justified punishment for their badness. ECT is still used for treating depression, as well as patients suffering from bipolar mental illness. Now he or she is sedated before the procedure, the convulsions hardly noticeable, and causing no fractures.

The ward doctor Yrjö Alanen, tall, slim, dark haired, serious looking, in his late twenties, was one of the young doctors who had gone to the USA, both to receive training in psychotherapy and to undergo his own personal analysis. Now he was working in Lapinlahti to complete his specialisation in psychiatry, and keen to offer psychotherapy to suitable patients on his ward. Full of his new insights, eager and enthusiastic, he wanted to teach us the basic ideas of psychoanalysis, and the new thoughts on mental illnesses. He explained Freud's and Jung's studies into the unconscious mind:

Painful experiences from our childhood are stored in the unconscious mind, and apparently forgotten. These forgotten memories then manifest themselves as symptoms of anxiety, neurosis, depression or physical ill health, and even as a total mental breakdown. He went on, 'The aim of psychoanalysis is to bring these childhood memories back into the consciousness. The patient talks, telling his or her story, the analyst listens, trying to discover at what point in the child's development there was a conflict between the child's needs, and what the environment provided.' He then explained that the earlier that point happens, the more adjustments the child needs to make. In order to get access to the unconscious, both Freud and Jung saw dreams as an important tool, as well as slips of the tongue, gestures, and 'active forgetting'. All these happened without our conscious control and can be interpreted by the analyst to reveal an unconscious message.

In the USA, Dr Alanen had seen the beginnings of Family Therapy, and had become interested in the study of interactions between family members. As a research project for his specialization in psychiatry, he had undertaken pioneering work in studying the mother/ child relationship of schizophrenic patients. He had been given permission to offer individual psychotherapy to a few selected patients and explore the use of Family Therapy.

I remember how excited I was when Dr Alanen told me, 'I have arranged an interview with the members of Mrs Kivinen's family. I would like you to join me and make careful observations of how the family members interact with each other. I have told them that a student will be present.'

Mrs Kivinen, a forty-year-old, short, thin woman with a pale complexion and mousy, tightly permed hair, had been admitted for severe depression, and an attempted suicide.

She had already had several ECT treatments, was no longer suicidal, but still looked depressed and downtrodden. Dr Alanen had decided to explore her home situation before she was discharged.

Her family consisted of Mr Kivinen, the husband, a carpenter in his early fifties, sturdy, quite tall, fair haired, and their son Lasse, twelve years old, still quite small, but facially a mirror image of his father.

Before Dr Alanen had a chance to introduce us, Mr Kivinen, turning to his wife said with an angry voice, 'You are the mad one. What are Lasse and I doing here?'

I can't remember much of the interview, but I do remember the surprised and embarrassed expression on Mr Kivinen's face, when Dr Alanen, turning to his wife, said, 'Have you noticed that every time you speak, your husband turns to Lasse with sneering, mocking smile, and neither of them listen to you?'

Mrs Kivinen looked up, encouraged by Dr Alanen's words, she said, 'Ever since Lasse moved to the Grammar School, my husband has spent all his time with him. He himself never had a chance to have a good education. Lasse used to be so good, now he ignores anything I say. He is rude, and calls me mad.'

Dr Alanen asked the three of them to stand up, turning to the father, and said, 'Your wife is still quite a bit taller and stronger than Lasse, so why do you think she is unable to control him?'

The three of them looked puzzled.

Dr Alanen then asked, 'On whose shoulders do you think Lasse is standing? There is no way Lasse on his own would be strong enough to ignore his mother's requests.'

Observations made in the interview were shared, and insights offered to help the parents to think of new ways of working together for the best interest of their child. Simply by observing family communications, a window was opening to a new approach to helping the 'problem' member in the family, be it a child or an adult. What I understood then was that, in the Kivinen family, father and son had joined together, like two adolescents, to undermine Mrs Kivinen, already an insecure person and lacking self-esteem. Her frustration and anger were then expressed in shouting and crying; this in turn was labelled madness.

Being allowed to sit in on these sessions was intriguing, opening my eyes to an entirely new way of thinking. I certainly wanted to learn more and was beginning to see clearly which way my specialisation needed to go, but I was not sure if that option even existed. At the end of my placement, I discussed with my tutor, Liisa, the possibility of specialisation in psychiatric nursing. Nothing was decided, but Miss Durchman had shown great interest in developing this new specialisation.

Autumn term 1952

Olympics over, life returned to normal, but with a difference: Helsinki and its people had had a taste of being part of an international world, and Finland had gained a new status amongst the nations. The Olympics had given the modern, post-war Finland a much-needed boost of confidence, and the country had received general laudations for the excellence in the way the games had been organised.

What a pleasure it was to return to this spick and span college, and have clean, freshly decorated rooms for our final year of training, thanks to the College having been used to accommodate the female competitors. The noise, laughter and excitement echoed along the corridor, as we gathered in the kitchen with our cups of coffee to share holiday news. Once news had been exchanged, our thoughts turned to wondering about our last two placements before the final six months of specialisation. We had gaps to be filled. I, for example, hadn't worked in an operating theatre, nor experienced the busyness in an outpatients' clinic. In addition, there was one bit of training that had been left for all of us to complete that term. As pairs, we were going to be sent to various districts, working under the area Health Visitors. The details of the plans made we would hear the following day. Miss Durchman had given a time slot to discuss and agree to the plans we might have made. I knew from Liisa that she had been busy constructing a programme for the brand-new specialisation in psychiatric nursing; Miss Durchman had been encouraging her.

We were first facing a month of theoretical studies, before being dispersed to do our training in home nursing. That month was going to give us time for forging our friendships. They had grown in importance as the time went on. Our strong bonds remained for years and years. Initially, we came together once a year, later less frequently. A group of sixteen came even to London. I was responsible for their programme: a city tour, a show, and a trip to Windsor. Our farewell dinner was in my home in Watford.

Home nursing

Occasionally, during the whole of our training programme, Seija and I had been in the same hospital at the same time, but we had never worked on the same ward. Allocations onto wards were done strictly in alphabetical order, so Pelkonen and Vaalas didn't have the remotest chance of ending on the same ward. Now, for the home nursing we had been given the opportunity to choose our partner. Obviously, student nurse Pelkonen and student nurse Vaalas were going to do their placement together. Our placement was going to be in the small village of Sammatti, about an hour's bus journey west of Helsinki. What could be better than spending two months in the country, far away from the college, and having my best friend as company?

We were lucky to be doing our placement in this historically important village. I am now going to make a diversion, and tell you about Elias Lönnrot, one of the most remarkable Finns. He was born in Sammatti in 1802 and died there in 1884. Probably every Finnish child recollects the etching of a little boy, sitting on a high branch of an oak tree, reading, in their elementary school book. In the background was a simple, little wooden cottage, depicting the home of the Lönnrot family; the father was the village tailor.

Little Elias was seven years old when Finland, having been a province of Sweden from the twelfth century, became a Grand Duchy under Russian rule, after the Napoleonic wars. This severance caused major changes in Finland and in Finns. A strong, patriotic movement began, first amongst the academicians, then spreading widely, promoting the use of the Finnish language as an equal to the Swedish language. An interest was awakened to discover more about the Finnish people, our ancient history, and our identity. The slogan, 'Swedes we are not, Russians we will never become, so let's be Finns', became a mission statement of Elias Lönnrot's youth. With a burning passion, he devoted his whole life to this aim.

Elias's exceptional giftedness was noticed from when he was a young child. Special educational opportunities were offered to him for gaining access to higher education. He began his academic career by studying languages at Åbo (Turku) University. Having completed his language studies, Elias continued his studies at Helsinki University, and changed to study medicine, becoming a qualified physician.

As a young bachelor doctor, he obtained a post as a district physician in Kajaani, a small town far in the North Eastern Finland. There was no health centre, so the young doctor saw his patients in their homes. Most of them lived in their tiny wooden crofts in remote parts of Kainuu, reachable only by walking. These home visits gave the young doctor an excellent opportunity to meet country people, sit down, have a cup of coffee, learn about their lives, and meet rune singers. He discovered the rich oral tradition of folk poems, and stories that had been, and still were, recited from one generation to the next. None of these had ever been written down. Lönnrot felt passionately the need to preserve the songs and stories. He sat in the farm kitchens, and jotted them down, then, by adding his own words to fill the gaps, collated and joined up the stories to tell of specific events.

Having discovered this rich national treasure, it became his passion to search for new rune singers. Lönnrot asked for some months' leave of absence from his job as a physician, and began his wanderings of miles and miles in the wilderness, stopping in small cottages to hear poems, and to write them down. He extended his search across the border to Russia, and later to Estonia. Thanks to his mammoth work, we Finns have our national epic, the Kalevala. It's as important to us as Shakespeare is to the British people.

The first version of the Kalevala was published in 1835. The title page stated: *'The Kalevala, or old Karelian poems about ancient times of the Finnish people'*. Lönnrot carried on with his work, and a more comprehensive version of the Kalevala followed in 1848. This version is still in use. The Kalevala has inspired, and continues to inspire musicians, artists, and designers, starting from composers like Sibelius. He gave the stories his powerful, musical interpretations, like 'Kullervo' opera or 'Lemminkäinen legends'. The artist Gallen-Kallela, a contemporary of Sibelius, depicted his images of the Kalevala people in paintings like 'The Defence of Sampo', 'Joukahainen's Revenge', and 'Lemminkäinen's Mother'. We adopted his images as true depictions of how people were, looked, and lived in ancient times. The Kalevala's importance to us Finns is unmeasurable. It gave us Finns a national epos, second to none, an identity, and a strong feel for the ancient history of the Finnish people.

Now Seija and I would have a chance to visit Lönnrot's childhood cottage, go to the library, learn more about him, and put flowers on the foot of the statue of him at the centre of the village.

Sammatti and its surroundings were not unknown to me. In the summer of 1946, I had spent a month in the area as a home tutor to a thirteen-year-old girl Pulmu. Mamma had made the arrangements with Pulmu's adoptive parents, a minister of the church and his wife, her close friends. My opinion hadn't been asked. Mamma had simply thought that it was an excellent opportunity for me to be spending my holiday in their spacious summer villa at the lakeside with a girl almost my age. For her this solved the problem of what to do with one of us during the long school holiday. I would earn my full board by giving German lessons to Pulmu. She had failed her German examinations and needed to re-take them for her to be allowed to carry on to the next class.

I didn't want to go but hadn't the courage to rebel. How I wished I had had. Maybe Jaakko's and my romance, in full fling at the time I left, would have carried on over the summer. He and I would have had a chance to say goodbye before Jaakko and his family moved away. Perhaps our friendship would have carried on by letters?

It's not surprising that I remember my time in Sammatti as a miserable one. Pulmu and I did not hit it off. In my eyes she was a spoilt brat, dim, overweight, and childish. Her company simply bored me. Teaching a lazy, stupid girl was no pleasure. There were consolations: the morning swim before anyone else was up in the crystal-clear lake was just wonderful, and secondly, the housekeeper, of the old-fashioned variety, served the best food I had tasted since before the war. Each main meal, beginning with the food being blessed by Pulmu's father, was a culinary treat. Pulmu's father, probably already in his late fifties, was a jovial, relaxed and kind man. We got on. At mealtimes he made sure that we all joined in discussions; he seemed genuinely interested in hearing my opinions, and he took the trouble to teach me new things. After my month in Sammatti, I did not see Pulmu again, though Mamma continued her friendship with Pulmu's parents.

On a sunny morning in mid-September Seija and I set off for our weeks in Sammatti. We might be lucky and enjoy couple of weeks of glorious autumn days before the greyness and rain of October set in. October in Finnish is *'lokakuu'*, the month of mud. Up to now Seija and I had travelled to many Christian Students' meetings together; this time it would be a totally different experience. The college had arranged our board and lodgings in a house close to the centre of the village, and quite close to the health centre. We were going to have an upstairs room, and were told that the landlord was a musician, a Helsinki symphony orchestra violinist.

The bus left us at the Sammatti village centre. We stood there, looking around for which way to go. We had been given a vague description of the kind of building to look for, up on the hill, overlooking the village and the lake. Seeing a pale-yellow, wooden building, surrounded by harvested fields, we assumed that might be our lodging, and headed towards the house, stopping midway to admire the landscape in the autumn sun. We had to admit feeling lucky that we would be working in this beautiful village, and in these attractive surroundings.

Mrs Levin, the musician's wife, stood outside, obviously she had seen us climbing up the hill, and was welcoming us. As she opened the door, we could hear Mr Levin playing violin. Turning towards us Mrs Levin said, 'I'm afraid you'll have to put up with my husband's practising his pieces for the next concert.'

We muttered something positive. What could we say? Perhaps we might be invited one evening to their living room, to sit down and listen to Mr Levin play? This never happened.

Mrs Levin led us upstairs, showing us our spacious room. 'I'll provide you with a main meal each day,' she said, adding, 'You'll have to self-cater for the other meals. I have provided you with an electric hotplate and a kettle. Hope this is OK?'

Seija responded, 'No problem, it is going to be fun to look after ourselves.'

Just as Mrs Levin was leaving, she added, 'As it's Sunday, we'll be eating in a couple of hours' time.'

We just dumped our cases on the floor, not bothering to unpack, and decided to walk down to the lake, and explore our surroundings. It was a perfect autumn day: a bright blue sky, light wind, and the air cool and crisp. The path took us across the okra coloured, harvested fields, then through a birch wood, the leaves on the trees had changed to golden, shimmering in the sun against the ultramarine sky. As we descended towards the lake, facing us, there was the red sauna building, and next to it, pulled to the shore, a rowing boat.

I said, 'One afternoon we might go rowing to have a look at the shore line, row close enough to see the many summer cottages, now empty. I would be interested to see if I recognise Pulmu's villa.'

We stood a while at the shore, admiring the reflections of the yellowing reeds on the clear, still water, then turning back; hungry and tired. Sadly, the water in the lake was already too cold to swim in, except from a sauna bath.

Monday morning early, we reported for duty at the health centre, met the two health visitors, and had our induction meeting. The district health visitors' main job was to take care of under school-aged children. In smaller districts, like Sammatti, the population was too small to employ both a district nurse and a health visitor, so the health visitor also provided long-term care for the chronically ill and the elderly, and short-term care for people after hospitalisations.

One home visit, to Mrs Pirkkko Virta, an elderly woman, has stayed in my mind. She was suffering from an inoperable stomach cancer and had reached the final stage of her illness. On the way to see her, the health visitor told me a little bit more about Mrs Virta's background.

'The farmer, Kalle Virta, died some five years ago quite suddenly of a stroke, leaving Pirkko, already then in her late seventies, to be in harness. In her healthy days, Pirkko had been a strong, capable, and controlling woman. She had to be totally in charge for some months, until their son Erkki was able to take over.' The Health Visitor continued, 'It wasn't an easy transfer of power, almost impossible for Pirkko to hand over the management of the farm to her son, and Anja, her daughter-in-law, she had simply dismissed and ignored.'

The Health Visitor explained, 'As you know, the tradition is that the farmer's widow carries on living on the farm. What tends to happen is that more often than not, the old mother carries on controlling her son, and the running of the household. No surprise to anyone that there has been quite a bit of tension between young Anja and Pirkko.'

Driving along the winding country road, the Health Visitor continued, 'Erkki married late, and remained the obedient son. This led to problems in the marriage. At one point, Anja nearly walked out. Unfortunately, Erkki, kind and gentle, had no skill in sorting out the difficulties.'

I just listened and said nothing, but wondered, was that the fate of sons, who had been brought up by strong mothers? What had Kalle, Erkki's father been like?

'The situation has now changed. Pirkko is bedridden, unable to get up on her own, she needs nursing care, and her attitude has changed from scorn to gratitude. Anja is pregnant, that is important to them all,' the health visitor concluded.

The farmhouse was a typical one, a low, one storey, red log building, with a spacious entrance porch. Walking through the hall, we entered into a big farm kitchen/ living room. I was overwhelmed by the unpleasant smell of vomit hitting me, so powerful that I wanted to run out and retch. The room was hot. Despite it being a warm autumn day, the woodburning stove was lit. In the remote corner of the room, shielded by a screen, I could see Pirkko's bed. I could not see her face, but heard her troubled breathing. Pirkko seemed to be sleeping.

Anja walked towards us, and whispered, 'Pirkko has no longer been able to keep any food in. After I have managed to feed her, she is throwing up immediately. For the last couple of days, she has been asleep most of the time. Erkki and I think that the end must be near.'

The only thing the Health Visitor was able to do was give Pirkko morphine injections to relieve the pain, and to offer her support to Erkki and Anja. She made sure she had time on her visits to sit and talk to both Pirkko and Anja. It had become part of the routine of the visits to accept a cup of coffee and let Anja talk. Some days Erkki joined them.

Anja had already placed coffee cups, sugar and cream on the sturdy wooden table. A fresh pot of coffee was brewing on the stove. Before pouring the coffee, Anja fetched newly baked 'pulla' (sweet buns) from the pantry. The strong aroma of coffee was somewhat diluting the smell of the vomit. Pirkko's laboured breathing was to be heard in the background.

Despite stirring my coffee, the cream just refused to blend in, and sat on the surface like a like solidified mass of snow in a shady place. Something snapped inside me. I had to rush out, be sick, couldn't stop vomiting. The whole scene held such a power, I didn't know why. Perhaps it was triggering forgotten memories of Mummi's last days? I could not explain what had upset me. All I know was that from that day onwards I never wanted to have cream with my coffee. I still dislike thick cream, even on cakes.

The main part of a Health Visitor's job, as the name indicates, is on the side of health and normality. Her days are spent seeing young children, checking their health, giving them vaccinations, and listening to mothers' concerns; all seemed easy, and enjoyable. I went on many of these happy, cheerful visits, and began to appreciate that health visiting might be an excellent choice to specialize in: living in the community, being pretty independent, and free to arrange your day to suit you. But it was not for me; I had already decided on psychiatric nursing.

In our spare time Seija and I spent time in the local library studying Elias Lönnrot's life. We discovered that he had married relatively late; his wife had been twenty years younger. They had four girls and one boy, the first born. The little boy died of tuberculosis before he was two. Sadly, Lönnrot's wife died of tuberculosis in her early forties, leaving Elias to care for their four daughters, the youngest only ten. At that point he and the girls returned to his home village to be looked after by a spinster relative.

The more I discovered the more my respect and admiration grew. Elias Lönnrot was truly one of the remarkable, great Finnish men. In addition to giving us Finns the Kalevala, he was the father of the written, modern Finnish language, inventing new words to replace the words modified from Swedish into Finnish, often simply by adding a vocal to the end of the word: telefon/telefooni, became *puhelin* or gaffel/kahveli (fork), became *haarukka.*

Lönnrot wrote the first Finnish/Swedish dictionary, he was a scientist, a botanist, a journalist, a hymn writer and a physician. He retired from his post of being a Professor of the Finnish language and literature at Helsinki University to devote the rest of his life to his passion for the Finnish language.

The weeks went by fast; some weekends we returned to Helsinki and had a chance to meet our families as well as our student friends; they in the full swing of their studies. By the end of October days were getting shorter, sunny days were rare, and the colourful autumn landscape that greeted us on our arrival had now changed to a darker, late autumnal one, with earthy tones of olive greens, greys and many shades of light and dark browns dominating the scene.

On the last Saturday, all packed and ready to leave, I suggested to Seija, 'Let's walk down to the lake once more.' The path was slippery and muddy. Here and there were puddles, reflecting light like prisms or spotlights. We proceeded with great care, passed the birch trees, now naked, just with one or two bright yellow leaves showing their brilliance against the grey sky.

We stood at the same spot as we had at the beginning of our stay, looking at the lake. How different it was now. Nature was preparing itself for a long rest. No fish jumping, no sounds, no wind. The world was tranquil, the lake still, lead-like, and the reflections of the withered reeds on the lake created a scene looking like a Japanese print. In unison we began humming: *'Säv, säv susa, våg, våg, slå,...'* (one of the many songs Sibelius composed to Swedish poems: 'Sigh, rushes, sigh, beat, waves, beat.') The song reflects the sadness of loss, and it captures the sound of the reeds. It was a goodbye moment to Sammatti.

Home nursing in Sammatti had been an enjoyable, even relaxing, and not a particularly challenging experience. Going around to home visits with the jolly health visitor, getting glimpses of people's everyday life, and, at times, sharing in their joys and sorrows had been great. There had been, for me, the sadness of Pirkko Virta's death. The long illness had given time for the family to come together, both to show their love, and for them to say their goodbyes. Kalle and Pirkko would be proud to see Erkki's and Anja's determination to continue running the farm in the way it had been done. The young couple looked forward to a good life for themselves, and for their baby, due to be born in late spring. Seija and I were ready to return back to the Nursing College, and to Helsinki life.

The Accident and Emergency Department of the Surgical Hospital

We experienced a complete gear change after the leisurely weeks: back to having to wear the blue uniform, a starched, white apron, and the white cap with its three blue bands, as a sign of our seniority. Back to alarm ringing at 6 am, and back to running to catch the tram. For the third time I would be working in the Surgical Hospital, no longer on the wards, but at the Accident and Emergency Department, known for being an extra hectic, busy place.

People arrived with all kinds of minor injuries: one toddler with a pea swelling in his nose, another had swallowed a coin, many domestic accidents with burns with boiling water or hot fat, and cuts with bread and other knives etc. Most of these weren't too difficult to deal with, but there were, of course, many more serious emergencies, some needing immediate operations like appendixes, some hospital admissions.

By end of November, as winter was approaching, there was a steady influx of people who had fallen and twisted their ankles or broken their limbs on the icy, snow covered, treacherous paths and roads. I assisted in putting broken limbs in plaster casts, stitching wounds, taking blood samples to be rushed to the laboratory, and wheeling patients for X-rays etc. Daily, there were serious incidents, heart attacks, accidents at work, and with machines.

One major incident has stayed in my mind. An ambulance, with its siren screaming, drove in right to the door. Nurses and doctors rushed out with a trolley, and the patient was carefully transferred onto it, and wheeled straight to the operating theatre as fast as could be mastered. I noticed a trail of blood on the floor. I saw the pale face of a teenaged boy, all colour had drained from his face, and he was unconscious, making quiet groaning noises; clearly he was in great pain. His right arm, covered with a sterile dressing, was almost totally severed. There was extreme urgency; there was no time to lose. The surgeons were going to attempt the miracle of attaching the arm back to where it had been cut off. There was panic, nurses running here and there, and the head surgeon giving orders. Medical students on duty and I were invited to watch the operation from the window in the anti-room. The operating team was ready, all in their sterile gear. They stood in silence, waiting for the anaesthetist to indicate that the narcosis was deep enough, and they could begin the repair work.

I am not able to describe the skilful, complex and painstakingly slow surgical procedure that took place in front of my eyes. Bones, muscles, blood vessels, nerves and tendons had to be re-attached. Luckily the cut had been relatively clean, so no bones had been crushed. The incredibly complicated operation lasted over seven hours; microsurgery was only just beginning to be developed from ocular surgery for its use to be extended in repairing severed limbs. How the surgeons managed to do it, I do not know. The end result was that the young lad had his arm back, with the hope of its function being substantially restored.

I went to see him when he had been taken to the ward. Pertti, aged fifteen, had been helping his father in threshing the grain. This he was used to doing. Why the accident had happened Pertti could not explain; all he could remember was the sharp pain, and he knew his arm had been caught in the threshing machine.

The operating surgeons followed the healing of the arm with great suspense, visiting Pertti daily. The most skilful team of surgeons had risen to the challenge to do all in their power to give young Pertti his arm back. The miracle happened, Pertti was so lucky. Once the scar had healed, he was discharge to continue with physiotherapy treatment as an outpatient.

Seeing the doctors and nurses having to deal with unexpected, challenging and even life-threatening situations day in and day out was impressive. My admiration rose sky high for the calmness with which the helping profession handled emergency situations, and their skill in working under such pressure. This was the last clinical experience in my training of nursing physically ill or injured patients, in fact, even as a qualified nurse I never returned to nursing in the traditional sense. By the time my weeks came to an end at the Surgical Hospital and its Accident and Emergency Unity we were at the beginning of January 1953, and ready for a week's break.

Skiing in Vuokatti

January is not the ideal time to go on a skiing break in the North of Finland, as daylight is still limited to a few hours. In spite of this, encouraged and assisted by Isä, Seija and I decided to use the break for a skiing trip up to Vuokatti, part of the municipality of Sotkamo, in Kainuu, the most northern province, before Lapland. The vast province of Kainuu was Isä's territory. Every summer he drove by car hundreds of miles to oversee the various swamp draining projects. Sotkamo was the centre from which he worked. South east of Kajaani, the Sotkamo area covers 3,000 square km. The region is famous for its forested range of seven hills; Vuokatti hill, at 345 metres being the highest. For years people have come to the region to enjoy its excellent skiing and winter sport opportunities, the well- maintained skiing tracks across the lakes and in the forests, some even lit. There is a fine Sport Centre, and an impressive ski jumping hill.

Isä knew the hilly terrain well, and gave us practical help, without which our trip would not have been possible. I had a sneaking feeling that he, an excellent skier, would have loved to join us, and be our teacher demonstrating the correct ways to come down the steep hills. Isä's keenness for our trip, was partly because he was curious to know the progress on our new summer cottage that was being built on the shores of Lake Nuasjärvi, in Vuokatti. The building work had begun in the autumn, and the house and sauna were expected to be ready for our use from the beginning of June. Unfortunately, Isä was not able to take the time off and join us.

Seija had never been so far north. I had been to Lapland on my cycling tour to Norway, and had, in my teens, made the skiing trip with my mates to Eevi's home, in the neighbouring province. Both events seemed a long time ago. During the previous year's winter break from the nursing college Seija, Minnami and I had been invited to Kaaki's home, near Kuopio. The terrain there had not been particularly challenging, being quite similar to what we were used to around Helsinki.

We did enjoy the sunny, carefree, early-spring days of cross-country skiing in Kiuruvesi. An extra bonus was being looked after by Kaaki's lovely mother. She, a typical wife of a vicar, was used to entertaining visitors with her excellent cooking in their spacious country vicarage, and we were treated as special guests. Kaaki's father, a dark haired, good looking man with a twinkle in his eyes, greeted me with special interest.

'How good to see you, Arna. I have been hoping to see you, as Kaaki has often mentioned your name.' Looking straight into my eyes, he said, 'Did you know that I christened you?'

I did know, but wanted him to tell me his memories of the event from so far back.

He explained, 'I was working then in Kuopio as a newly qualified theolog. The christening took place on a glorious July Sunday, warm, with a cloudless blue sky. I remember that I had to take a boat to get to the island where the ceremony was held. A lovely day, that I do recall,' Kaaki's father added.

I then added my bit. 'From a photo, I know that the christening took place in 'Honkaniemi', a villa that belonged to my Great Aunt Eva Nylenius, who taught English in the Kuopio Grammar School for Girls. She was a great support to my mother.'

Kaaki's father then turned to Seija. 'I don't know your father very well, but as two clergymen we have met several times. Next time, I'll make a point of speaking to him at length.' The two fathers met, and were hoping that Jussi, Kaaki's brother, and Seija would become a pair. An excellent match, in their opinion.

Well, now back to the skiing trip to Vuokatti. Looking forward to our adventure, we were both slightly anxious and worried about hazards that might occur. On a cold January evening, we set off with our skis and belongings by a night train. The ten-hour journey went surprisingly quickly in the comfortable sleeper compartment. At seven in the morning there was a knock on the cabin door. The conductor wanted to see our tickets and informed us that the train would arrive at Vuokatti in an hour's time. Looking out of the window, I was surprised to see the darkness around; the main lightness to the black and white landscape came from the snow. The sky was dark grey, with only a thin glimmer of light at the horizon. I had not given much thought to the decreasing amount of daylight the further north you went. We soon discovered that our skiing hours were limited to four, or a maximum of five a day. Well, it was another new experience!

My good, kind Isä had arranged with his foreman, Mr Saari, to meet us, as well as to prepare and heat the lumbermen's room for our use. In the summer months our room housed casual labourers, working on the swamp drying projects, but in winter the room stood empty, as the same men had their camps on the sites in the forests. They were working there cutting down trees, trimming them to logs, and gathering the logs into piles.

As promised, there outside the station, a well-built man was waiting, smiling, and walking towards us. Offering his hand, he introduced himself as, 'Esko Saari,' without removing, just touching, his fur hat, covering his ears, as he welcomed us to Sotkamo. Mr Saari was dressed in a fur-lined leather coat, had thick leather mittens, and boots coming up to his knees. He seemed both amused and surprised by our choice to come up north at the darkest and coldest time of the year.

'It's your good luck, that you did not come last week,' he said. 'Here in Sotkamo the temperature went down to minus thirty for several days, too cold even for us Kainuu people.' After a short silence he continued, 'The camp is warm and comfortable. All has been taken care of, as Forestry Officer Pelkonen requested.' As Mr Saari was driving us some five kilometres towards Sotkamo, he explained that his private home was next door to the building in which we were staying. 'My wife and I are here to help you with any problems, don't be afraid to ask and to use us,' adding, 'We would be pleased to offer you a simple evening meal in our home this evening.'

The kind offer was gratefully received. We certainly had not planned to cook a meal on the first evening. In any case, the plan was to manage with as little cooking as possible.

Mr Saari placed our skis in the porch of an olive green, two-storey, wooden building, and explained that Isä's office was on the ground floor. The rooms were standing unheated and unused in the winter. 'Your room is upstairs. See you tonight, about five,' he said, as he left us to settle and unpack.

Climbing upstairs and opening the door, we entered a large, quite sparsely furnished room: three bunk beds, with the two lower beds ready made for us with starched, white sheets and thick, grey army blankets. Two towels, one small and one large, were laid on each bed. A woodburning stove, already lit, stood in the corner of the room, and next to it a large wooden box full of logs. A colourful rag rug and two comfortable chairs had been placed in front of the stove. We guessed these were extra items, added for our benefit. What a pleasure it was going to be to sit in front of the fire, to read, talk or do nothing, just stare into the flames.

On the window wall was a wash basin, attached to a wooden draining board. Near the window was the eating area: a long wooden table, with wooden benches on each side of it. I could see the lumbermen sitting there, relaxing, sharing jokes, and drinking home-brewed beer or vodka after a hard day's work on the marshes.

In its simplicity, the room was warm and welcoming.

The sun, colouring the snow pink and pale mauve, was just rising above the hills. Amazing, where had the time gone? We had better get used to the short daytime light, and get a move on. It was already ten o'clock. We needed to get some essentials from the shops, about four kilometres away, at the centre of Sotkamo. With rucksacks on our backs, off we went on our skis along the ready-made ski-track, not knowing whether we were crossing fields or lakes; the white winter-scene didn't make that separation.

Our shopping list was simple. For breakfast: porridge oats, milk, ground coffee, bread, butter and 'pulla'. For the evening meal: tea, rye bread, cheeses, cold meats, tins of soups, and fruit, if any was available. Our main, hot meal we planned to eat at the Vuokatti Sport Centre. From Isä's description, I knew that Sotkamo, situated between two large lakes, was on the route from Kajaani, going south east, towards the border with Russia. The main road ended after sixty kilometres in another village, Kuhmo, now world-famous for its Chamber Music Festivals, held annually in July. At the centre of Sotkamo was the market square with no stalls, but I could imagine that in the summer it would be the heart of the town. Clustered on three sides of the square were wooden houses with shops on the ground floor. The first floors were used as accommodation. By the time we had shopped, and had walked to the end of the village, towards the impressive looking, wooden church, the light was diminishing. We turned around but decided to attend the Sunday service during our stay.

Back onto our skis. The frost was intensifying, the temperature dropping rapidly, and twilight descended. Before our eyes, the white scene was being transformed into an increasing blueness, and the surrounding undulating hills to differing shades of purple. My toes and fingers were freezing.

It was good to be back in our warm camp, and to start getting ready for our visit to Mr and Mrs Saari's home. We were hungry. As we rang the bell, we heard a dog barking, and heard Mr Saari's command, *'Maahan'* (lie down), before he opened the door. Mrs Saari, a brown haired, short, round woman, in her late forties, welcomed us with a broad smile. She ushered us into their rustic, cosy, homely living room: rag-rugs covered the wooden floors, the fire in the woodburning stove was lit. The room was like so many other Finnish rooms: a pull-out settee, an occasional table in front of it, two armchairs, a bookshelf, and a radio on a side table. On the walls, a couple of landscape paintings, most likely by amateur painters, and a *ryijy-rug,* a woven, long-tufted tapestry.

Ryijys, date from as early as the 9th century, and originally they were used as coverlets in sledges. Later a ryijy was used as a prayer rug during wedding ceremonies, and then afterwards displayed on the wall in the newlywed's home. In the late 19th century, ryijy-rugs changed from being simply practical objects and folk art to an artform, the designs drawn by famous artists like Akseli Galleen-Kallela.

Sitting round a long wooden table in their large farm-type kitchen, we ate a simple meal of reindeer stew. As we were eating, Mr Saari told us of the life in Sotkamo.

'In the summer you would appreciate how beautiful place Sotkamo is. It's surrounded by seven hills and has lakes on both sides. The shallow main lake, Sapsojärvi, has a long, sandy beach, ideal for children, as you have to wade in a long while before it gets deep.' He continued, 'Sotkamo people have a saying: "God created the world in six days, then, on the seventh day, as a crown to His creative work, God created Sotkamo."'

We talked of this and that. Turning to me, Mr Saari mentioned how appreciated Isä was by the lumbermen, and explained, 'Unlike some other Forestry Officers, your father is so at ease and relaxed with the lumber men. There he is, as one of them, sitting on a log, smoking his pipe, chatting, quietly smiling, and sharing jokes. He loves sharing his coffee break with the men.'

I was not surprised; that was the kind of man Isä was.

It was late. *'Monet kiitokset.'* (Many thanks) and *'Hyvää yötä'* (Good night), we said in unison.

Happy and tired, we walked to our lodgings. The temperature had dropped; the snow on the path was frozen solid and made a crunching sound under each step we took. Before we opened the outside door, we stopped and admired the night sky with its thousands and thousands of stars. Not since I was evacuated to Kuopio during the Winter War had I seen a sky as full of stars.

The next morning, as soon as the pale winter sun had risen above the hills, we were ready for our first skiing trip. As we opened the front door the freezing cold hit us, luckily not minus thirty, but certainly approaching minus fifteen. We were prepared, had greased our faces, had thick, waterproof anoraks, and woollen bonnets to cover the ears under the hoods, thick waterproof skiing pants, fur-lined leather mittens, and skiing boots.

The plan was to ski towards the forest on the other side of the lake, and aim to get to the top of Vuokatti mountain while the light was still good. Crossing the lake was easy. Our well lubricated skis glided along the track with minimal effort. Even in the pale winter sun the whiteness was dazzling, but the northern wind was merciless on the open plain.

Once on the other side, the land rose gently and the track led us to the snow laden forest of pines and fir tree. What a delight to feel free from nursing and hospitals: to feel the snow flurries kissing my cheeks, take in the biting cold air with every breath, and enjoy the pure wonder of the glittering winter world.

After we had skied in the forest for nearly two hours, hunger began to make itself known. It was time to find the Sport Centre. First, we spotted several log cabins scattered around, available to rent all the year round, and then, further along, the Sport Centre, a simple wooden building, amongst the pine trees. We spent some time skiing along the tracks in the forest before finally having our lunch.

The meals offered were: pea soup or Karelian stew, warm *piirakka* (a Karelian pasty made of a thin rye crust, and filled with rice or mashed potato, served with egg butter), and various cold meats or smoked fish, and for pudding, pancakes with cloudberry jam.

After a good, filling lunch of pea soup and pancakes, we began our climb along the marked track to the top of the Vuokatti mountain. The wind had dropped, the world around us was still, the trees majestic, no sound, except ours, as we pushed forward on our skis. Going up the hill the track became steeper and steeper, and the effort became more and more strenuous the higher we climbed; every muscle in my body working to its maximum capacity. Finally, we reached the top of Vuokatti. What an astonishing sight! We were in the ancient land of mythological figures; the trees, bushes and rocks had turned into unrecognisable creatures by the snow falling on to them since the beginning of November. The shapes sparkled like diamonds in the sun, and threw unrecognisable shapes of blue shadows on the snow. We stood still in wonder. In front of us was the panoramic view of lakes and lands fusing into one white vastness against the backdrop of undulating forested hills: the stems of the trees making vertical dark marks, forming a pattern on the snow. In the distance, the sky merged with a chain of blue hills.

A quick cup of coffee in the red mountain hut, then it was time for our return journey. By then the sun was beginning to disappear behind the fells. No lingering, the twilight was gently changing the white world into pastel shades of cold blue and purple. It was time to speed back to our camp.

Each day we tried different tracks. Sotkamo area offered one of the best cross-country skiing experiences with its hilly pine forests, its well-made, much used and even, lit tracks. The skis simply followed the marked route, making the danger of hitting trees less likely. Skiing in the dark along the lit tracks felt like entering a fascinating fairyland.

On our last day we made a second trip to Vuokatti mountain. Our plan was to ski away from Sotkamo towards Vuokatti to make a detour and try to find the half-finished building of my family's new summer cottage. This time we decided to come down from Vuokatti mountain a faster, different, and more challenging route. We would use the slope of the ski jumping structure to make a shortcut. This was a serious mistake as far as I was concerned. We faced an open slope, with nothing to slow you down, and high speed. At this speed one of my skis came loose from its binding and hurtled down the long slope. I fell. The ski-less leg sank deep into the soft snow; the other ski, with my boot firmly fixed to the binding, twisted itself around my leg. With *'sisu'* (stamina, guts, hard effort) I pushed the two ski sticks as deeply as possible into the snow and managed to get myself into an upright position. But the problem remained: How to catch up with my run-away-ski?

I need not have had worried. Having been more skilful in the use of her ski-sticks to break her speed, Seija was already at the bottom of the slope, watching my clumsy efforts at getting up, laughing aloud, and holding my ski in her hand. I was left with the only option: to use the one ski to sit on, and use the ski sticks, and my bottom, to break the speed. This time there was no cause to worry about tearing my skiing pants.

After this little interlude, we headed west towards the shores of Lake Nuasjärvi through the undulating, tree-lined cross- country track. Lake Nuasjärvi is as part of the main waterway running from far beyond Kuhmo, in the east, and in the west, through lakes and rivers, to the port at Oulu, on the shores of the Gulf of Bothnia. In the old times, the route was used to transport timber and tar.

Once we reached the lake shore, the unfinished, wooden building was easy to find. There it stood on a peninsula; the wooden structure blending in with the few trees surrounding the building. Quite a few trees had been cut down to open up the site, and to give the house plenty of light, and a good view of the lake from three sides. The frontage of the house was facing west.

Standing there, looking at the lake, an enormous expanse of white, turning more to grey as the light was fading, and reaching as far as Kajaani, I fully appreciated how important this place was going to be for Isä. It would be his earthly paradise. This house was the first property, not counting the island cottage, that he had ever owned; how proud he'd be. A true compensation for the loss of Kaihoniemi. Now he could have his family around him whilst undertaking his overseeing trips to the worksites. God had been on Isä's side and made the impossible possible. It was a true miracle, and a new dawn for Isä.

This is the story: Isä had for years, long before the loss of Kaihoniemi, longed to have a summer cottage in the area, where he spent his summer months working. On his travels around Kainuu, he kept on looking for suitable lakeside places; facing the evening sun was one essential requirement. He spotted his ideal site on the shores of Lake Nuasjärvi, with no other cottage in sight. After making enquiries, he had to accept that the particular site had to remain an unattainable dream. The land belonged to the Kainuu Energy Company, and they would never sell their land. Then came the war, the loss of Karelia, and the resettlement of Karelian farmers. By law, Kainuu Energy, like all other landowners, was forced to give up some of their land to the resettlement of Karelians. Feodotti Makkonen, from near the border with Russia, became the new owner of the Kainuu Energy land. He built his new farmhouse on another peninsula on the shores of Lake Nuasjärvi.

Isä, once back in his permanent job, was aware of the changed ownership of 'his' peninsula, and saw a faint chance of his dream becoming true. As a fellow Karelian, he approached Feodotti and asked, 'Don't you agree that stony peninsula is no good for farming?'

Feodotti agreed.

'What about selling it to me?' said Isä.

Feodotti thought for a while, and then he replied, 'I'll count the trees first, and then I'll give you a price.'

After the trees were counted, the deal was done. Feodotti, even agreed to build the cottage, and the trees that had to be felled were made into planks for the building. In the summer 1953 the house would be ready for Isä to start his new, ideal summer life. How well I could understand his happiness, a happiness that lasted to the day of his death, in 1977.

As I stood in the snow, I felt quite detached from the idea of summers in Kainuu. I now have my *'Metsäkirkko'* (Forest church) on the shores of Lake Nuasjärvi, my own house, a precious gift from Isä.

Mamma was going to be delighted with an ever-changing lakeview. She would spend hours watching the daily dialogues between the lake and the sky, in all their variations, and be inspired as an artist. The light would be fantastic. By midsummer, there was nearly twenty-four hours of light, the sun only briefly disappearing before rising again.

After an eventful day of skiing, we were tired, happy to be relaxing in front of the woodburning stove, and settled to enjoy a cosy evening. Staring into the flames, we talked about love, and shared our fantasies of our future lives.

Seija, still tied to her father's high moral standards, was living with her unreal, romantic fantasies, expecting a miraculous falling in love, and to be carried away on the wings of love by her Mr Perfect. My dream was to find a partner, a doctor or clergyman, and work with him as a team in Africa. My fascination for Africa had remained. The immediate priority was to complete the nursing training, become qualified, and become financially independent. It had been instilled in me that, to be equal with men, you need to have financial independence. Once that was achieved, there was no need to rush into a marriage. Mamma's firm belief was that God would be guiding each of us. The right man, and marriage would come naturally in its own time.

Psychiatric Nursing – Final six months

Energised by our winter break, Seija and I returned to the college, keen to face the last lap. Seija had decided to specialise in internal medicine; a good basic choice for her. She was planning to continue, in a year or two, with a postgraduate course in social work. My path was clear: specialising in psychiatric nursing would take me deeper into the world of mental health and illness. I had had a small glimpse into this fascinating world through psychology lectures earlier on my course, and then learned much more during my placement in Lapinlahti. I wanted to find out about the current thinking on the causes of mental illness, and the links between the body and mind. One example has stayed with me, told by one of the young psychiatrists. It demonstrated clearly how physical symptoms can act as messengers of a person's mental dis-ease, which they are unable to verbalise. One of the psychiatrists gave the following, fascinating example: 'An elderly man's wife died of a sudden and unexpected heart attack. The man, physically fit but emotionally very dependent on his wife, was in a total shock. Every time food was offered to him, he was unable to swallow. Caring for his father, the son accepted this as an initial reaction to the loss, but as the symptom continued, the man was admitted to the hospital for investigations. He went through many tests and examinations. No physical reason could be found for his symptom. Still unable to swallow, the doctors decided to send him home. A rubber tube was inserted straight into his stomach, and arrangement were made for a district nurse to call three times a day to feed him. His son arranged for his father to receive counselling. In these sessions the widower began to put into words the enormity of his loss, and accepted that his loss had been too great for him to be able to 'swallow'. Once this link was made, the body no longer needed to be a messenger. The man started eating. Interestingly, the death of his wife had opened up the memory of the earlier traumatic loss of his sister years ago. That loss had to be 'swallowed', the grief had become a taboo subject in his childhood family; even her name was forbidden to be mentioned.'

I was so lucky to have had Liisa as my tutor already earlier in the course. With her enthusiasm, her inspiration, and her encouragement, she had made it possible for me to be one of the first students to seek specialisation in psychiatric nursing. She had worked in Nikkilä mental hospital, and had there seen new ideas being experimented with in treating chronically mentally ill patients. Liisa was keen to train a group of qualified nurses to bring a change in attitudes to mental illness. Up to now only short training courses were available for nursing assistants, who worked in mental hospitals. These practical, less academic, courses accepted both men and women as students. At present the only qualified State Registered Nurse was the sister, even though she had had no special training in working with mentally ill patients.

Before we started our final six months, each Sister Tutor arrange a meeting to share the plans they had devised for their students. Entering Liisa's room, I was utterly surprised to see Helinä, a girl from my course I had not worked with, already there. How interesting that she was going to do the six months' specialisation with me, I thought. Her interest in psychology and mental health matters had never come up during our training.

Helinä, a farmer's daughter, oozed health and strength. She had been seen by her father as the brightest of the three children, so she, rather than her two brothers, had been allowed to carry on in the sixth form, and take her matriculation examinations. I sensed an ambition in her, a thirst for knowledge. Helinä did not see her future as a farmer's wife. Though, in my opinion, she already looked like one: sturdy, tallish, masculine; her complexion permanently tanned. She had brown eyes, short dark hair, big hands and feet. Helinä came across as a sensible, down to earth kind of woman. I looked forward getting to know her better, and perhaps discovering another side to the robust person I saw.

This was Liisa's plan: We would begin by going back to Lapinlahti hospital. This time, Helinä was going to work on an unlocked female ward, and I, on a locked male ward. An experience of working on the neurological wards was to be included. We would learn how organic illnesses, such as tumours, strokes and Multiple Sclerosis, were affecting the mind as well as the body.

Then Liisa had planned for us a four-week residential stay in the large Nikkilä Hospital, situated some fifty kilometres east of Helsinki. Liisa had worked there, and had excellent connections; the matron being her good friend. Nikkilä was going to be the most challenging part of our placement. Most of the patients were chronically mentally ill, needing lifetime psychiatric care or long-term hospitalisation.

Liisa had thought out our programme with great care, and had engaged the best of the young psychiatrists to lecture and give seminars to us. She had made a note of my request to have a chance to work my last weeks on the children's ward in Lapinlahti Hospital. After the meeting, Helinä and I had a coffee. We talked of the plans we had just heard, and agreed enthusiastically that, with Liisa as our tutor, we were going to have an excellent, exciting and challenging time. Helinä and I looked at each other and said, 'Think how ridiculed we are going to be by friends, when we tell them: "Sorry, we won't be available for a month. We'll be locked up in Nikkilä!"'

Lapinlahti, locked ward

It was in July that I had last walked the familiar route to Lapinlahti. Now, in the beginning of February, the world looked very different: snow covered the ground, the trees were dark and skeletal, and the sea frozen. Nobody around, no birds singing, just cold, frosty silence. The closer I got to the hospital the more my anxiety increased. I had heard tales of violent patients, and heard ghastly stories of insulin shock treatments.

Nervous and scared, I rang the bell of the locked male ward. Standing there waiting for the door to be opened, I could hear my heart pumping: A key was being pushed into the lock. A friendly looking, tall, well-built male nurse stood there, introducing himself as Tapio Lehtinen. Smiling reassuringly, he said, 'Welcome to this mad house. You'll be ok here.'

He locked the door behind me with his big key. Being locked in felt truly uncomfortable; at least his friendly manner had reduced my anxiety.

As we walked further in, I wondered, how do the proud, independent Finnish men experience being locked in? I could imagine them being angry and rebelling. The thought of being locked in must add to their paranoia. As we passed the dormitory, a sickening, sweet smell hit my nostrils. Maybe my expression revealed disgust, as Nurse Lehtinen was quick to give an explanation.

'The smell, unfortunately, is part of the Insulin Shock Therapy: a mixture of bodies dripping with sweat and the smell of the sickly glucose. Glucose is given to the patients to waken them from their coma.' He added, 'You'll find out tomorrow; Insulin Therapy is given every morning.'

I wasn't looking forward to that experience.

The Ward Sister walked towards us, introducing herself as Greta Anderson. She was a tall, thin, grey-haired woman, probably in her early fifties. Her name told me that she was a Swedish speaking Finn, and her looks indicated that she came from the better off, educated, and cultured class. I wondered why she had chosen to work in Lapinlahti? Maybe she had known Baroness Sofia Mannerheim, perhaps even been one of her students.

Miss Anderson's steel-grey eyes looked straight into mine, as she held out her hand, and with a strong grip, clasped mine. 'Welcome, I hope you'll enjoy working on this ward.' She then explained, 'It will be a very different experience from the ones you have had in your nursing training with physically ill patients. I need to warn you: unexpected things might happen. Some patients hear voices, some talk to themselves, and some can be violent. Do not be surprised if some patients ignore you or some might want to touch you.' She noticed my worried look and rushed to reassure me. 'There are always nurses around. You'll be safe'. Then she added, 'Most of the patients suffer from schizophrenia; we have patients who have had a manic episode in their manic-depressive illness and need hospitalisation.'

We walked past a room where a young man was lying in a rigid pose, slightly raised from the bed.

'He is in a catatonic stupor, and can remain immobile like that for hours, even days,' said Sister Anderson.

We carried on. I noticed a young man, looking familiar, talking to himself. I knew I had seen someone very like him: tall, about 190 centimetres, a noticeably large head, flaxen, straight hair, light blue eyes. He was mumbling to himself as he was walking back and forth along the corridor, taking no notice of us. He simply stared at me, and carried on talking to himself.

Sister Anderson stopped him and turning to me, she said, 'Meet Risto Jalas.'

Hearing his name, I had no difficulty making the connection. His father was a well-known conductor, Jussi Jalas, and his mother, Margareta, one of the Sibelius's five daughters. Risto Jalas, indeed came from a truly famous musical family: his grandfather was none other than Jean Sibelius.

Sister Anderson explained, 'Many famous people spend some weeks here in Lapinlahti, so do not be surprised if you see some while you are on this ward. I am reminding you, that you have, like we all have, made a promise of secrecy, not to reveal the names of our patients.'

I have kept my promise all these years up to now. The two persons I'll mention, died a long time ago, and their mental illnesses were widely known.

Twenty-four-year-old Risto Jalas, an exceptionally gifted young man, had studied Law. He had had his first psychotic episode as a teenager and had been diagnosed as suffering from 'dementia precox', a form of schizophrenia affecting adolescents, often young males. In spite of his mental illness, he had gained his Law Degree in record time, but had never been able to work. Since his teens Risto had been in and out of Lapinlahti hospital for periods of treatment. He died in 1956.

When I met him, he was going through an acute psychotic episode. He heard voices, had both hallucinations and illusions, and was locked in his own psychotic world. This time he had been admitted for a period of observations and treatment with the new drug Largactil rather than Insulin Shock Therapy. I did not have the skill to find a way of communicating with him. I was immensely sad to see this talented young man so alienated from normal life.

Insulin shock therapy

In 1927, Austrian-American psychiatrist Manfred Sakel introduced Insulin shock therapy as a physical method in treating mentally ill patients, particularly those suffering from schizophrenia. The treatment was used extensively in the 1940s and 1950s. By the early 1960s it had fallen out of favour; schizophrenia was treated with neuroleptic drugs, alongside the first experimentations in psychotherapy. In my previous time in Lapinlahti hospital, I had been shocked to see the administration of electroconvulsive therapy. In Insulin shock therapy the patient was injected, repeatedly, with large doses of insulin, aiming to produce a coma.

Seeing it administered, I was revulsed rather than shocked. The treatment was, in my opinion, both inhuman and exceedingly humiliating for the patient. The procedure was ugly and could be dangerous. No studies had been made of the physical effects of putting a person repeatedly into a coma. What was known was that the treatment could sometimes cause brain damage or, and, on very rare occasions, death.

Lying in a row in a big dormitory, the patients were waiting to being injected with large enough doses of insulin to produce a coma. As the glucose level went down the patients became drowsy, started sweating, became restless, tossing, rolling, and twitching around, often needing to be strapped down into their beds. Finally, they fell unconscious, and went into a coma. This state was allowed to last for about an hour or so. A rubber tube was pushed through their nostril into the stomach to terminate the unconscious state. Then, slowly, a condensed solution of glucose was poured into their stomach. The awakening from the coma had to be monitored carefully. Sometimes patients had convulsions, were disorientated, and aftershocks occurred, and at times it was difficult to wake the patient up. The final part of the treatment involved two male nurses dragging the sweat- drenched, sleepy patient into a bath. The bath certainly woke the patient. Perhaps, once clean, they felt more human. One of the unpleasant and unattractive side effects of all that glucose being fed into the patients for weeks, was the weight increased, often to gross obesity. There was no scientific proof why insulin therapy worked, but it did. I witnessed the improvement in patients suffering from acute psychosis; their symptoms improved enough for them to be able to return home after a few weeks.

Lapinlahti, as I mentioned earlier, was for short-term care only. The patients were either admitted for a period of tests and assessment or they were going through an acute mental breakdown. Providing two doctors, one of them a psychiatrist, had certified a person being mentally ill, and of danger to himself or those around him, the Finnish Mental Health Act allowed compulsory admissions to be made. Under the law he/she could be kept locked up for thirty days. After that a new order had to be obtained or the patient had to be released to go back home.

These compulsory admissions were deeply disturbing. I can well remember on one occasion witnessing a man in his late thirties brought in by two policemen. He was shouting, swearing and kicking in his attempt to free himself from the policemen's grip. The man was Lauri Viita, a famous poet and writer. He was suffering from an acute psychotic breakdown and was admitted to the locked ward for insulin treatment.

Lauri Viita, the son of a carpenter, had followed his father's footsteps. He became a carpenter, working on building sites. He had been writing stories since he was a schoolboy and had been encouraged to continue writing. During lunch breaks he, in his powerful voice, began to give poetry readings to his work mates testing out how they were received. He soon discovered how appreciated these readings were, and this encouraged him to have them published. His first anthology of poetry, *'Betonimylläri'* ('Cement Mason'), was published in 1947. The popularity of the anthology exceeded all his expectations. It was praised for its originality, its rhythmic style, and economical use of words. Soon he was able to become a fulltime writer. A year later his multi-layered poetic tale 'Kukunor' was published. That same year, he married Aila Meriluoto, an already well-known, much loved poet, who in 1946 had published her first collection of poems *'Lasimaalaus'* ('Stained-Glass Window'). Straight away she gained fame with her lyrical poems.

The marriage between these two poets/writers was a sensation, and a talking point in all circles. People wanted to know everything about them, about their romance, and what brought two such opposite poets together? Lauri Viita's style of writing was frugal, his language powerful, sharp and realistic, whilst Aila Meriluoto's poetry was delicate, ethereal and sensitive.

Aila Meriluoto came every day to visit Lauri Viita. They created their own private world, ignoring what went on around them, openly and passionately embracing each other, and whispering loving exchanges. I wondered, looking at them, was it being such total opposites that had drawn them together? He: dark, almost black hair, a weather-beaten skin, a determined jaw, a thin mouth, and deeply set, dark eyes. His strong, chiselled features could have been carved from a block of wood. He was not particularly tall, but he oozed masculine power. She: fair-haired, with a pale complexion, and pale blue eyes, was petite, small boned, like a little bird. She came across as delicate and vulnerable. Seeing these two love birds caressing each other one could never have guessed the difference in the same man, Lauri Viita, when he was in his psychotic and most frightening rages and became violent. He hated insulin treatment. His resistance was crushed by two strong male nurses holding him down and strapping him into his bed. He became unrecognisable and disorientated when he woke up from the insulin induced coma. His will to fight was broken down eventually; he gave in, was tamed. He lost his aggression, and became an expressionless, passive zombie; no longer the man I knew as Lauri Viita. The daily large doses of glucose poured into his body made his masculine appearance change; he became grossly overweight, fat and ugly.

Once the insulin treatment was over, he managed to lose weight. His psychotic episode was over, and he was able to return home. The marriage did not last, passion ran out, and violence increased. They divorced in 1956. Aila Meriluoto gained custody of their four children and moved with them to Sweden for a period. Her comment about Lauri Viita, 'He was not a writer; he was a cataclysm.'

Lauri Viita carried on writing, but the writing no longer had the same radical passion as his earlier works. His last book '*Entäs sitten Leevi*' ('So what, Leevi') was published a few months before his accidental death, caused by a drunken driver, in December 1965.

Working on this locked male ward was a disturbing experience, partly due to my fears and prejudices. I had never before met psychotic, seriously mentally ill persons. I did not find it easy to relate to the patients. I was baffled, anxious, and felt awkward. One thing became clear to me: mental illness is rarely an organic disease, and medication doesn't cure the illness, but at least the symptoms can be controlled with modern drugs. Being on this locked ward left me with many questions and uneasy feelings, not only about the treatments used; more disturbing was keeping patients behind locked doors, as if they were criminals. Particularly disturbing was to see a violent patient locked into a room to calm him down. No effort was made to try and understand what might have provoked the reaction.

I thought already then that there had to be a reason why so many creative Finns had mental breakdowns. The society, as it was after the war, demanded conformity, obedience, and hard work. Quite small sidesteps from what was considered to be the norm were frowned upon, and labelled madness. But who was mad? Was it the individual who was searching for new understanding or was it the rigidity in the environment, demanding a certain type of behaviour? I was left with many questions and few answers.

Liisa frequently popped onto the ward and was keen to discuss any concerns I had. The main and most important teaching was done in the weekly, lively tutorials Helinä and I had with her. We both were so keen to learn more, understand more. We were lucky to have the young psychiatrists as our teachers. They shared with us the latest research projects in America, and their new insights and understanding. Liisa, Helinä and I were determined to become torchbearers for more humane treatment of the mentally ill.

Nikkilä Hospital

Built in 1914, Nikkilä hospital was an elegant, Art Nouveau style building. It had beds for three hundred mentally ill and mentally defective persons (now referred to as persons with learning difficulties), needing long-term or life-long care. The hospital was situated in Sibbo village, an hour's bus journey east from Helsinki, and was surrounded by acres of land. This gave an opportunity to build several small houses for patients, as more beds were needed almost immediately.

Gradually, as Nikkilä grew, it became a self-sufficient village, with a bakery, a laundry, its own heating system, and a fire brigade. The farm run by the hospital produced grain, meat, milk and butter, and the nursery grew enough vegetables and some fruit to even sell to other people living in the village. Some of the patients were cared for by these locals like foster children. The mentally ill patients were free to walk around and were accepted as part of the community.

Helinä and I had an eye-opening, happy and interesting stay in Nikkilä. We took part in the various activities available for the patients and were spared from working on the locked wards. On the very first day I was sent to the weaving workshop. The spacious room had eight large looms. The weavers, all patients, were old-looking country women in long skirts, and scarfs covering their heads. Some talked to themselves, some, at times, left their looms, as if hearing a calling voice, and walked around, until ushered back by one of the nurses.

I was encouraged to sit down at one of the looms and guided by the nurse, I started weaving a linen tablecloth. Concentrating on the task at hand, I had not noticed a young, blonde, good-looking man in a white coat, approaching me. He introduced himself as, 'Raimo Lindquist, I am the hospital psychologist.' We chatted easily and in a relaxed manner for a while. He seemed knowledgeable, and keen to show it. I have to admit, I was surprised and taken back when he came up with the suggestion, 'I would like to give you an IQ test. May I come tonight to the nurses' home to test you?'

I simply said, 'Perhaps later,' and carried on with my weaving.

Raimo wandered off. The nurses had been following our exchange and as soon as Raimo had left the room, one of them said, 'Be aware of Raimo. He is one of our patients. He is good at fooling new people with his fantasies. He is a psychopath and is very clever.' I was then told that he used the hospital like lodgings and was free to come and go. Raimo certainly managed to convince me that he was a psychologist.

The hospital had outdoor sporting facilities, an indoor gymnasium, and a ballroom, where weekly dances were held. Nurses were expected to attend, and dance with the patients. Helinä and I naturally joined in the fun. Is dancing a sin? had been a question troubling me since my conversion. I had not attended dances held at the students' union, though, of course, I wanted to, but in my circle of friends no one danced. Now I felt free from any conflicts. It couldn't be a sin to dance with the patients, as dancing was part of the therapy offered.

One evening Seija came to the dances with her brother Jussi and their cousin Ilkka, a student of biology. Jussi had been allowed to borrow his father's brand new Peugeot car for the evening. The three of them were keen to join the dance, Seija perhaps slightly reluctantly, but the two boys had decided to enjoy themselves, and to have a good story to tell their mates. They asked the most unlikely partners for a dance. Of course, I danced with Jussi and Ilkka, and loved it, but mainly with the patients. Raimo was there, charming as ever, no sign of any mental disturbance, and an excellent dancer. I felt so free and happy that evening. It had been real fun.

Having a day off the following day, I was able to join my guests in travelling back to Helsinki. Jussi had just recently passed his driving test and was keen to show off. I think we were all slightly manic; the evening had seemed quite absurd. We were laughing and singing and Jussi's driving became reckless. The more we asked him to slow down, the faster he went. No speed limit, no seat belts. The country lane was narrow and bendy; the speed made even Ilkka scared. Suddenly we saw lights, a car was coming towards us. Jussi slammed the brakes on, and swerved into the hedgerow, and managed to avoid a full-blown collision with the oncoming car. A near miss, but Jussi was left with the unenviable task of explaining to his father the scratches on his brand-new car.

The weeks in Nikkilä hospital had been happy. They had convinced me how much can be done for mentally ill people with the right attitude, and with the wish to get to know each patient as a person. Many of them no longer needed psychiatric care, but had nowhere to go, and were too institutionalized to live without the hospital's support. Earning their living, they worked on the farm or in the various workshops. The whole Sibbo community had become used to patients from Nikkilä hospital and had made friends with them. The villagers attended their funeral services and cared for their graves.

Nikkilä hospital was a pioneer in its readiness to try new treatments and activities. During the time Liisa worked there, they explored the benefits of art therapy. The very first art therapist was Rafael Waardi, then an unknown art student. He became very involved in working with the patients, and soon discovered how much the patients enjoyed this new activity, and what interesting, often revealing images they produced.

Liisa realised Waardi's talent, saw in his works Bonnard's influence, and she used the opportunity to buy some of his paintings. This was a fantastic investment for Liisa, as Waardi became a famous, much admired artist, and his works increased greatly in value. He was commissioned to paint the official portrait of Finland's eleventh president Tarja Halonen, in power from 2000 to 2012.

By the early 1990s Nikkilä stopped functioning as a hospital, and the whole hospital area was redeveloped. The beautiful main building, as well as the smaller buildings, were converted to luxury apartments, and the land redesigned as a public park.

The Children's ward in Lapinlahti

Returning to Helsinki to do the final weeks of my nursing training, and work on a children's ward, filled me with happy anticipation, partly, of course, as the finishing line was already in sight. The familiar path had, like me, changed into its summer clothes: the birches, the maples and linden trees, all in their unique, delicate shades of light greens, even the dark fir trees were happily showing off the brightness of new growth. The sea, reflecting the clear blue summer sky, had warmed enough for the swimmers to flock the beach. Once inside the hospital gates a multitude of colour, and a great the variety of flowers greeted me with their 'summer is here' message.

My mood matched nature's: happy to be young, happy to be alive, and happy to celebrate the wonder of summer. The children's ward, quite separate from the adult wards, was on the first floor. The small unit, with only twenty beds, was designed to offer short-term care for children to be assessed, and for plans to be worked out for their long-term treatments. The ward doctor Marja Koski was one of the psychiatrists who had been psychoanalytically trained in the USA. She had the reputation of being especially good with children. She had a skill in relating to them, and seemed to understand a child's non-verbal communications. She was popular with the nursing staff and we, the students, had been lucky to listen to her seminars.

I was met by the ward Sister Mirja Virtanen and Doctor Koski. The Sister said,

'You are the first student we have ever had. It will be interesting to see how it works out for you, as well as for us.'

'You'll be happy here,' Dr Koski said, smiling reassuringly. She added, 'First, we'll tell you something about all the children, and the work we do on this ward, and then about Kasper. He was admitted a couple of days ago for a lengthy period to assess both his welfare-and his educational needs. His circumstances are quite exceptional. You'll be surprised to hear Kasper's story.'

Working in a mainly Swedish speaking area, east of Helsinki, the Education Welfare Officer had discovered Kasper on his travels checking that all seven-year-olds were attending school. He knocked on the door of a little cottage and there was no response. He was just going to walk away when he heard some faint animal-like sounds. He stood still and waited. The door was opened by a frightened peasant girl, insisting that she didn't have a child. Whilst they were talking, he heard banging on the cupboard door. The E.W.O made the young girl open the door. There, curled on a wooden bench, holding his hands across his face, sat a young, almost naked boy, looking both starved and frightened. The boy refused to come out. He was not forced. He was left sitting with the cupboard door open, while the E.W.O informed the mother that Kasper needed to attend a school, as he had had his seventh birthday, adding that she was breaking the law by keeping him at home. Seeing how frightened the mother became, he reassured her that he was there to help her, and nobody was going to punish her. His job was to find out what would be best for Kasper. In the end she agreed for her child to be taken to Lapinlahti for a period of assessment. Kasper was the illegitimate son of this young, simple peasant girl.

As the society was then, both in the eyes of the people in the village, as well as in her own eyes, she had committed a punishable sin by becoming pregnant. As she had feared, once her pregnancy was noticed, she had to suffer finger-pointing accusations and gossip. The baby was rarely seen, and people lost interest. She had decided to keep her child hidden as much as possible from the judging eyes. Some kind neighbours, being aware of his existence, brought food and clothes to the mother. Being now seven, Kasper had come to the notice of the local Education Department through the gossip in the village.

As I was extra staff on the ward, Dr Koski's had made a request to Sister Virtanen to allow me to be Kasper's special nurse. My task would be to build up a relationship with Kasper, play with him, and continuously teach him. The language he and his mother spoke was Swedish. It was agreed by all involved, that I would use Swedish in my communications with him.

The Kasper I met was not who he had been when he was admitted to the ward. He had been cleaned up, his tangled, brown hair had been cut short, and he was properly dressed in very unflattering hospital clothes. Having seen very little sun, his complexion was pale, almost white. His fluttering eyes were looking around for signs of danger. He looked frightened and bewildered sitting there in a room of his own. Kasper refused to look at me, but at least he no longer covered his face with his hands. The first few days I simply sat with him, showing him picture books, talking to him, and giving names to what we saw. We played catch the ball and many other simple games. Dr Koski and the Sister were pleased with Kasper's progress.

Meanwhile, a social worker was seeing the mother, who had serious problems and needs herself. Her intelligence level was low; she had no skills, and, so far had survived by helping on a local farm, receiving farm produce as her pay. Kasper had been locked in the cupboard while she worked. Her neglect of Kasper's basic needs was a serious matter, and court proceedings were pending. The most likely outcome was going to be that Kasper was taken into care by the local authority, and a childcare officer appointed to make sure his welfare needs were met.

The summer days were sunny and warm. I asked, and was given permission, to take Kasper into the hospital gardens. There was so much new to see, touch, and even taste. He was like toddler, picking up sand, trying to put it into his mouth, he pulled leaves from the plants, feeling their texture, and he found pine cones to play with. I showed him how, by pushing small sticks into them, he could turn the pinecones into toy animals. The first time he made his own animal his high-pitched, joyful laughter was heard a long way off.

Within weeks the difference in Kasper was remarkable, almost miraculous. The frightened, pale and under-nourished boy had gone through a transformation. Now the boy running towards me had colour in his cheeks, his body had changed, his muscles had become firmer, and he was gaining weight. He had begun to speak; he wanted to learn more words, and was constantly pointing at objects around him.

The initial fear had been that Kasper might have serious learning difficulties, and that he might need a special residential school and very few existed in the 1950s. The assessment was ongoing; the signs were quite encouraging. Kasper was learning fast, but he had a lot to learn before it was feasible for him to be able to attend an ordinary primary school.

We were now in early July, the hottest month of the summer, and Finland had *'helle',* a heatwave, quite common during the summer months when temperatures stay for days and days over 25 Centigrade. Kasper's favourite spot on the ward was standing at the window, from where he could see the sea and the Hietaniemi beach. What about a special treat for him? An outing to the beach? When I put this suggestion forward, both Dr Koski and the ward Sister had their reservations, but as 'helle' continued, it seemed a good time to agree to my request.

Dr Koski was keen to find out how Kasper would cope with this totally new experience.

I had become very fond of Kasper and wanted our outing to be a success. I knew that Kasper reacted with panic to an unfamiliar situation. What would be the best way to prepare him for our adventure? How much warning should I give him?

One morning, as Kasper was again standing by the window, I simply said, 'Kasper, today I would like to take you for a walk to the beach.'

Hearing this, rather than panicking, he turned around and started dragging me towards the door, expressing his feelings by clapping his hands, and jumping up and down, demanding: '*Gå nu, vi gå nu*!' (Go now, we go now!)

I have to admit I was slightly anxious. Had I taken on more than I could handle? Kasper could be quite unpredictable. I explained to him that he needed to hold onto my hand at all times. Happily, hand in hand we ran down the wooded path, both keen to reach the water. Running at speed, we came to a sudden a halt, and fell into the soft sand at the end of the path. Having let go of my hand, Kasper was quicker at getting up than I, and started running towards the water at full speed. There was no way of stopping him. I, in my uniform and with shoes on, ran after him, and waded up to my knees before I caught him. He was so full of joy, splashing salty water on himself and on me time and time again. It was fun, but I was now the one who was panicking. What if he tore away from me again? What if he fell? He couldn't swim. Would I be able to rescue him? I tried to take a stronger hold of him, suggesting that we could come back another day, but telling him that we needed to go back. Reluctantly, Kasper agreed. Both of us were soaked through and through. We began the slow climb up the path towards the hospital.

Luckily, the Sister was off duty, and we sneaked in. One of the auxiliary nurses took Kasper into her care, gave him a wash, and changed him into clean, dry clothes. I changed into my summer dress; we were not allowed to wear our uniform outside.

The only problem was that my wet uniform needed a proper wash, and I needed to have a plausible explanation to take it to the college laundry, and to be given a clean uniform. It was easier than I feared. Luckily, the manager of the laundry room asked no questions; she simply handed me a fresh one.

There were only two weeks left; then my three years of nursing training would be over. Dr Koski had asked me to start preparing Kasper for my departure in good time. We read stories of losing a friend, and we played games like hide and seek. I disappeared, and Kasper had to find me. The games gave me an opportunity to talk of us moving on, and going to new places, where we would not see each other.

'Saying goodbye is sad, but I'll not forget you, Kasper. Soon you'll be going to a school, and you will find many new friends,' I told him.

Dr Koski informed me that she was keen to experiment with play therapy, something she had never done nor had she been trained as a child therapist. She had read of the work done in England, and wanted to explore how Kasper might express his feelings in his play. Unfortunately, I never found out what happened to Kasper. At the point when I left Lapinlahti, this was the likely outcome: Kasper would be placed in a Children's Home, while a suitable foster home was searched for. Kasper would be given individual tuition until his language skills were good enough for him to be able to cope with a group of children. As an outpatient, Dr Koski was going to continue seeing him for play-therapy. She was very hopeful, and of the firm opinion that Kasper would eventually be able to join the main stream.

The final session with our excellent tutor Liisa was both joyous and special. Helinä and I were invited to her flat in the teachers' block of the nursing college. As we stepped into her living room, my eyes turned to admire two large prints of Bonnard's paintings in delightful, pastel colours, both portraying women in a room, with subdued light. Liisa pointed to two oil paintings by Rafael Waardi she had bought while working in Nikkilä hospital. In them one could clearly see Bonnard's influence.

On the round table three plates were laid. As a surprise, Liisa had prepared a light supper for us: 'Gravadlax' (salt cured salmon), new potatoes and a cucumber salad, followed by strawberries and ice cream. Just delicious. We ate, laughed, and talked and talked. We did not know it then, but the three of us would become friends for life. All we decided, right there, was to carry on meeting. We would become the torchbearers of a new understanding of mental illness; we would bring psychodynamic ideas both to psychiatric nursing and into the general thinking of illness.

The following year, five student nurses chose psychiatric nursing as their specialisation. Then there were eight of us, all as enthusiastic, all keen to carry on meeting, even if our jobs were going to take us away from Helsinki. The last time we all eight met was 1987. Liisa and Helinä remained life-long, very special friends.

Celebration party and Graduation Ceremony

During the final months, the topics we returned to over and over again, were firstly, where and how to celebrate our graduation, and secondly, our plans for the future. Many lasting friendships had been made during the years. There were fifteen of us who were planning to celebrate together, but how, that was the question. Then, one day, Minnami came up with the answer:

'I asked my parents if they would agree to you all coming to my home for a party,' she told us. 'My mum agreed without hesitation, dad thought a while, then he said, "Why not, they'll be very welcome."' She then gave us a formal invitation. 'You with your partners are invited on the evening before the graduation ceremony to my home for a celebration dinner and a party.'

It was going to be a great way to celebrate. We were delighted, and sent our warmest thanks to Minnami's parents, Heikki and Anna Herlin. Minnami's family was one of the wealthiest in Finland. In 1924, Minnami's grandfather, Hugo Herlin, had bought up a small engineering firm, and decided to change it to specialise in making elevators. He named his firm, simply, KONE Oy (machine). In no time the KONE lifts became well known, first in Finland, for their reliability, and their excellent after-care service, then, gradually, KONE grew to be one of the main international lift makers in the world, and made the Herlin family billionaires. Minnami's father, Heikki Herlin, took over KONE Oy from his father in 1941. He modernised the company and established his own style of management. He and his wife Anna were part of the Oxford Moral Rearmament Movement, and Heikki Herlin's aim was to run his company on the OMRM principles: honesty, fairness and discipline. I am sure this was one of the reasons for the company's success.

As soon as we had digested Minnami's fantastic invitation, the planning started. My immediate worry was whom I should invite as my partner. Mr Right hadn't arrived, and there was nothing exciting about the two candidates available; my longstanding mate Olli or Olavi Järvinen, still around even though I had rejected his proposal, and still believing that I was God's chosen one for him. After my marriage, he told one of our mutual friends, 'Arna was the girl God had meant for me. This arrogant Englishman came and pinched her from me.'

Many years later, Olavi, by then married, had heard from Seija that I would be coming to visit her. With Seija's permission to call, he turned up, clutching a deep red rose in his hand. He suggested we go for a walk, so we could talk in private. It was a cold winter's day. We walked in the harbour area. Olavi confessed that his love for me had never died. He often thought of me, and was happy to gain up-to-date information about my life through Seija. I felt sad and felt that hanging on to this youthful attachment to me was robbing his wife of his full love. I admitted to him that I had handled his deep and genuine love very badly and insensitively, and asked him to forgive me. The meeting left me wondering why he needed to hang on to this unrealistic fantasy of romantic love. It stayed there all his life. When my husband died in 1999, he sent me a book of poems, and a touching letter. On that occasion, his care moved me deeply.

In my usual impatience or panic, I went ahead and invited my mate Olli, though, in my heart, hoping that someone more dashing might appear at the last minute. So many of my student friends were going steady. I felt quite desperate not having a boyfriend whom I really fancied. There must be something wrong with me,

I thought, feeling really downhearted, and lacking trust in myself as an attractive woman.

One evening, in my unhappiness, I turned to Mamma, telling her of my worries. She showed little understanding and didn't see my genuine unhappiness. Her first response was, 'God will, in his time answer your prayers.' Then, flippantly and laughing, she came up with her suggestion, 'Why don't you marry Eino Pinomaa?'

I felt deeply hurt and insulted by Mamma's insensitivity, and her frivolous attitude. She had shown no attempt to put herself where I was, soon to be twenty-two years old. I should have known better. This is going to be the last time I ever turn to her with my personal problems, I promised myself.

Of course, I knew Eino Pinomaa well, and there was nothing wrong with him. We had both attended Käpylä Grammar School. His father was the vicar of Käpylä parish, and Mamma's good friend, we were related, and I had attended his confirmation classes. In school Eino made no impact. He was known as the clever, serious and studious one; lean-built, average height, dark haired, and wearing glasses; he had seemed shy and withdrawn. Certainly not someone I would ever look at twice as a possible boyfriend. We had met quite regularly at the Christian Students' meetings and exchanged greetings: 'Hei' (hello). 'Mitä kuuluu?' (What's your news?); that's all. He was studying theology.

In my group of student friends, many had found their life-partners, mainly from the medical candidates. Minnami had begun to go out with a law student, Eero-Pekka Paavolainen, Kaaki was planning to get married to Raimo, and, in a casual way, even Seija, as virginal as before, was seeing Kaaki's brother Jussi. This pleased both sets of parents. An ideal match as far as they were concerned.

At one of the Christian Students Union meetings, a theology student I hadn't seen before, appeared. He was expressing refreshingly liberal views, different from the pietistic ones, and seemed confident, free and relaxed. I wanted to know him better. I hadn't failed to notice his good looks: Tallish, slim, blonde hair, big blue eyes, a straight nose, and a tanned complexion. When he smiled, he showed off his brilliant, white, rather big teeth. I felt immediately attracted to him. After the meeting, I approached him, commented on what he had said; our conversation was in full swing before we had introduced ourselves.

'Timo Saarelma,' he said, as we shook hands, and added, 'I have been so busy with my studies, no spare time for meetings. Now I am on my last lap, I have just handed in my graduation paper.'

It turned out that his lodgings were near the nursing college, so walking back to our bases together was quite natural. From then on, we met weekly at the Union meetings, each time discovering more and more about each other. Timo had applied for, and was hoping to hear that he had succeeded in getting, a scholarship from the Lutheran Church in America to continue his theological studies in the USA. I have to admit, the news was a big blow to my budding dreams and fantasies.

Luckily, that was in the future. I had become more and more sure that Timo would be just the young man I wanted to accompany me to Minnami's party. It took some courage to ask him. An unnecessary worry. It was great to see Timo so genuinely delighted by the invitation. 'With the greatest pleasure,' he said.

My impatience had put me in a dilemma: How would I find the right words, or a convincing lie, to explain my need to cancel my invitation to Olli? Should I pretend to be ill, or say, 'So sorry, Olli, but I am not able to attend the party, something urgent has come up in the hospital, and I have to be on duty.' That wouldn't do; Olli would know straight away that I was telling a fib. I can't remember what I said or what words I might have used to soften the blow. All I do recall is how deeply hurt Olli looked. I felt mean and horrible and was sure that God was going to punish me, but I didn't care. I was so happy to have Timo as my partner.

I needed a party dress. The new fashion, the midi dress, had just reached Finland. Mamma came with me to search for a suitable material. We found raw silk in my favourite colour, bluebell blue. Aunt Law's friend was pleased to make me a midi outfit. The dress turned out stunningly beautiful and very becoming.

The Herlins lived in Kulosaari, an island part of Helsinki suburbs. The highway from Helsinki eastwards goes through the island, which is linked with bridges to the mainland on both sides. In the 1950s, Kulosaari was where the Helsinki nobles lived, in their inherited, massive wooden villas. One of these, a grand three-story villa, close to the Bay of Finland, with large park-like grounds, was Minnami's home.

Anna and Heikki, both tall and handsome, were in their large drawing room waiting like a regal pair to welcome us on our arrival. They spent a short while talking to each couple before guiding us to their garden, to be offered a welcoming fruit drink. Minnami's dark-haired and beautiful mother, Anna, came across as warm and friendly, whilst her good-looking father, Heikki, seemed more reserved in his friendliess. They lingered amongst us for a while, before withdrawing indoors.

We carried on walking around the park, introducing our partners to each other, and enjoyed the warm and balmy evening. We began to feel hungry, so Minnami's invitation to follow her inside, was very welcome. In their elegant dining room, a 'fine dining' three-course meal was served. I do remember the happy atmosphere, a lot of laughter, chatting, and jokes were shared, but have no memory what we ate, except that, for our dessert, we had the sweetest strawberries I had ever tasted.

This was the first occasion to talk with some of the boyfriends I had met only briefly. A new acquaintance was Minnami's boyfriend, Eero-Pekka Paavolainen, a law student, tall, good looking, and with dreamy brown eyes. I was slightly surprised to see Minnami's choice. For her powerful personality, Eero-Pekka did not seem strong enough. But who would be? At least, his background was suitable for the Herlin family, especially to Anna. Eero-Pekka's family came from Karelia, and from a line of famous creative people, mainly writers and poets. He and Minnami became a steady pair.

The evening was just great. All the girls looked lovely in their new party dresses. Seija's dress was made of pink organza; the colour suited her perfectly. She looked beautiful, like a rose bud. 'You can look at me, and admire me, but if you come too near the thorn will sting you.' This was the message, she had internalised from her father's attitude to sex.

I received many compliments, and I felt confident both about my looks and the dress. I knew the blue colour flattered me and made my eyes even bluer than they were. Timo was great company, mixing easily and in a relaxed manner with everyone. He, as a theologian, knew Raimo, and had shared seminars with Jussi. My friends commented, 'He could be your brother; he looks so much like you.'

Had I fallen in love with my own image? That thought came much later.

Happy and proud as I was to have had Timo as my partner, the disappointment was that he didn't give me any obvious signs of wanting to be anything else except a really good friend. I, on my side, had begun to have fantasies of our relationship developing to a more meaningful one.

On a rational level, I had an explanation: knowing that he would be going to USA in the autumn, Timo had no wish to get involved with me or with any other girl at this point. He wanted to be free to explore the new world without commitments. That explanation was of no help on the feeling level. I had fallen in love with Timo.

Ready for the following day's graduation ceremony, we left Minnami's home in a jolly mood. Timo escorted me back to the college, took my hand, held it in a strong grip, and thanked me for a wonderful evening. We parted with the knowledge that at the beginning of September, before Timo's leaving for the USA, we would have a chance to see each other for some weeks.

Graduation Ceremony

Three years earlier, at the beginning of their journey into the hospital world, a group of young, eager, and anxious nursing students had gathered in the big auditorium of the Nursing College, where the Director of the College, Miss Aino Durchman, gave her welcoming address. Now these same students were sitting, in alphabetical order, in the same auditorium, waiting for the graduation ceremony to begin. This time, feeling proud of their achievements, dressed in their sparkling white, brand-new uniforms, and in headgear, equally brilliant white, and with no bands on it, they were looking forward to the life ahead with confidence.

The auditorium was filling up with parents and close relatives, some clutching bouquets of flowers in their hands. Glancing back, I recognised many of the parents, but there was no sign of mine. They had not seen my graduation as an important enough event to break their holiday up in Vuokatti. Naturally, I was deeply upset. Did my achievement mean so little to them? Mamma, in her heart, knew the importance of the occasion, and she had sensed my disappointment. Feeling guilty for letting me down, she had turned to Isä's cousin Sister Aino, Deaconess Aino Miettinen to be their representative at the ceremony. She had willing agreed; she was proud of me. Sister Aino, in her long-hemmed deaconess costume, and her tiny, white, starched headgear was easy to spot. Miss Durchman rushed to greet her. Sister Aino's attendance was a great personal honour for her.

Before I carry on with the graduation ceremony, I would like to tell you a little about why Sister Aino was such a well-known person in nursing and medical circles. I have mentioned her before. After my grandfather's death in 1902, she, as a teenager, agreed to become the home tutor to Ester and Laina, provided her own two brothers Eino and Aito were included in the teaching group. My personal memory from 1937 is when Sister Aino, dressed in her dark deaconess outfit, was having driving lessons from Isä. I, six years old, was in the car with them. We ended at the police station, as Sister Aino's bumpy, learner driving had caught a policeman's attention. Isä had to give an explanation as to why he was teaching Sister Aino to drive. Together they gave a feasible reason. They were cautioned, as Isä was not qualified as a driving instructor.

Aino, born in 1885, started studying mathematics, physics and chemistry at Helsinki University in 1913. Before completing her studies, and aiming to spend her life for the benefit of others, she decided to change direction. She enrolled as a student at Helsinki Deaconess Institute, where her talents were immediately spotted. Soon after her qualification, in 1918, Sister Aino was appointed as the head of the Student department. In twenty years in that position, she completely overhauled the training programme. Her aim was to offer the deaconess students the best possible education.

Already in the early 1920s, Sister Aino saw her life's task as changing the care of and the attitude to children with learning difficulties. Her radical proposals for creating a small, self-sufficient community, where these children would be lovingly cared for and could work in agriculture, were received with resistance and open hostility, even from the medical profession. In 1927, she took into her personal care two Downs Syndrome boys. This was the beginning of the work done by her and the Deaconess Institute for children with learning disabilities. She was sent to Denmark to study their advanced work with these children.

From 1938 onwards, Sister Aino devoted herself entirely to this work, and transformed the lives of so many young people with learning difficulties. She made them feel proud of themselves and their achievements. She helped to create a community where they were happy and safe. She continued her work for twenty more years after her retirement. Sister Aino's life's work is well recorded in several books. She is seen as a pioneer and a visionary. In 1976, at my parents' Golden Wedding Celebrations, I saw Sister Aino for the last time. Sitting next to Isä, wearing her deaconess uniform, she looked frail, but her presence radiated love and wisdom. Four years later she died, at the age of 95.

Back to the Graduation Ceremony. Miss Durchman spoke at length of her vision in nursing. Her aim was for the nursing qualification to be seen as academically equal to a University Degree. She was proud to tell the audience that our group was the first one for this new training programme. Turning to us, she thanked us for having been such fine students. Then she went on to add some words of wisdom for the journey awaiting us. Calling us, in alphabetical order, to the podium, she presented to each of us the Certificate of the Membership of the Finnish Association of Nursing. As a sign of being a fully trained nurse, Miss Durchman pinned a silver badge with a blue cross onto our uniform.

The formal part over, we moved into the sunny, spacious hall to meet up with our relatives, and for coffee and cakes. Seija's parents, Pauli and Maija Vaalas were there, and were delighted to spend time with Sister Aino. They had met each other on several occasions in the church circles. A few years later, Pauli Vaalas was elected as the Director of the Institute of Deaconesses. Then he became fully acquainted with Sister Aino's life-work, and came to admire her wisdom and humility.

Sister Aino and I said goodbye, and I thanked her for having given me of her time. She took hold of my hand, looked straight into my eyes and said, 'Arna, may God bless you, and the work you are going to do.'

The most important chapter of my life, up to then, had come to end. That same evening, I took the night train up to Vuokatti.

Kajasti, our Summer house in Vuokatti, built 1953

Heikki and Arna, Summer 1955

Heikki and Arna, Summer 1955

Heikki, Summer 1955

Chapter Seven

Young Adulthood. Working as a qualified nurse 1953 – 1955

Celebrations over, training finished, and my first salaried job waiting for me. Now on my way up to Vuokatti for a well-earned holiday. I should have felt on top of the world, but no. Instead, I felt a peculiar emptiness, a kind of void, and slight apprehension. I needed the break to sort out thoughts and feelings before returning to Helsinki.

Isä met me at the station, gave me a good, strong hug, and congratulated me.

'I expect to be well looked after by you from now on,' he said, jokingly.

In his light-hearted comment I sensed a relief. No longer was he going to be responsible for me, financially or otherwise. For the first time, over the three years, it dawned on me that I had taken his support for granted and had not even thought of thanking him. Isä had been good to me. At twenty-two, it was high time to become independent, be responsible for my life, and the decisions I made. How very different studying had been for Isä: no financial support from his widowed mother, a loan from the state, a loan that he was paying back up to the Winter War. All his life he had lived with money worries.

Leaving the station, we passed a few scattered houses. Isä pointed at one, and said, 'Family Moilanen live there, they keep some life-stock. We get our milk and butter from them.' He added, 'Juha was very happy to discover that they have a son of his age; the two lads get on well together. This has made a huge difference to Juha's happiness here; at first he'd felt quite lonely.'

No more houses, the village road changed to a sand track, and moved on through a pine forest, now so different and uninteresting from the white, magic winter world of a few months ago. A slight yellowing in the nature had begun. In Kainuu, by August, the best of the summer is over.

As we left the forest, I could see glimpses of 'our' lake to the left. The track narrowed to no more than a wide path, cutting across a marshy meadow before coming to a stop. We had reached our destination: the only summer cottage visible on the shores of the sandy beach of Lake Nuasjärvi. I stepped out from the car with curiosity to see the transformation of the half-finished cottage of the winter trip, to a brand-new, fully functioning summer dwelling. The first building facing me was a red log building, the *sauna*, large enough to have a separate dressing/bedroom, sparsely furnished with two beds, a table, and a chair. Doors from the sauna and the dressing room opened to a veranda on the side of the lake. There, one could sit and relax with a drink between the dips in the lake and the hot sauna. For a perfect completion of the sauna ritual, you linger on, your body and soul cleansed, feeling in total harmony with yourself and nature and look at the setting evening sun.

Up a gentle slope, there it was, the new house, partly hidden by a few birches, and camouflaged by its light olive-green colour. In the corner facing the lake was a large veranda, a summer living room, where meals were served in all weathers.

Mamma, Laila, and Juha with Taru stood on the steps ready to welcome me. We had a joyous and warm reunion, each of them keen to show the house, and tell me what they had discovered in the area. Mamma was delighted that there were plenty of '*mustikka*' (blueberries) on our plot, and in the nearby forest. To her great delight, she had found in the ditches a good supply of the rare '*mesimarja*' (arctic bramble), enough for her to make *mesimarja* liquor, an expensive rarity. Juha and Laila praised the sandy beaches, stretching long ways on both sides from our plot, ours to explore; no other cottages anywhere. In the distance one could see Makkonen's house and farm.

Isä, proudly, and with a hint of a smile lingering on his face, showed me around. Both Aunt Laina and Lyyli had already been on an inspection visit to this, for Isä, replacement for Kaihoniemi. They had been impressed with the location and the great lakeview. Aunt Lyyli had made suggestion of a name for the place and house: '*Kajasti*' (a new dawn is breaking). An excellent name and accepted by those present.

In no time Kajasti had become Isä's earthly paradise: He had drawn the plans, he had overseen the building process, and now he was the owner of Kajasti. Truly, a new dawn had arisen. For the first time in his life, Isä was able to carry on working during the summer months without being separated from his family. Now, after a working day, he had time to go for a swim, lay the nets, and heat the sauna. Summer evenings up in Kainuu lingered on and on.

Basically, life in Kajasti was the same as it had been in Palosaari; no electricity, no telephone, no running water. There were improvements and differences: a well with most delicious water, a good cellar under the kitchen floor, and a house with a good size kitchen, a large living room with a bedroom alcove for Mamma and Isä, and a box room with a bunk bed for Juha. The loft was an open space, but could, later, be divided to one double and one single bedroom. The major and most important difference was that the house was on the mainland, reachable by car, and only seven kilometres from Sotkamo, with good shops, a market, a library, and a Health Centre.

Unfortunately, the arrival to this remote place, where the rest of the family were well settled and happy, didn't do the same trick for me. I was longing to be back on Paradise Island, seventeen and dreaming, instead I was in an alien place, both in actuality as well as within myself. One clearly marked path had come to an end, an unknown, and unmarked path was a question mark. Too much had happened, too many emotions had been stirred up; I needed to be alone.

Walking down to the lake gave me a moment to look around. The landscape facing me was so different from the ones in more southerly parts of Finland. There, lakes are scattered with little islands, the shores dotted with red saunas, and the forests filled with birches. Now, the waters of Nuasjärvi opened up more like a sea than a lake, and the expansive view was unhindered by islands. The forested slopes were dark green with fir-trees, the land rising higher and higher, to undulating blue hills. The stillness of the wilderness facing me gave no solace, it simply echoed my sombre mood.

It was great that I had a profession and I could practise anywhere in the world. But in my personal life there was uncertainty, lack of confidence, and soul searching, taking away from the joy of my professional achievement. During the spring months, gradually, I had become more and more attracted to Timo. He ticked all the right categories; I had fallen in love with him. I was convinced we could have made an excellent pair, but Timo's plans to carry on with his studies in America, had taken me with complete surprise, and had robbed me of the hope of our relationship developing into something more serious. Having met someone special, why should he be disappearing to the other end of the world? I knew that Timo was fond of me as a friend. Maybe with more time, I would have won his heart? Being shy, inexperienced, and full of doubt about my attractiveness, I passively and fatalistically, accepted that Timo was not meant for me. Minnami's party had made it clear. My heart ached, and was left to suffer in this alien landscape.

It was not only my heart that ached, I had started to suffer from spasmodic stomach pains, occurring, mainly, after meals. My diaphragm became rock-hard and tense, and the pain radiated upwards to my shoulder blade. One day the pain went on and on, kept worsening without any relief. I was in serious agony. Labour pains can't be as bad as what I am going through right now, I remember thinking, but at least then I would be rewarded with a baby!

It was obvious that I needed medical help. Isä agreed to drive to Sotkamo Health Centre. Luckily, a female doctor was on duty and came out with Isä. After a thorough examination, her provisional diagnosis was gallstones. She prescribed medication to be taken immediately when the pain started, to release the tension. She urged me to have a full investigation, and X-rays to be taken as soon as I was back in Helsinki.

Once the pain was diagnosed, and controlled by medication, my mood changed. For a few days *'helle'* (heat wave) returned. The sandy beaches and swimming in the lake were there to be enjoyed. This was the healing and inner cleansing experience I needed. Relaxing in the water and in the sun, I understood how much pain had soaked into me in those years in the hospital world. I could feel myself letting it go, letting it float away; it was no longer for me to carry.

As the days grew shorter, the sunsets, against the darkening August sky were becoming more spectacular, more colourful and dramatic. With the large open water in front of us, we were able to see the sun sinking behind the thin horizon line, leaving the clouds in their brilliant colours and their reflections on the still lake for hours and hours. On many early mornings I was Isä's rower in picking up the nets. As the sun was rising, we were able to see the morning mist evaporating, gliding silently and gracefully, as 'corps de ballet'.

The Kainuu landscape was not one to sooth or jolly you out of your sadness. The rugged beauty, instead of pulling me out of my melancholic mood, added its own. The dark fir trees, standing tall in the barren soil and harsh climate, told a tale of their survival with 'sisu', merciless honesty, echoing my mood; life wasn't a bed of roses. Seeing, on a stormy day, the power of waves hitting the rocks in the corner of the cape, finally pulled me out from my sombre mood and gave me renewed strength. I began to look and listen, see and hear what this landscape revealed of its history. Its primeval spirit had begun to live and speak. Here, the ancient people of Kalevala had lived, worked, loved and fought. Here, Elias Lönnrot had wandered miles and miles, summer after summer, collecting their stories, through oral memories passed on from generation to generation, and remembered by a few rune singers. This was the landscape that at the turn of twentieth century, Akseli Gallen-Kallela and Eero Järnefelt immortalized in their powerful, nationalistic paintings. Jean Sibelius, at the same time, had found sounds to express the spirit of the primeval Finland in his forceful music.

The month in Kainuu was a watershed for me, both internally and in my relationship with my family. Family holidays were over; I was no longer a child, nor did I need my parents to provide for me. Next summer I would only visit Kajasti briefly; I would be travelling; where I didn't know. There was a hint of melancholy in the air; the short summer was soon over and nature as well as people was changing into a different gear. A new life was about to begin. But first, a family outing for us to enjoy together: Eva-Brita's wedding.

Piittu's Wedding

Early on a glorious, late August day, the five of us left Kajasti, heading towards Kuopio and Halmenjoki to attend the wedding of my cousin Eeva-Brita (Piittu) Dahlström and Rauni Mollberg. Seeing the groom's name on the wedding invitation was a shock to me. Who was he? Where had he popped up from, without Piittu telling me? I had met her early in the spring, when she was going steady with her schoolteacher boyfriend Kalevi. Piittu told me of their plans to get married within eighteen months. What had happened to Kalevi? More interesting, this the new man, Rauni. Who was he? Where and how had the two of them met?

We arrived at Halmenjoki in good time. There was enough room in the large villa to accommodate us all: Laila and I shared a room, Juha shared a room with his cousin Eero, just a year older, and my parents had their own bedroom.

Aunt Laina had stepped in with the purchase of the material for a midi length dress for Laila, now eighteen. She had chosen a check patterned, pale green taffeta. The dress suited her perfectly, emphasising her slim figure. The colour deepened the colour of her grey-green eyes and was becoming for her complexion. I was pleased to have another opportunity to show off the bluebell dress, knowing what a success wearing it had been.

There was time to have a chat with Kaarina, Piittu's older sister, and find out details about Rauni, and the whirlwind romance. She told me that Rauni Mollberg, aged twenty-four, an upcoming actor/director and filmmaker, had been engaged by the Kuopio Theatre last autumn. After one of the shows, Piittu, a keen theatre goer, had been introduced to Rauni, and his friend actor/director Seppo Wallin, now the best man at the wedding. The romance between Rauni and Piittu had flared up in no time.

It did not surprise me that Rauni, a filmmaker, would have noticed Piittu and her lively, expressive, and photogenic face. Petite and pixie-like in a classical sense, she wasn't as beautiful as her mother, but in profile, with her straight nose and her thick brown hair pulled back, she looked like an ancient goddess. Uncle Kaarlo and Aunt Eva, and the whole bourgeois Dahlström clan had been shocked to hear of Piittu's unorthodox choice for a husband. Uncle Kaarlo hadn't minced his words in expressing his strong disapproval. As a businessman, he had no time for art of any kind, and saw actors as no good loafers. Rauni's working-class background did not help. His father was a caretaker of a block of flats in Hämeenlinna, a small town in the South West, where Sibelius had been born.

Once Kaarlo came to accept the inevitability of the marriage he, with Aunt Eva, decided to give their daughter the best wedding they could master. Halmenjoki, with its extensive grounds and its lakeside setting, was an ideal choice for the venue of a summer wedding. Aunt Eva had performed a miracle in transforming the massive, log-walled living room into a festive sanctuary for the wedding ceremony. A temporary altar had been erected in front of the side window. Through the birches, glittering in the sun, you could see a glimpse of the lake. An organist had been hired, and a harmonium had been brought in for him to play the wedding march as well as accompany the hymn singing. As you entered the room, a gentle, delicate fragrance hovered in the air, and drew attention to the numerous flower arrangements of sweet peas, grown in the Dahlström's commercial garden. An arch of small birches had been erected at the entrance for the bride and her father to walk through towards the altar, where the groom and best man stood to attention.

Waiting for the ceremony to begin, I recognised, to my astonishment, that the pastor conducting the wedding service was Jussi Simonjoki, now a newly qualified clergyman. I had had no inkling of him being a friend of

Rauni or Piittu. The organ began to play Mendelsohn's 'Wedding March'. All eyes turned to see Eva-Brita and my Uncle Kaarlo ascending the steps from the garden, and coming through the arch, walking towards the altar. Piittu looked stunningly beautiful in her tightly fitted, long white dress, carrying a bouquet of small roses and sweet peas. I sensed a vulnerability in her that I had not noticed before. Why? Was it a premonition of the life facing her? Rauni, walking towards her, had an amused expression on his face, as if he was both acting a part in a play, and an onlooker of a show. Disappointingly, he was a very ordinary looking, typical Finnish man of medium height, and mousy coloured hair. His manner was confident, almost arrogant, and relaxed. Whatever the couple might have been thinking in their hearts, in the presence of all of us, they gave their vows promising, 'For better or worse to love each other...'

A buffet meal in the garden followed. I had been placed between Jussi and Seppo Wallin, the best man. He had studied acting with Rauni, and he, Rauni, and Jussi had done their military service together. That answered the question of why Jussi was the pastor conducting the wedding ceremony. As soon as we had filled our plates, Seppo started talking to me, ignoring the other guests at the table, and looking straight into my eyes with embarrassing intensity, as if he had seen a vision. I had to admit that his gaze and attention both disturbed and flattered me. He seemed a most interesting person, and I was glad to be sitting next to him. He was a good-looking 'Don Juan-type', and his looks guaranteed hero roles in films. His long-term plan and hope was to spend more time in writing than acting. He was writing poems in his spare time.

It was time to move to puddings, Seppo got up, exchanged a few words with Jussi, and then left the table, walking towards the forest. Jussi and I started chatting, and he decided to share with me what Seppo had told him.

'In that dreamy, blue dress Arna's ethereal beauty overwhelmed me. I just couldn't take my eyes off her,' adding, 'I need to get up, be on my own. I want to find words for what has taken place within me.'

Hearing what Jussi told me, I too wanted to understand what had been happening between Seppo and me. My interpretation was that Seppo had seen in me his own fantasy figure of a virgin girl, pure and innocent. The vision had both disturbed him and inspired his creativity; he needed space to process his feelings, find words, perhaps, write his poem. I fitted the image of his dream maiden. Hearing this was music to my ears.

Seppo returned. The walk had helped him separate fantasy from reality. We carried on talking; the intensity in his way of looking at me was no longer there, but he suggested that we meet when we were both back in Helsinki. I was left with the hope and expectation that Seppo would contact me. I have to admit that Seppo had disturbed and fascinated me; I was really, really hoping to see him again. He carried on working at the Kuopio theatre. We never met again. At least I was left with a happy memory of having been an inspiring muse for Seppo. I have followed his career all these years. He became first, a very well-known actor, and later, far more famous for his work as a writer and director of TV plays.

The happiness in Piittu's and Rauni's marriage was short lived, though it took almost twenty years before they divorced. They had two children, Eira, born in 1957, and Heikki, born three years later. Eira has become famous in her own right, as a writer and director of television documentaries. She has in her writings revealed the hell of the Mollberg family life, and describes Rauni as a cruel, harsh father, at times tender but more often violent. His class hate, scorn and ridicule were directed towards the Dahlström family, and Piittu got her share of this hate, being too conventional and bourgeois. She became submissive, suffered from depression, and spent, on and off, longish periods in a mental hospital. Heikki had a troubled life, and suffered a psychotic breakdown when he reached the age of twenty.

In his theatre work Rauni Mollberg was highly respected and admired. His fame as a film director grew year by year; he received honours and rewards; he was made Art Professor. Rauni's outbursts of violent temper were well known, and those working with him were afraid of him. He died in 2007.

In late autumn 1974, my husband Peter and I received an invitation from the Finnish Embassy to attend a late night showing of Rauni's first feature film, 'The Earth is a Sinful Song', at the Festival Hall. The film had stunned critics and audiences alike, and received many awards both in Finland and internationally. Filmed in Lapland, and using ordinary people as actors, it told an earthy, erotically charged, blood-soaked tale of a young village girl's ill-fated affair with a Lapp reindeer herdsman. Rauni had, with his stark, realistic naturalism, stripped away life's illusions, showing scenes of unseen raw cruelty. We, Peter and I, arrived at the film show from an evening dress function; he wearing a dinner jacket, and I in full evening dress. The contrast between the raw, earthy and authentic film and us two could not have been greater.

Autumn 1953

Returning to live at home with my family felt like a step back in time. After the three years of college life, sharing merriments and afflictions, stories and gossip, I missed my colleagues, missed the communal living, and missed the freedom from parental control. Luckily, before starting my new job, I had a few days to catch up with my two closest friends, Seija and Minnami, and hear their news.

Seija had made an interesting choice. She would be working as a second nurse at the Helsinki County Prison, located at Katajanokka, the headland of Helsinki peninsula, and an elegant part of the city. One can see from some distance the impressive, gold-domed, red-brick Uspenski Russian Orthodox Cathedral, the hallmark of Katajanokka. Behind the cathedral, are a cluster of art nouveau buildings, with large apartments for the wealthy and/ or famous to reside in. The prison, situated in the far end of the peninsula, was built in 1837, and had then been surrounded by small wooden houses, burned down some time ago. Now a high brick wall with a massive iron gate separated the prison from its surroundings.

There were two nurses working in the prison. They took care of prisoners' minor ailments, gave first aid, and assisted the doctor on his daily visits. The prison had one small hospital ward, offering short-term care while patients were waiting to be transferred to an appropriate hospital for treatment for their illnesses. Seija's colleague had an attractive apartment within the prison, but Seija commuted daily from her home, beyond Kulosaari. I tried to imagine what Seija might be feeling each morning as she entered the prison through the massive, locked gate and heard the lock shut behind her. She was facing a strange, closed world. I was looking forward to hearing Seija's tales.

Minnami had had enough of hospitals and nursing. She had no intention of working as a nurse so she enrolled herself back to Helsinki University to study for a Master of Philosophy degree, with Psychology and Art History as her subjects. Eero-Pekka Paavolainen and she had become steady pair, and had become engaged. In the summer of 1954, I had the pleasure of attending their splendid wedding at Kulosaari Casino.

Though Minnami and Eero-Pekka looked an imposing, fine couple, the marriage was not a happy one, and ended in a divorce after some ten years. They had three children, a daughter born in autumn 1955, and six years later twins, a boy and a girl, were born. Minnami completed her degree, and started her personal analysis with a famous analyst. She worked as an administrator for the Finnish Psychotherapy Organisation for several years, until, after her divorce, she moved to the art side, and became a co-owner of an art gallery. Each time I visited Finland we met, right to the time close to her death. She was an exceptional person; gifted, sensitive, beautiful, cultured, and knowledgeable, but deeply troubled. She never recovered from her son's suicide, at the age of twenty.

At Piittu's and Rauni's wedding Jussi had told me Kaaki's latest news. She was back at her childhood home, staying with her parents until her wedding, planned for the autumn of 1954. She had begun collecting items for her dowry. The Finnish custom was for the bride to have a chest full of linen; all items with the bride's monogram embroidered onto them. Kaaki was no needlewoman, so her mother was busy doing the embroidery. Jussi had also informed me that Kaaki had started working as a staff nurse at the local cottage hospital.

After our shared experience in specialising in psychiatric nursing, Helinä had become my close friend. She had decided to continue her studies at the Nursing College for another two years in order to gain a social worker qualification. Being a farmer's daughter, she wanted to work in the community and felt that nursing on the hospital wards was not for her. Working as a social worker, seeing families in their own homes and environment gave her an opportunity to use her psychotherapy specialisation in helping them with their social and emotional problems. It turned out to be the right choice for her. She met, and later married, a young, newly qualified Forestry Officer Erkki Romppanen. Being employed by the Department of Forestry, he was posted to Suomussalmi in Kainuu, and there in Suomussalmi Helinä started her pioeering work in mental health. She was employed by the Social Services Department as a Social Worker with special responsibility for mental health. All these years we have corresponded, and met up during my summer holidays in Kainuu area.

Auroora Hospital

This Helsinki City hospital was built in 1914, originally for infectious diseases. When isolation hospitals, thanks to vaccinations and penicillin, were no longer needed, Aurora Hospital was changed into a general hospital, and it incorporated two psychiatric wards for adults. Scattered around the main red brick building were several smaller buildings. In one of them, a psychiatric children's ward for children from aged three to eleven had been recently opened. I was lucky to have obtained a staff nurse's post on this ward.

On the first of September I began my first salaried job in Aurora Hospital working with emotionally disturbed children. Very soon after I had started working on this ward, a London-trained child psychotherapist, the first one, was appointed to give therapy to some of the children. I remember well the excitement of the arrival of Mrs Jokinen. She had spent three years in London, being in analysis with a Kleinian analyst, and simultaneously being trained by the world- famous child analyst Melanie Klein. This originally Austrian psychotherapist had been working in Vienna before settling, in 1926, in London. Based on Freud's theories, Mrs Klein had created her own Kleinian analysis for children and adults. Unlike Freud, she concentrated on the experiences in a child's very first years of life, experiences that had become unconscious, and not verbally available. Melanie Klein was of the opinion that much of the suffering in later life was a result, and a repetition, of these early painful experiences. Using and observing a child's free play, she gained insight into the child's fantasy life. She then interpreted what she had understood to the child, and encouraged the child to act out her/his feelings through play.

In spite of her Finnish name, Mrs Jokinen did not look Finnish. She was slightly over-weight, her black hair pulled back from her face in an untidy manner, her eyes were very dark, her nose big. Middle-aged, she did not wear a white coat, but instead favoured colourful, flamboyant, floating dresses. A faint smell of garlic lingered around her. Looking so different and being so free and easy-going both as a person, and in her style of dressing, she did not go down too well with some of the members of the staff. There was curiosity, and a certain hostility towards her work with the children. The normal routine on the ward was disturbed by her arrival.

In equipping the therapy room for seeing children, Mrs. Jokinen had been given a free hand. She wanted it to be similar to the one Mrs Klein used. Separate from the ward, the room had a washbasin, a sandpit, a dolls' house, small human figures, representing family members in three generations, and small animals. Drawing material, paints and plasticine were also provided. An important aspect of the therapy was that each child had his or her own named box of toys and figures, chosen by themselves. I was fascinated and intrigued. At any opportunity I talked with Mrs Jokinen, hoping to learn more.

A four-year-old boy, Erik, had been admitted for an assessment. Erik's mother had died quite unexpectedly some months before. In that general upset and sadness in the family, no one had taken much notice of Erik, until he became more and more listless, almost stopped speaking, and refused to leave the house. The family doctor, after discussions with the father, referred him to our ward. We tried to make a relationship with Erik, talk to him, sit next to him, but he remained withdrawn, and did not want to speak to or join the other children in play.

One evening, when I was on night duty, I asked Eric to come and sit with me in the office. I gave him some crayons and a piece of blue paper. Bending over the paper, he took a red crayon and began hesitantly and slowly to make marks, taking his time to draw a flower. Then, he picked up a black crayon and using jerky, rapid movements, carefully avoiding the flower, he covered the lower part of the paper black. He was in his own world; I did not disturb him. Bending even further down over his drawing, he then picked up a white crayon, and, gently, covered his red flower with white. Looking up to me, he said, '*Sataa lunta*' ('It's snowing').

I did not need to be a child therapist to understand Erik's communications: his black anger, his red love, and the freezing cold, the white snow covering his living red flower. Hesitantly, I began to talk about his drawing, I suggested, perhaps, he wanted to cover something precious with the white snow. Cautiously, we moved on to talk about his mum, how much he missed her, how sad and angry he was. His frozen feelings began to thaw; his eyes filled with tears. Sitting there with this sad little boy, is one of those moments I'll never forget. He took his drawing with him, and hid it under his pillow. Maybe I had been able to help him just a little. Erik remained on the ward for some time, gradually looking much happier, and eventually joining the other children in their play. Mrs Jokinen decided to offer him therapy sessions. In the safety of the therapeutic relationship, he was able to begin work with and through his shattering loss.

I can still remember the joy of receiving my first pay packet, all 380 marks (thirty-eight pounds) for a month's work, in cash. I had never held so much money in my hand; I felt rich; I could spend it on what I wanted. On my way home, the first thing I bought was a meringue cake, the best cake I knew. I wanted the whole family to celebrate with me. Then some flowers for Mamma. By the time I had bought a navy-blue, 'Sunday best' dress, and beautiful high-heeled shoes, the money had almost disappeared. Another long month to wait. But it had been great to receive money I had earned with my work.

In early December, having by then settled down in my job, and really enjoying my work, I received a request from Miss Durchman to come and see her. Not a total surprise; I had met Liisa some while ago. She had told me of her decision to undertake a two-year post-graduate course in administration, this qualification was needed to be able to apply for a post as a matron. She had decided to apply for leave of absence, and keep her good teaching job for the two years as a safeguard.

Casually, she had remarked, 'Perhaps you would be interested in my teaching job?'

I took her suggestion more as a joke and forgot all about it until the call.

Well, it was not a joke. Miss Durchman offered me Liisa's job and gave me a few days to think about it. I was happy in the job I had chosen, and had no wish to give it up, but the offer was quite a challenge. In the end I decided that it would be foolish to refuse this opportunity of a promotion to a job with far greater responsibility than I had as a staff nurse, and a much higher salary.

By February 1954, I was back at Helsinki Nursing College, now with the huge difference of being a teacher rather than a student. The teachers I had bowed to were now my colleagues, and invited me to call them by their Christian names. In the first few weeks, I found this almost impossible. To call Miss Durchman 'Aino' was simply too difficult, so for a while I avoided addressing her at all.

I had assumed that I would be moving into Liisa's wonderful apartment, but no, Liisa was allowed to keep her flat. I had to be satisfied with a large single room on the ground floor of the students' quarter. At least it had its own access from outside. I was free to come and go as I pleased and invite friends without anyone checking who visited me. I was pleased to have my own life and only go home for visits, often taking Mamma flowers, and to Juha small gifts and a little extra pocket money, each month. He was now twelve, attending 'Normaali Lyseo', a highly respected Grammar School for Boys. He was causing concern to my parents. Isä had caught him smoking, and Mamma, shocked, had rushed to make an appointment for the three of them with a psychiatrist.

Apparently, one of his first questions had been, 'Metsänhoitaja (Forestry Officer) Pelkonen, may I ask you, do you smoke?'

Isä admitted that he did. The psychiatrist's stern advice had been, 'To set an example to your son, you need to give up your smoking habit. Come back once you have done that. I'll then talk to Juha.'

Isä did, Juha did not. Instead, he became extraordinarily skilled and careful in hiding his smoking.

The new job was a major step towards independence. I looked after myself in every sense. No longer could I get free meals at the college or in the hospital, but I was able to buy meal tickets for the hospital. At the college I was able to prepare simple meals in the communal kitchen. Managing my finances and working out my income and expenses was difficult. Often, I overspent, and had to turn to Mamma for assistance. Professionally, I was in charge of planning my week, and working out how to divide my time between the Psychiatric Hospital and the Nursing College. At the hospital my task was to go around the wards, spend time with each student, teach and observe them, as well as discuss the student's progress with the ward sisters. Back at the college I was giving theoretical seminars, arranging psychiatrists to give series of lectures, and writing reports to be discussed at the weekly meetings with other clinical nursing teachers, and chaired by Aino Durchman.

Initially, I was scared stiff, afraid that I would fail in my job. I can well remember my first seminar, standing there in front of the students, all almost my age, feeling embarrassed, my voice faltering, and my knees knocking. Then on top of it all, I ran out of what to say. Wishing the floor would swallow me, I stood there like a fool, seeing the staring eyes of the two dozen students waiting for me to continue speaking. I had no alternative except to say, 'Sorry, this is my first lecture. I'll promise to do better nexttime.'

On that occasion I used the rest of the time inviting the students to share their prejudices about mental illness. A good bond was established, and I learned that discussions were a better way of teaching than formal lectures; they could be left to the psychiatrists. The next group, coming to Lapinlahti for eight weeks, I handled with more confidence. I began to enjoy my work.

Timo had left for the USA early in the autumn. We had met and agreed to write to each other. I had sent him a little parcel for Christmas and had had a friendly thank you letter back. He was happy with his studies and enjoyed being in the States. Olli was still around, keen to be with me in spite of the hurt I had caused him in the summer. He was getting on with his studies as well as singing in the YL choir. We went to concerts and the pictures. One evening in the spring, after a walk, I invited him into my room for a coffee and cakes. We had sat there talking, each sharing plans and hopes. Suddenly, and quite unexpectantly, he got up, took a powerful hold of me, and gave me a deep, forceful, and penetrating kiss. I was shocked, I had had no time to push him away. I had never in my life been kissed like that or any other way by any of the boys I had been going out with. The aggressive force of the kiss felt like a rape. Once I recovered, my temper flared up. Olli had crossed an invisible boundary he had no right to cross.

Olli defended his action by saying, 'Can't you understand that I have waited and waited for a sign of love from your side? I have loved you for years and years.'

Still furious, I replied, 'I'll never, never love you in the way you want. You'll be my very dear friend for always, but nothing else. You'll be the godfather of my first child, I promise.'

He walked out wounded; our relationship changed for good.

Olli's choir YL went on a tour to Germany. There he met the girl. She had picked out Olli from all the dashing young men in the choir, had waited for him after the concert, and had made sure to get him. She succeeded. Knowing how badly and hurtfully I had treated Olli, I was so pleased for him. He had met a girl who had chosen him, who had fallen in love with him, and, who, eventually, became his wife and came to live in Finland.

Scandinavian tour

Since my teens I had been corresponding with a Danish girl, Margareta, a farmer's daughter from Zealand. In the spring, in one of her letters she had, yet again, invited me to come to Denmark, first to spend some time on the farm, and then she would be my guide, and we could go to Copenhagen, and other places of interest. This time, her invitation was just what I needed. Having already decided that a week at Vuokatti would be enough this coming summer, the invitation was the beginning of my plan for a Scandinavian tour, my 'Hero's Journey'. I was going to travel alone, first to Sweden, then Denmark and Norway. I was confident that the tour would open new vistas and boost my confidence. An excellent plan, except for one major defect, I had not managed to save enough money for such an extensive trip. Discussing my plans with Mamma, who saw herself as much as a Scandinavian as a Finn, she encouraged me to go ahead, and offered to give me a loan for the missing funds. Late in July, I took an overnight boat from Turku to Stockholm. I was ready for an adventure, and a feeling of delight and freedom filled me as I boarded the boat. In the evening sun, the boat slowly glided past the Finnish archipelago, moving towards the open sea. What a wonderful way to spend a summer night. In the early hours of the night the boat reached Mariehamn, the capital of Åland islands, an autonomous territory under the Finnish rule, unfortunately the brief stop gave no time to explore the island.

As the morning sun rose, we reached the archipelago on the Swedish side, with bigger villas, and far more expensive motor and sailing boats moored on the shores than on the Finnish side. Before my next connection I had several hours to explore the beautiful city of Stockholm, with its fourteen islands, linked by bridges. Walking around, some vague memories of the city returned from my childhood. This time, I decided to take a sightseeing tour by boat around Stockholm.

As we passed the prison, the guide, seeing the brooch with a Finnish flag on my blazer, said, 'I see we have a Finn amongst us. You might like to know that the prison is full of Finns. Many are known for their attempts to escape.'

I felt insulted, removed my Finnish flag, and decided to speak English from then on in Stockholm, and not to reveal by my accent. After the war thousands of Finnish workers had gone to Sweden searching for jobs and a better life. The flood of too many Finns, and the behaviour of some of them, had gained the Finns a bad reputation: getting drunk, fighting, not speaking Swedish, and being petty criminals. I was pleased to move on.

Denmark was a totally new and delightful experience. Margareta met me at Copenhagen Station. Straight away I felt the difference between the Swedes and the Danes. The one-upmanship, formality and stiffness were exchanged for friendly, relaxed openness. This was confirmed on the bus journey to her home; passengers were chatting, the driver joined in, jokes were shared, and on and off laughter filled the bus. We stopped outside a small house; the driver got out, leaving us puzzled and waiting.

After a while he returned with a gleaming face, and said, 'It's Birger's birthday today. How could I drive past his house, without wishing him "happy birthday"? Of course, I had to have a quick drink with him.'

A bus driver in Finland wouldn't dare to do anything similar, I was sure.

I had imagined that I would manage with my Swedish in Denmark. That wasn't so. Initially, Margareta and I had some difficulties in understanding each other. We had managed in our correspondence, each writing in our own language, but the spoken Danish was as alien as Russian would have been. After a while I was able to pick up familiar words, even though the pronunciation remained a mystery. Margareta's family were very welcoming, her father showing me around the farm and the piggery, spotlessly clean like a factory. I had never seen as many pigs and little piglets, all to be grown and slaughtered for bacon.

Margareta was an excellent guide, and we spent our time sightseeing.

One day we took the local train to Roskilde, a small town known for its twin-towered Cathedral that held the tombs of many Danish monarchs. The main reason for our trip to Roskilde was a visit to the famous Sankt Hans Mental Hospital, built in 1620. Margareta had, at my request, managed to make an appointment with the Matron. As a teacher of psychiatric nursing, I was interested to gather material for my seminars, and interested to see how chronically ill were cared for in Denmark. Many of the treatments were similar, but there was a shock waiting. We were taken to a ward with the most disturbed patients, and shown patients in straitjackets to restrain them. Having never seen someone in a straitjacket, I was shocked and horrified that such a cruel, medieval method was used still in 1950s.

The days staying with Margareta and her friendly, easy-going family went fast. It was as if I knew them before meeting them, as Margareta had written so much about them during the years. Sadly, I discovered that as young adults, we now had little in common; she well settled in the farming world, waiting to find her right partner, I keen to explore the world. But we had a great day at Tivoli, the famous amusement park right in centre of Copenhagen. There we were back being two happy teenagers, laughing, going on the huge wooden roller-coaster ride, screaming in fear, then rewarding ourselves with a delicious Danish sandwich, followed by ice creams. I really fell in love with the humorous, relaxed Danes.

The route of my Scandinavian tour had been influenced by friends I could visit or stay with, as travelling on my own without contact points seemed too scary, as well as aimless. After my stay with Margareta, I moved west to meet Gunhild, my Norwegian friend. She had, since our last meeting in 1952, qualified as a teacher, and was spending part of her summer holiday on a further training course in music. Luckily for me, the course was held in Denmark, in a boarding school on the Jutland Peninsula. That was where I was heading next.

Being on my own on the train, I concentrated on looking at the flat, almost treeless landscape, the yellow ripening grain fields, the open vista of blue, cloudless sky, and the frequently visible sea, sometimes blue, sometimes green. Danes and their land became one. The unrestricted views explained their happy, relaxed way of being, so different from the other Scandinavians.

I counted how many ferry journeys I would have taken before I was back in Finland. Two so far: from Finland to Sweden, then from Malmö to Copenhagen. The next ferry ride was waiting in a little while: from Korsör, across Storebaelt, the 50 mile stretch of water, to the island of Fyn and the town Odense. There I would stop for long enough to visit Hans Christian Andersen's house. His fairy stories had been so much part of my childhood, I just had to see where he had lived. The sadness of the matchstick girl, and many other of his sensitively told stories had made me cry. For crossing the strait from Fyn to Jutland, a bridge taking trains and cars had been built in 1935. As the train approached the shores of Jutland, the landscape became hilly, with open heaths and peat bogs, and far fewer dwellings.

My destination was Arhus, where Gunhild was waiting with her teacher friends. I shared meals with the group and as a listener, joined them in their musical programmes in the evening. I met Paul, a Dane, an excellent violin player, and guessed that a romance was brewing between him and Gunhild. Indeed, they married a year later.

This brief stay strengthened Gunhild's and my friendship, and it has lasted through all these years. The marriage with Paul ended in a bitter divorce three years after their fourth son was born. Gunhild, a year older than me, is still leading an active life with her second husband Aage, some twelve years younger. We have visited each other's countries innumerable times, and she and Aage have come with their caravan to stay in the grounds of my summer house in Finland.

Staying in the school had been quite awkward. There was no accommodation for guests, I wasn't even sure if guests were allowed. I shared Gunhild's small room, and had to share her, rather too narrow, bed. I can still remember how tense I was, and so afraid that I might in my sleep roll over and touch her, equally afraid that she might touch me. I had hardly slept those two nights I stayed with Gunhild. Now thinking about it, I link my tenseness and awkwardness with my confusing thoughts about bodies, sex, and my fears and longings.

Since the cycling trip, in my teens, I hadn't been back to Norway, and was looking forward to seeing the country with its fjords and mountains. Another night-long ferry journey from Aalberg took me to Oslo. Standing on the deck, seeing Denmark disappear, I saw a young Viking approaching me, not another Hans-Ludvig in looks, but pleasant looking, with brown hair, a tanned face, and a relaxed manner. If I am honest, of course I was hoping that my trip would include meeting someone interesting, who would keep me company, and add sparkle to the trip.

Moving close to me, he said, 'Hi, I am Leif. Where are you from? Are you on your way to Oslo?'

I answered him, telling briefly of my trip. We kept each other company for the rest of the ferry journey. Quite a relief, after struggling with Danish, that I could understand his Norwegian, and he my Swedish; our chatting was easy and free flowing. I was pleased to hear about his life. Leif came from the coastal town of Bergen and was studying at Oslo University for an engineering degree. He had been to Denmark working on a bridge project.

The ferry provided an excellent buffet meal, and you were allowed to fill your plate as many times as you wished. Leif and I spent a long time sitting in the warmth, eating and chatting. He insisted on paying for both of us.

The approach to Oslo was along a narrowing fjord, the land rising sharply on both sides, no small islands. As we reached the harbour, the water opened up, and at the end of this widening fjord, in the valley, was the city, surrounded by wooded hills.

Leif and I parted on arrival. He was heading to catch his train. Pity there wasn't a chance to carry on learning to know each other better. No need to exchange addresses, just a strong, friendly handshake and, *'Hej, hej, tack för trevligt sällskap.'* ('Cheerio, thanks for thegood company.*')*
My hostess in Oslo was Ragnhild, at least ten yearsolder than me, and Gunhild's friend. The two of them hadvisited us on Paradise Island. Ragnhild and Mamma had got on famously; they shared the same type of evangelical Christianity, and had carried on corresponding. Ragnhild, having heard of my trip from Mamma, offered tolook after me in Oslo. I was happy to take up Ragnhild's offer to stay in the old people's home where she worked and avoid

months and months of paying back my loan. I was pleased to see that I had my own room.

Oslo was a city I was keen to visit, but now I can only remember the visit to Holmenkollen, the wooden ski jump, and the famous skiing area from where one could see Oslo and its surroundings. Secondly, the visit to Frogner Park and Frogner Manor, then known as the Vigeland Park. Within the grounds of the park was a permanent sculpture installation, created by sculptor Gustav Vigeland (1869-1943), and consisting of 212 granite and bronze sculptures, mainly of human figures. As you cross the central bridge, on both sides there were these figures in different human pursuits: dancing, running, wrestling and holding hands. A stunning site. Further into the park, we came to the most popular sculpture Monolitten (the Monolith), a totem of thirty-six figures. Oslo, then quite a small city, left me disappointed, I would have needed much more time, and knew how much more there would have been to explore.

After Oslo I had no more contacts, and no free accommodation. My journey continued to Trondheim, where I would stay in a youth Hostel. I had reserved a window seat on the train to be able to enjoy the fantastic views of mountains and fjords. Indeed, the views were majestic, though at times claustrophobic, with mountains on both sides, and the train crossing on bridges over narrow fjords. The scenery was as impressive as I remembered it from 1948, but with the difference of being safely transported, and able look without having to manoeuvre sharp bends and soft, sandy roads.

Again, I was lucky to have an interesting travel companion, this time, a middle-aged Norwegian man, keen to inform me about life in Norway. During the seven-hour journey we had time to cover many topics. I learned many new things, and my admiration grew for the Norwegian people living in such a challenging landscape. My travelling companion's special interest was Norwegian food. He insisted that I order 'römmegröt' (a porridge made with sour cream, served with jam and cinnamon) for my breakfast in Trondheim, and suggested I taste other Norwegian specialities like *'fiskebollar'* (fish dumplings), made of minced white fish, eggs, flour and milk, served with white sauce. Gladly, I accepted his offer of coffee and sandwiches, filled with *'mesost'* (goat cheese, brown in colour, slightly sweet and caramel-like). As soon as I tasted the cheese, I remembered having had *'mesost'*, as a special Saturday treat, in Sweden as a child.

Trying now, some sixty-six years later, to remember more details of this extensive round trip, has been quite impossible, so much has been forgotten. I do remember entering the impressive Nidaros Cathedral, a Gothic monument in the centre of the Trondheim. I was glad to be alone in this medieval, holy building, built over a 230-year period. I was thinking of the effort and faith building this cathedral had taken; fires destroying it, and then rebuilding it again, at least twice. After the Reformation, Nidaros Cathedral became a Lutheran church, once again destroyed by a massive fire in 1701. In 1869 Nidaros Cathedral was rebuilt, using the original building techniques. Restoration work goes on. The stained glass rose window, part of the extensive renovation of the cathedral, filled the holy space with mysterious blue light. I sat there in stillness, needing to be alone, and allowed myself to feel overwhelmed by all that I had seen, what I had taken in with all my senses: in rapid succession, three very different Nordic countries, with their different people and their three different tongues, and the effort it had taken to understand what was being said. Suddenly I felt very tired, and, for the first time, longed for the journey to come to an end. Perhaps, I had had some romantic fantasies. There was a slight disappointment on that score; but the overwhelming feeling was of pride and pleasure. I had had the courage to face the challenges of travelling alone, a massive journey that had widened my view of the world, left me determined to explore more.

There was another very long, tedious train journey ahead, at least now moving east, to Sweden, to the coastal town Umeå. No need to strain myself in understanding what was said, I could just relax and take in the changes in the landscape. Mountains became lower and rounder, no fjords but the long and wide river Ume, and its shores began to remind me of Finland.

Through the Umeå tourist office I found a friendly, retired couple offering a room in their home at a very reasonable price, including a good meal, and a lovely bed. A safe place for the night. The following morning, the final ferry crossing from Umeå to Vaasa, and from Vaasa I finished my journey by taking a train to Vuokatti.

How lovely to arrive back home, and to the warm welcome from Mamma, Isä, Laila and Juha. I had missed them. Isä had heated the sauna, Mamma had baked her famous oat biscuits, and Laila and Juha had been waiting for me to join their card and other games. I felt so, so happy. The landscape that had depressed me the previous summer, with its dark, graphic lines, and austere beauty, had grown on me. After the time spent travelling, and constantly moving to new scenery, its steadfastness brought peace and tranquillity. In that tranquillity I had time to relive my 'Hero's Journey', linger with people I had met, revisit places, and make comparisons between the three countries: Denmark and its people left a happy feeling of a country where life seemed easy, people happy, humorous and relaxed. I enjoyed the stay on the farm, and the generosity of Margareta's family. Sweden, this time, just a thoroughfare, but the time there long enough for the wartime memories to begin to well up, memories I wasn't ready to remember. Norway, with its majestic, inaccessible, and so extremely beautiful mountain scenery, and the people I met, left a feeling of being close with them. Norway, like Finland, was a young independent nation, having separated from Sweden in 1905. A poor country in 1954, with hardworking, honest and serious people. My two Norwegian travel companions, each in their own way, took me further into the Norwegian way of life. Leif told me of the nearest municipality to Bergen is called Arna, and has the highest, (987m), mountain, Gullfjellet within its area. He had added that in old Norse 'Arna' meant 'eagle', and his name 'Leif' in old Norse meant 'heir' or 'beloved'. I felt really at home with the Norwegians and would gladly return there any time.

The nature in Vuokatti had its own moods. After a heatwave it is not unusual for an almighty storm to blow up, shaking the tranquillity and peace, and providing a frightening drama. This happened soon after my arrival. The lake was welling up with oceanic, giant waves, hitting the rocks with full force. The lightning flashing non-stop across the sky, the thunder booming, amplified by the Vuokatti mountain, and trees bending double in the storm. A bolt of lightning hit a big tree near the sauna building; luckily the falling tree missed the sauna. After the storm, calm returned. My holiday weeks, jammed full with new experiences, were over. My first independent holiday had been a challenge and a success.

August 1954 - August 1955

Enriched by my holiday experiences, I was happy to return to my work and life in Helsinki. Teaching no longer scared me, in fact, I liked my job. It gave me considerable independence and regular working hours. The seminars I had prepared for the last term would need some reworking, new details to be added, but basically, they were done.

For the first time in many years, I was able to commit myself to attending the weekly rehearsals of the considerably enlarged *'Akateeminen Laulu'* (The Academic Choir). Thanks to our new choir master Tauno Hannikainen, many new students and postgraduates were keen to join the choir under his leadership. We had a busy autumn ahead of us. Rehearsals were at times tedious, singing big works required hours and hours of slow building up. The breaks in singing gave time to chat, mainly with other mezzo-sopranos. Progressively, we experienced the joy of hearing how great the choir's singing of a major work sounded. After each rehearsal, I walked back to the college elated. The performance of Mendelssohn's oratorio 'Elijah', with the Helsinki Symphony Orchestra, was scheduled for early January. Then, in the spring term, the next major piece to be tackled would be Verdi's Requiem.

On the home front, there was the happy news of the birth of Rainer's and Anna-Liisa's second son, on 20th August. Already during Anna-Liisa's pregnancy he was nicknamed Kalle, and remained Kalle, even though he was christened to Eero. Kalle was a sunny, lovely and mischievous baby. The problem for his parents was his refusal to adjust to normal sleeping hours, and to use nights as his waking time, when he was at his liveliest. I loved babysitting, particularly as, the older Kalle grew, the more interactive he became. He had a great sense of fun from a very young age, and knew how to amuse me.

Laila had taken her matriculation examinations in the spring, but had failed in one subject, Finnish. After retaking and passing her Finnish examination in August, she was ready to begin her University studies, with English as her main subject. She had a most wonderful and enthusiastic teacher in English, and thanks to her, Laila had fallen in love with the English language. She gained the highest mark, 'laudatur', in the matriculation examinations. Her career path was clear, she would begin her studies for a Master of Philosophy degree, with English as her main subject. She would aim for nothing less than mastering English to near perfection, working on correct intonation and pronunciation. She carried on playing viola in *Helsingin Naisorkesteri* (the Helsinki Women's orchestra), touring with them in Scandinavia as well as in Finland. By now Laila had grown to her full height, 167 cm, and was an attractive auburn haired, sporty, Ingrid Bergman look a-like, young woman. Laila's friendship with Helena, her best friend since she started secondary school, had been spoilt when a new girl, Anneli Lindros, joined their class in the sixth form. Straight away, Anneli began monopolising Laila, and Helena, deeply hurt, was pushed aside. Unfortunately, I never learned to like Anneli, but I could see why, with her unconditional admiration and motherly care, she was someone Laila so badly needed, and she captivated Laila. They became inseparable best friends.

Isä and Mamma bought Mummi's flat from Aunt Eva and Aunt Ruth. Laila and I moved in there in autumn 1956. After I married, in the spring of 1957, Anneli moved in to share the flat with Laila. When Isä sold the flat a few years later, Laila and Anneli, with Laila's lovely border collie, Sunny, moved to a rented a flat in Kulosaari. In 1973, the two of them, and Sunny, were on their way to Kuopio to spend an autumn weekend with Isä and Mamma. Their car crashed, and Anneli died instantly. Laila was the driver, with no other car involved.

The cause of the accident has never been fully understood or explained. The one possible explanation offered is that Sunny, in the back of the car, had become restless when he saw sheep in the field, and Anneli, to calm the dog, had removed her seat belt and turned around and Laila had lost her concentration. The car rolled down a steep bank to the field and Sunny jumped out, unharmed. Anneli did not survive, and Laila was very badly injured.

This accident scarred Laila both physically and mentally for the rest of her life. She spent a long time in the hospital; initially being shielded from, and unaware of, Anneli's death. The following summer Laila, still recovering, came to England. The two of us went for a little holiday on the South

Coast. I wanted to give Laila a chance to talk to me, and to show her some of the beautiful English countryside. Laila was full of unforgiving feelings of guilt, and in a state of deep, deep mourning. She was, in my eyes, a 'shadow' person, private and secretive, as if she needed to walk, unnoticed, on the shadow side of life. She was highly gifted, ultrasensitive, and a great nature lover.

Professionally, Laila achieved both a high position and high regard. She worked as a translator in the Canadian and Israeli Embassies, and ended up in the Finnish Foreign Office as the head interpreter and translator. Laila's main language was English, she was fluent in Swedish, and managed with French and Italian. She dressed stylishly but unobtrusively, behaved correctly, like a lady, and aimed for perfection in her work. She was President Kekkonen's interpreter, and present as an interpreter when Queen Elizabeth and Prince Philip visited in Finland in May 1976. At the Queen's request, she translated the recipe for *'Kainuun lohisoppa'* (Kainuu salmon soup), and had the honour of sending the recipe to Her Majesty.

I am so grateful that I had the chance to spend several summers with my sister after Peter's death. Together she and I planned the summerhouse to be built on our land inherited from Isä. I bought Laila's share, with the understanding that she could both use it, and spend time with me there. We had good times together. We had a chance to clear up childhood hurts, often caused by me. Laila, unlike me, was quite obsessive about sticking to rules and instructions, and was critical of my careless attitude. Helena, now back in picture, and Laila could give me an evening's entertainment with their stories. It was great to see Laila totally relaxed with Helena, showing her most wonderful sense of humour. In the summer of 2013, Laila was too ill to come up to my house, so I met her in Helsinki for a shared meal. It was the last time we met. Laila died of cancer in May 2014, six months before her eightieth birthday.

Back to 1954; Juha was now thirteen, and clearly a teenager with his own secret life. I had a feeling that he was going out with a gang of boys, and they were up to no good, but I had no evidence. Girls had become of interest; not so easily available when you attended an all boys' school. I heard from Seija that the friendship between Anna-Maija and Juha continued until he moved to Kajaani with my parents in 1956.

My work in Lapinlahti was going well. Five students had indicated their wish to specialise in psychiatric nursing; their specialisation was going to begin after Christmas. Planning their programme and working with this group would be a new and exciting challenge. Liisa continued to be my friend and mentor, and had agreed to help and advise me. She knew these five; they had done their eight weeks' placement during her time in Lapinlahti. Liisa, Helinä, who specialised in psychiatric nursing with me, and I decided to invite them to join our 'Psykoklubi', thus expanding our group to eight. We met in Liisa's flat at regular intervals. They were great evenings: noisy, exciting and inspiring. Our task was to put the world right, creating tolerance and understanding towards the outcasts in society. As I have mentioned earlier, 'Psykoklubi' existed for years and years. The last time we met was in the summer of 1987. In addition to Liisa and Helinä, I kept in touch with a fourth member of the group, Helena Sommers, until she was no longer able to communicate by writing. She became blind and seriously handicapped. Helena, like Helinä, carried on her training, becoming a Health Visitor, and spent her working years as a Health Visitor in a small village in Lapland.

During the autumn term of 1954, Aino Durchman wanted to see each teacher individually to give us her feedback, and to listen to our plans for the future. Two of my colleagues were planning to go to the USA for further training, and then work for the World Health Organisation. One of them, Terttu Tela, I met again in London. She had met her husband while she was working in the Far East.

I was still in awe of Aino and felt tense and self-conscious sitting in her room facing her. She tried her best to make the discussion informal and emphasise that we were colleagues. We sat in armchairs, and Aino offered me a cup of coffee with 'pulla'. She began by wanting to hear about my visit to the Danish Mental Hospital, and the discussion moved on in a relaxed manner.

Aino, then, asked me about my professional plans. Not waiting for my answer, she said, 'You are doing so well in Lapinlahti. I assume you have decided to become a qualified teacher and go on a teacher's training course, in a year's time.'

She then went on to tell me about the discussion she had had with Venny Snellman, Finland's then most highly regarded pioneer in the world of nursing, with the title *'Sosiaalineuvos'* (Social Counsellor), given to her by the Finnish state in 1953.

I had met Venny Snellman once, soon after she received this title, and heard her, pointing at me, asking

Aino, 'Who is the attractive doctor's wife?' Aino had explained who I was, and what I did. Apparently, Miss Snellman had been impressed by what I had said in the meeting, and Aino had praised me. Together she and Aino had been plotting, there and then, a career plan for me in nursing, even eventually taking me to Miss Snellman's position.

Aino reiterated what she had said earlier. 'The first step you need to take to promote your career is to take the two-year course and become a qualified teacher in nursing.'

I thanked her for their trust in my ability, but inside, I was utterly taken aback, shocked, and rebelling. Who were these two to be making plans for my life? What could I say to Aino, except, 'I do enjoy, teaching, but I'm not ready to consider going on a two years' training course next autumn, sorry, Aino.'

The talk with Aino did upset me, and left me confused and angry. In no way, at twenty-three, was I ready to be making such long-reaching career plans. I might have appeared confident and capable, but I didn't even know who I was; I felt both immature and insecure. Luckily, Aino could not read my thoughts. What I did know was that I had no desire to become one of the spinster teachers the college was full of. I had to find a way out from the path being earmarked by Aino for me, before it was too late.

Heikki

'Pikku Joulu' ('Little Christmas', 'First Advent') was approaching, and at one of the choir's rehearsals it was decided that we would have a 'Pikku Joulu' party, with food

and dance. We had little chance to get to know each other at our weekly rehearsals; the party would give us this opportunity. A 'Pikku Joulu' party was arranged, using one of the large Student Union halls as the venue. As soon as the music started, one of the new postgraduate choir members strode towards me. I had noticed him amongst the tenors, even picked up his excellent voice. We hadn't had any occasion to enter into conversation, except a weekly exchange of the greetings, *'Hei'! 'Mitä kuuluu*?'

There he stood, this tallish, attractive looking man, with dark blue eyes and brown, curly hair. Looking straight into my eyes, he bowed in front of me and asked, 'May I have the honour of dancing with you?'

At the end of the first dance he said, 'May I reserve the next dance with you too?' This was repeated and we danced together most of the evening. He did not let me go, just holding onto me, waiting for the music to start again. It was wonderful to be led by a partner who held me firmly and danced confidently, so different from the shy young men I had danced with before. Great to be carried away on strong arms.

Between whirling around, we introduced ourselves. My dancing partner's name was Heikki Kuusi. By the end of the evening, I had also learned that he was a musician, a violinist, studying privately with a well-known violinist; this added to his plus points. For me, violin music had been something special, Isä had played violin; now Laila had his instrument. I remembered the eleven-year-old Karelian child prodigy, Heimo Haitto, who during the war years had conquered the hearts of all young girls, and how the whole nation had followed his progress to fame. After the war, he received a scholarship to continue his studies in USA. Heimo settled there; only returning to give concerts in his fatherland.

Delighted to accept Heikki's offer to walk me home, I was keen to find out more about him and his life. Walking arm in arm in the cold winter night, Heikki said, 'Were you aware that we, the male singers, have been playing a game? Each week, looking at the women sitting in front of us, we have been choosing our favourite. Not all the blokes have been keen to take part in this innocent fun. From the start, there has been only one choice for me, that is you, Arna.' He added, 'All autumn I have been waiting for a good opportunity to speak to you, but you have been in such a hurry to leave after the rehearsals. I have waited my time. I am so happy about tonight.' I was utterly surprised to hear that we, the female singers, had been so closely observed, but of course I was flattered by Heikki's revelation. This our first evening together was just wonderful. Before we parted, we agreed to walk home together again after the next rehearsal.

When Heikki told me his surname I knew straight away that he came from a well-known, upper middle-class family. His father, Aarne Kuusi, was a High Court Judge, whose name was frequently mentioned in the newspapers. From Helinä I had heard that Aarne Kuusi's wife was mentally unstable, suffering from manic depression, and needed, at intervals, hospitalisation in Lapinlahti. I had not nursed her but knew the ward on which she had been. It did not take long before Heikki wanted to tell me about his mother's mental illness. 'It has been a large shadow on our family, leaving its marks on each of us, the six children, as we were growing up.' I did not mention that I already knew their family secret. I just listen to him, showing empathy.

Gradually, I heard about his siblings: Matti, the oldest, was now a Professor at Helsinki University, teaching Finnish Literature, specialising in folk poetry, and highly respected in the academic circles. He was nine years older than Heikki and his twin brother Olli, an architect. Pekka, the second son, had made his career in business. He was the Managing Director of Alko (the national retailing monopoly of alcoholic beverage in Finland). Then came two girls, Katri, a Domestic Science teacher, and an author, and Helena. Out of the siblings Heikki was the least successful. He had begun studies in garden architecture and design, but had given up his university studies before getting his degree, and had decided to concentrate on music. His aim was to become a professional violinist in a symphony orchestra.

Very soon after we met, I discovered that Heikki was eight years older than me. Then came the shocking news that he was a married man with a four-year-old son. According to Heikki the marriage had been unhappy from the start. He had moved out from their marital home some months before we met. He added: 'The divorce proceedings have not begun, as my wife is still hoping to patch up the failing marriage for the sake of our son Timo.' I was speechless. I needed to digest what I had heard.

Heikki not being a free man became an enormous obstacle in our budding romance. Could I, as a Christian, carry on with the relationship with clear conscience? I stilled my guilty feelings with Heikki being separated before I came into his life.

An additional difficulty was the physical distance caused by Heikki having succeeded in getting a temporary position as a violinist with the Oulu Symphony Orchestra. Oulu, a town further north than Kajaani, made casual meetings impossible, and our meetings less frequent than we would have wished. Luckily, he returned almost weekly for his violin lessons. The violinist's post was a temporary one, so by the spring Heikki was working as a designer of gardens on one of twin Olli's building projects.

The months that followed the 'Pikku joulu' party took me to a wonderland. I was living in a dream where I was the princess, admired, loved, and put on a pedestal; swept away on wings of love. Heikki was a full-blown romantic dreamer, bringing wonderful bouquets of flowers, expensive surprise gifts, like a dainty gold wrist watch, hidden in a huge box of chocolates. He, like a true troubadour, often surprised me with violin serenades and love songs under my window.

On one of our walks in the spring sunshine, we bumped into Heikki's brother Pekka. Having been told of my existence, he was pleased to meet me. There was no embarrassment from his side. '*Hei, kiva tavata*.' (Hi, nice to meet you), he said, then invited us for a cup of coffee in a nearby bar. Confident and sure, he took hold of the conversation and asked me lots of questions, smiling and polite, but revealing little about himself or his thoughts. As the First of May celebrations were approaching, Pekka said to Heikki, 'Come to my office, I'll give you a bottle of Alko's best champagnes for your 'Vappu' celebrations.'

We did celebrate in style. With our balloons, wearing our white caps, and hand in hand, we joined the mingling crowds. Our hearts singing with the happiness of being in love and feeling the joy of eternal youth. We walked slowly in the balmy, white spring night along the road next to the sea, rejoicing the increasing light and warmth, ending in my room at the college. I had prepared a delicious light supper; the champagne was chilling in the fridge. On entering the room, I opened the window, took a deep breath, and allowed a waft of fragrance from bursting spring to float in. Heikki stood next to me, bending over to caress my cheek. We looked into each other's eyes.

This is happiness, I thought, but simply said, 'Time for champagne.'

Only once, at Piittu's wedding, had I tasted champagne, and then wasn't sure if I had liked it. This time was different. The spring night was long and sweet. We took sips of the now heavenly drink, we talked, read poems, and we rested on my bed, cudddling just a little. Heikki was gentle, sensitive, and considerate. He was careful to move at my tempo, treating me as if I was a fragile china doll that would fall to pieces unless he handled me with the greatest care.

In late May I became ill with glandular fever and ended up on the sick ward at the college. The doctor examined me, gave his diagnosis, expressed his concern for my low weight (49 kg), and prescribed a daily portion of porridge for breakfast.

By now I had told Mamma, not Isä, about Heikki. At first, she was shocked and upset, hearing that Heikki was still legally married, but then, surprisingly accepting. The tone in her voice had changed when I mentioned Heikki's surname. She knew the cultured background he came from, knew that the family's Swedish surname had been Granfelt before it had been translated into the Finnish, Kuusi (spruce). Mamma, a culture snob, was well acquainted with Heikki's mother. These facts reassured her about Heikki. I used the opportunity, and asked her then, 'May Heikki come to Vuokatti with me?' She agreed with my request, providing Isä also agreed.

One day, unannounced, my parents marched into my room on the sick ward. First, Isä, as upright as ever, and looking really stern, Mamma following a few steps behind. We had barely exchanged greetings before Isä launched, what felt to me, his well-prepared, attacking speech.

'Arna, what on earth are you thinking about, going out with a married man? You have to stop seeing him. I can tell you right now, you will be hurt; it'll all end in a shame and disaster. You should know better.'

I was utterly unprepared for this angry onslaught from my beloved Isä. I burst out crying. Sobbing, I replied, 'How would you know what I feel? You have never been in love; you don't know what it feels to be in love.'

I could sense Isä softening, and his expression had a hint of wanting to say to me, 'Arna, what do you know about Karin and me, your parents?' Maybe he was recalling his and Mamma's passionate love story. He knew, and understood too, that he no longer had any authority over me.

Undiplomatically, stubbornly, and stupidly, I announced, 'I want to invite Heikki to Kajasti for my summer holiday.'

Isä's anger arose again: 'On no account, absolutely not, Heikki can't come to Kajasti. He is not welcome.'

I replied, 'It is important for Heikki and me to spend our holiday together.'

I could see Mamma coming on my side, making suggestions, but Isä repeated: 'I mean it, Heikki is not welcome to Kajasti.'

I wasn't going to give in so easily, so in defiance I replied, 'Well, in that case I'll not come either. Heikki and I, we'll be going to a hotel instead.'

I could see Isä was thinking hard how to respond. He certainly did not want his daughter going to a hotel with a married man. That was unheard of in those days. What would people say?

My parents were silent for a while, then Isä turned to me and said, 'Arna, I do care about you. I can see how much Heikki means to you. What I have decided is this: I'll go on one of my business trips for several days. There are several swamp-drying projects within my area I need to inspect. It's easy for me to stay overnight in the camps with the men. If you still insist, feel free to spend time in Kajasti with Heikki. I do not want you to go to a hotel. I'll not be at Kajasti when he is there.'

I wanted to hug him, but spontaneity is not part of our family culture, so I simply thanked him. I knew in my heart what this sacrifice and change of mind had meant to my proud Isä. I also knew how worried he was about me getting hurt in this relationship with an older, experienced, and married man.

Aino Durchman was putting pressure on me to begin the Postgraduate course for qualification in the autumn. So much happening in my private life had made it both easy and necessary to find a way of buying time before making any long term career plans. The solution I came up with was to take six months' sabbatical leave and travel to England to study psychiatric nursing there. The Finnish Nursing Council encouraged me and worked out the study plan. I would be leaving for England at the end of August. Aunt Ester, now 62 years old, was still in London, working at the Finnish Embassy until the end of the year. Then she would be transferred to the Foreign Office in Helsinki to work there for the years before her retirement, at 65. It would be great to make use of her knowledge, and have her guidance while she was still in London. I was also encouraged by Laila, who had travelled to London in May as soon as the University term had ended. She needed a three-month's study period in a language school in England for her University studies. She just loved London and had instantly fallen into the English way of life, encouraging me to come.

More importantly, I was fully aware that my relationship with Heikki could not continue, unless he was able to move on from simply being separated from his wife to actually starting legal divorce proceedings. I couldn't carry on living in sin long term. I needed to find out if he would have the courage to take the necessary step if I wasn't physically next to him? Only by removing myself far away, would I find out. I had already discovered that Heikki had been the weaker twin, allowing Olli to be the one he followed. Olli had made a good career, had a successful marriage. Heikki was impulsive, had left his studies in the middle, and spent money over-generously, when he had it, and then ran short. There had been occasions when I had had to rescue him by giving him money. This was OK for two lovebirds, but in the long run it would not work.

We had many serious discussions and reluctantly, he accepted my plan: my absence would give him time, and, from my point of view, would test his seriousness about our relationship. This agreed, we allowed ourselves to be immersed in experiencing being in love and being loved.

Maybe, Seija's plans for the autumn had a minor influence on me. With this whirlwind romance going on in my life, I hadn't spent much time with her. When we met, she shared her news about planning to apply for a job at the famous Karolinska Hospital in Stockholm. She had a cousin, also a nurse, living in Stockholm, and another married there. This made her adventure relatively safe, and she spoke fluent Swedish. Seija had confessed that at times, working amongst the prisoners felt uncomfortable. 'I am getting too much attention and unwanted comments,' she said.

Later, she added to her story. She had become great friends with one of the prison wardens, a young married man. 'He is clearly very fond of me and keeps on suggesting that we meet after work. I have to admit that I look forward to seeing him each morning. He is an interesting man. I am afraid I might fall in love.' She added, 'Don't worry. Up to now it's all been proper. Just imagine what my father would say.' Yes, I could very well imagine what Pauli Vaalas would say, and saw that Seija's option of escaping to Sweden was the best one for her.

With the sea and open countryside all around, Helsinki is a charming summer city. Early in June, Heikki and I we were walking in Seurasaari, as we often did. The long, white night was enfolding us into its magic. The full silver moon was casting its spell on the landscape, forming a shimmering bridge across the water. Heikki picked me up into his strong arms, danced with me, swung me around, and then, with me in his arms, jumped over one rock to the other. Spellbound, we melted into the dream state with the summer night. Never having been truly in love, I was now experiencing it so powerfully, so beautifully, so romantically, and even more perfectly than I had dared to dream.

In the week leading to midsummer celebrations, Heikki was attending a summer course for musicians in Orivesi, a small town 200 kilometres north of Helsinki. The Klemetti Institute was famous to musicians, their summer courses highly valued. Some of their teachers were well known musicians, such as the composer Tapani Rautavaara, the violinist Anja Ignatius, and the singer Maria Heidi.

Surrounded by well-kept parkland, the Institute, a white, imposing, wooden villa, sat on the shores of a lake. The beautiful, idyllic setting was typical of Finland at its best. Heikki had invited me to join him for the midsummer weekend. I had worked out my outfit with great care. My new, sky blue summer dress emphasized my slender figure, and my little white, veiled hat completed the picture of a Doris Day look-a-like. As far as Heikki was concerned, I passed as a film star. He was delighted and proud to introduce me to his musician friends. Later in the evening, we wandered along the lake side, found a secluded spot for our private midsummer celebration. Having taken his violin, Heikki started serenading me with Schubert's love songs. In a state of timeless reverie, we embraced each other.

Overwhelmed by the magic of the white summer night, our hearts were bursting with the wonder of love.

Heikki and I took a train up to Vuokatti, with nobody meeting us. Isä had kept his promise and stayed away for the time we were there. Mamma, Juha and a summer maid were the only ones there. Mamma was amazingly welcoming, and, true to her style, brought God into conversation as soon as possible.

'I am praying for you both,' she told us, 'and asking for God's wise guidance for you.'

Heikki very courteously thanked Mamma for allowing him to come. Later, he asked her for permission to create a sunken garden on the slope, as an appreciation for her kindness to us. He spent hours and hours digging, moving soil, and rearranging the stones he had dug up. Then, together we went looking for suitable wild flowers and bushes to plant in the garden. Mamma was really pleased with Heikki's creation and witnessing our love softened her heart. Heikki charmed her, and she became very fond of him.

We spent one very special week at Kajasti, explored our surroundings, its beaches and the wilderness. We rowed to one of the small islands, not really suitable for landing, but wonderful to cross the water and row there. The uninhabited, golden beach around the corner was our hiding place for lying in the sun, and swimming in the nude. One afternoon we were disturbed by the rattling sounds of twigs being broken: Juha, aged fourteen, was spying on us, and this time he was discovered.

Heikki returned to Helsinki before me. I wanted to spend some days with my family, especially to have a chance to see Isä. This was my only opportunity to see him before leaving for England. Fully realising the sacrifice he had made, I wanted to thank him for allowing Heikki to come to Kajasti. I had, with one ear, heard Isä's and Mamma's repeated warnings about Heikki, but let them go out through the other.

I did have my own doubts about Heikki's and my future. I felt guilty, and knew that, in God's eyes I was committing a sin. Was going to England an escape from decision-making, and a coward's solution? I had taken the attitude, that, if God so decides, all will work out for the best for me and Heikki; I would just passively let things happen, and accept what God's will.

My departure date, 24th August, was approaching with speed. The nearing separation tinged our times together with sadness. On my side, there was a budding excitement that I didn't want to share with Heikki. All was in order for the forthcoming journey. The Finnish Nursing Association had arranged my study placement in a psychiatric hospital in Portsmouth. Laila had advised me to book a first-class passage on Russian ship called 'Baltica', the same boat she had used. She had even recommended that I order Green Chartreuse at the bar, and had added that she had been served by a charming barman. Aunt Ester was coming to meet me; I would stay in London as her guest for a week.

The Aleksanterinkatu flat was empty. Why shouldn't Heikki and I spend the few last days together there? So that's what we did; the most precious days for us, filled with the joy of being together. On one perfect summer day, we took a short boat trip from the harbour. Standing at the rear of the boat, seeing Helsinki disappear, Heikki held me close.

It felt like a rehearsal of what would be happening in a few days' time, except he wasn't going to be next to me then. With his beautiful voice he started singing Oskari Merikanto's song: *'Sinä kullanmurunen, kullan puhtahimman, Minä vasken palanen, vasken ruosteisimman. Minä kultahan kun sulan, vältän ruostumisen pulan. Sinä kullanmurunen, kullan puhtahimman.'* ('You, my piece of gold, of purest gold, I, a piece of brass, a rustiest piece of brass. Melting into your gold, saves me from rusting. You, my piece of gold, you, a piece of purest gold'), followed by other love songs.

On the last day, before my departure, we went to the market next to the harbour, and bought some live *'kräfta'*(crayfish), dill, new potatoes, and strawberries. Heikki was an expert; he knew what to do. He filled the bath, and let the living creatures gently into the water, until it was time for their death sentence. Meanwhile I took care of laying the table: red candles, napkins, paper plates decorated with 'kräfta' motive, and a Japanese style flower arrangement of red, spiky dahlias as the centre piece. In the kitchen a big pot of boiling water was ready, potatoes were on the boil; it was for Heikki to transfer the happily swimming creatures into their boiling hell. Within seconds their life ended, turning them from muddy grey to fire-engine red, as a final protest against their death sentence. The final evening was beautiful, slightly wistful, and filled with love. Neither of us could sleep, we clung to each other, wanting to remember and re-remember the closeness. There was, somewhere within, an unvoiced fear that our dream might end. Heikki and I had lived a more beautiful love story than I had ever hoped for. I couldn't wish for more.

****

My story has reached its beginning and ending.

The goodbyes, with the hope of meeting again, had been said, and many questions had been asked, and left to wait for answers.

My voyage, from what I knew to something unknown, was beginning. With increased speed Baltika, the Russian ship, was heading towards the open sea. I was still standing on the deck, my long blonde hair blowing over my face, concealing the tears streaming down my face. I buried my face into Heikki's red roses to feel his loving presence.

The Finnish coastline was gradually diminishing. Behind me and in front of me was the vast open sea.

Acknowledgements

I am most deeply indebted to Philip Lawder, writer and poet, for being my mentor, giving me guidance and encouragement throughout the whole writing process. Without his kind and appropriate advice as well as his professional expertise, the book would not have been completed. His wife Jeannine has been a background support; thank you Jeannine.

Thank you to Colin Robinson for his masterful work on the cover and the photographs.

My sincere thanks to the writer and editor Siobhan Curham for her gentle editing, and for her skilful editing comments.

I want to extend my thanks to The Pinner Writers Group for their support in the early stages of the process.

My special thanks to my brother Rainer Pelkonen, who both assembled and published the rich and important correspondence that my mother had had the wisdom to save, covering the years from my parents' courtship, in 1925 to my father's death, in 1977.

With Rainer's permission, I am quoting some extracts from the letters in my book.

My longstanding friend Seija Tikkanen has been with me every step on the way, sharing and recalling our common memories; heartfelt thanks to her.

Lastly, my children and grandchildren have been the main inspiration in wanting to write this story, which would otherwise have ben forgotten. Each has helped me in their own way, but special thanks go to Callum and Kim for technical help.

Thank you to all who have followed me on this journey.

About the author

Arna Davis was born and educated to postgraduate level in Finland. She moved to the UK in 1957, after her marriage to Peter Davis, PhD. They settled in Hertfordshire, bringing up three children. Arna was widowed in 1999. She has four grandchildren.

Arna continued her studies in UK, first in Social Sciences, then in Psychotherapy, leading her to qualify, and work, as a Jungian analyst for many years. She gained an BA (Hons) degree in Fine Art in 1995 as a mature student and has exhibited in the UK and Finland.

Having published chapters in professional books on psychotherapy, this is her full story.

Printed in Dunstable, United Kingdom

71144921R00231